Diversity in America

Diversity in America

Vincent N. Parrillo

The William Paterson College

PINE FORGE PRESS

Thousand Oaks, California ◆ London ◆ New Delhi

For information, address:

 Pine Forge Press
A Sage Publications Company
2455 Teller Road
Thousand Oaks, CA 91320
(805) 499-4224
E-mail: sales@pfp.sagepub.com

SAGE Publications Ltd.
6 Bonhill Street
London EC2A 4PU
United Kingdom

SAGE Publications India Pvt. Ltd.
M-32 Market
Greater Kalisah I
New Delhi 110 048 India

Special Editor: Gillian Dickens
Designer: Lisa S. Mirski
Typesetter: Joe Cribben
Cover designed by: Paula Shuhert and Graham Metcalfe
Production Manager: Rebecca Holland

For permission to reprint the map on page 20, grateful acknowledgement is given to Alvin M. Josephy, Jr. (The Indian Heritage of America, *New York: Knopf, 1986).*

Printed in the United States of America

1   2   3   4   5   6   7   8   9   10—99   98   97   96

Library of Congress Cataloging-in-Publication Data

Parrillo, Vincent N.
    Diversity in America / Vincent N. Parrillo
        p.   cm.
    Includes bibliographical references and index.
    ISBN 0-8039-9049-9 (pbk.: alk. paper)
    1. Pluralism (Social sciences)—United States—History.   2. United
States—Race relations.   3. United States—Ethnic relations.
I.   Title.
E184.A1P329   1995
305.8'00973—dc20   95-16608

To my friends and acquaintances, both in the United States and abroad, for the enrichment their diversity has brought into my life.

About the Author

Vincent N. Parrillo is an internationally recognized expert in the field of immigration and multiculturalism. He has spoken on these subjects on numerous occasions throughout Canada and Europe to government officials and public and university audiences under the sponsorship of the U.S. Information Agency. Listed in the *International Who's Who in Education* and past recipient of the Outstanding Educator of America Award, Dr. Parrillo is Professor and Chair of the Department of Sociology at The William Paterson College of New Jersey. Two of his most recent, related books are *Strangers to These Shores: Race and Ethnic Relations in the United States* (4th ed.) and *Rethinking Today's Minorities*.

About the Publisher

Pine Forge Press is a new educational publisher, dedicated to publishing innovative books and software throughout the social sciences. On this and any other of our publications, we welcome your comments and suggestions.

Please call or write to:
Pine Forge Press
A Sage Publications Company
2455 Teller Road
Thousand Oaks, California 91320
(805) 499-4224
E-mail: sales@pfp.sagepub.com

Contents

3   Diversity in Colonial Times / 35

4 Diversity in the Early National Period / 57

Preface

This book is about race and ethnicity in the United States and the interaction of gender relations within that context. Because of this special focus, my use of such terms as *diversity* and *multiculturalism* does not include sexual preference, the aged, or the physically challenged, as some others may do for a different purpose. Although this book delves deeply into the subject of multiculturalism, it is not a paean to either anti-assimilationists or anti-pluralists. It is instead a moderate approach to a volatile subject with the goal of demonstrating that multiculturalism is neither a new social phenomenon nor a threat to American society.

All of us know something about diversity in America. We probably learned a little about it in our past, bear witness to it in our present, and may hold expectations about it for the future. Yet although many extol the legacy of our immigrant heritage and/or lament the injustices of our race relations history, to many we seem to be on the brink of a societal unraveling. As in generations past, voices rise up against immigration, against foreign language retention, against "nonproductive" or "nonassimilating" racial/ethnic groups, and against racial/ethnic leaders espousing separatist policies or actions. Similar concerns can be heard in Australia, Canada, and much of Europe, where unprecedented migrations of diverse racial/cultural groups have also made an impact.

These responses were the catalyst for my writing this book. All of my discussions on the subjects of multiculturalism or diversity—with my students and colleagues, with government officials, university students, or the general public during my various lecture tours abroad for the U.S. Information Agency, or with listeners/viewers when I appeared on numerous Canadian or U.S. radio/television call-in shows—played a role that impelled me to write this book. Between the polemics of voices advocating policies that challenge the dominant culture and those denouncing multiculturalism as a threat to society, are, I believe, the ambivalent but concerned feelings of the vast majority.

As a sociologist aware of the patterns of dominant-minority relations, I wanted to dispel misconceptions about our past, misunderstandings about our present, and anxieties about our future that appear to be so prevalent. This book is written for the general reader, but rooted in the sociological perspective. It is thus an effort to look at American diversity objectively, not with a revisionist or a special advocacy position.

Both pluralism and assimilation have been dual realities throughout the often raucous history of intergroup relations in the United States. This book is an effort to show that, in many ways, what we witness today is a continuation of those dual processes, that the social dynamics we observe are not new, including the efforts of minority separatists and the outcries of alarmists. In fact, most Americans can find examples of the duality of pluralism and assimilation in their own family histories.

When my mother's Irish forebears came to the United States, for example, many native-born Americans looked on them and their compatriots with scorn and dismay. By then, the large presence of Irish Catholics had been a reality for a couple of generations, but other Americans remained convinced that this "inferior" group tainted the "purity" of the American character. Undaunted, the Irish persevered, overcoming religious bigotry and flagrant discrimination, to become an integral part of American society.

Andrew Kohns, my maternal grandfather, typified the Irish immigrant saga. A peasant from County Monaghan, he came to America in the late nineteenth century and settled in Paterson, New Jersey, where he and thousands of other immigrants worked in the city's textile mills. He became a political leader and one of his greatest satisfactions as an American was personally escorting presidential candidate Woodrow Wilson to a major political rally in Paterson in 1912.

Andrew and Mary Kerr Kohns had fourteen children, several of whom died young, and they also adopted three newly orphaned kin. Betty, my mother, was their second-youngest child and, as a beautiful woman, had many Irish American suitors. All of her older sisters married Irish Americans, each a successful middle-class businessman. But Betty, resisting family pressures to do likewise, broke the endogamy pattern in 1937 when she married my father Vince, a second-generation Italian American who was the second of three sons born to Nicholas and Giovanna Infante Parrillo. Like Betty's mother, his mother died when he was a youth.

Nicholas had been a highly respected Italian community leader and publisher of an Italian weekly newspaper before his death in 1929, but Vince's family background hardly impressed Betty's family. They were aghast at her even dating Vince, let alone marrying him, convinced that he and his family—in fact, all Italians—were beneath them. Although restrictive immigration laws a decade earlier had drastically reduced the flow of new arrivals from southern, central, and eastern Europe, these groups—particularly Italians and Jews—remained stigmatized as personifying all that was wrong with America. They had replaced the Irish as the subcultures deemed "unassimilable." Betty, though, was an independent and open-minded person who rejected such prejudices.

Her job as school secretary in Paterson's north ward brought her into daily contact with youngsters and parents from all backgrounds, so possibly this interaction helped break down some barriers. I think, though, her acceptance of others was heavily augmented by a vacation in Cuba before she met my father. Her fascination with the Hispanic culture began there and was furthered by later visits with my father to the Caribbean, South America, and Spain.

The oldest of five children, I grew up exposed to more than just my dual cultural heritage. We lived on the northern edge of Paterson in a neighborhood that straddled a tight-knit Dutch community on one side and a mixed second-generation German/Italian/Polish neighborhood on the other. Not surprisingly, my boyhood pals were of all four backgrounds as were my first dates.

My family lived nine blocks from the Black neighborhood down the hill that, in my boyhood, I would often walk through, without incident, on my way to or from the movies downtown. When I reached Paterson Central High School—through classes, sports, and other extracurricular activities—my social world expanded to include many African American and Jewish students, along with many other second-generation White ethnic students.

As the years passed, this mixture of race and ethnicity among my closest companions continued and expanded as I moved through high school, college, graduate school, and into academia. On my wedding day in 1972, my closest friend, an African American, served as best man in my marriage to Beth, a Scots-English Presbyterian. Dennis remains one of my best friends among others who are Czech, English, German, Greek, Irish, Italian, and Saudi Arabian; their religions are Christian, Greek Orthodox, Islamic, or Jewish. What is important here is not just that I have such diversity within my social circle but that each of these persons has also welcomed me into his or hers.

In my lifetime, I have witnessed the influx of African Americans and Puerto Ricans into urban areas, the arrival of Korean, Cuban, and Vietnamese refugees, and the immigration of millions of Asians, Latinos, and Middle Easterners. Their difficulties in acculturating, their determination to succeed, and their struggles to gain acceptance are in many ways similar to those on both sides of my family in years long past. So too are the criticisms, social ostracism, and discrimination today's newcomers all too frequently encounter, although no one in my family suffered from the racism that many people of color still encounter today.

As an American of mixed ethnic heritage, my biography is far more representative than it is unique. Hundreds of millions of American biographies contain homogenizing/integrating elements across racial, religious, and ethnic lines. Often these did not come about quickly or easily but, taken together, they form an interwoven tapestry that is forever a tribute to the American spirit. Despite the isolationists and separatists, despite the radicals and reactionaries, despite the skeptics and pessimists, assimilation continues as a powerful social force, keeping alive the country's motto of *e pluribus unum* (from the many, one).

Witnessing the millions of Americans living in poverty, in cultural isolation, or out of the mainstream, one might reasonably argue that the preceding statement is too sweeping and ignores harsh reality. Yet the imperfections of American society do not negate the social forces within it, nor the means its members have to accelerate the process. This book offers both a sociohistorical perspective and a sociological analysis to provide insights into American diversity and into how the forces of pluralism are a necessary counterpart to the forces of assimilation.

This book is a reworking and a significant expansion of an article that appeared in the December 1994 issue of *Sociological Forum*. I want to thank Steve Rutter, publisher and president of Pine Forge Press, for his encouragement and strong support for this project. I am also most appreciative of the efforts of some other fine people at Pine Forge Press— Sherith Pankratz and Rebecca Holland, who were helpful in the book's development, and Gillian Dickens, who guided it through the production phase. I am especially grateful for the valuable comments and critiques from the reviewers, who helped shape this book into its final form:

Kevin Delaney, *Temple University*
Ellen Rosengarten, *Sinclair Community College*
Susan Hoerbelt, *University of South Florida*
Peter Rose, *Smith College*
Raul Fernandez, *University of California, Irvine*
Maura Toro-Morn, *Illinois State University*

Also providing some helpful suggestions were Richard D. Alba, Charley Flint, Ronald Glassman, Geoffrey Pope, and Peter Stein, and I thank them for their input.

I hope this book provides the reader with a greater understanding about our multicultural past and present. If so, perhaps more of us can break down the barriers of social distance that separate us, becoming more aware that diversity is not the problem. Intolerance by anyone—assimilationist, multiculturalist, or undeclared—is the problem.

1

Perception and Reality

Emblazoned in virtually every individual's mind is the knowledge that the United States is a nation of immigrants. That realization—taught in our schools and reinforced in political speeches, particularly on the Fourth of July—serves as a source of nationalistic pride for everyone, even those who trace their ancestry back to seventeenth-century colonists.

The American Dream—that promise of freedom of choice, education, economic opportunity, upward mobility, and a better quality of life—inspires many to come here. It also serves as the underpinning for basic value orientations that are the foundation of American beliefs, behaviors, definitions of social goals, and life expectations.

Today, immigrants continue to arrive in pursuit of that dream just as others have done for more than two hundred years. Yet these newcomers frequently generate negative reactions among native-born Americans despite their common pride in belonging to a nation of immigrants. In all parts of the country we find frequent expressions of fear, suspicion, anxiety, resentment, hostility, and even violence in response to the immigrant presence.

Immigrants are not the only group triggering a backlash. African American and Native American assertiveness often provoke resistance. Challenges to the status quo by feminists and gay rights activists regularly induce adverse responses as well.

Why this contradiction? If Americans value their nation's immigrant heritage and ideals of equality and opportunity, why do they begrudge those traveling the same path to the same destination?

Answers come readily from the critics. It's different now. Earlier immigrants came here, learned the language, worked hard, and became Americanized. We're getting too many immigrants. They take away jobs from Americans. They drain our tax dollars through health and welfare benefits and schooling for their children. They don't want to assimilate or even learn English and therefore threaten to unravel the fabric of our society. Too many people today just are too lazy and want a handout. Too many want undeserved privileges at the expense of everyone else. They want the rewards without earning them.

Complaints by the citizenry in everyday conversations are partially fueled by the media or by public pronouncements from reactionaries and immigrant bashers. Sometimes, though, even respected scholars are in the forefront. Noted historian Arthur M. Schlesinger Jr., for example, has denounced "the cult of ethnicity" (an insistence on maintaining vibrant ethnic subcultures) as a forerunner to the imminent "balkanization" of American society. His reference to the continuing hostility among the Bosnians, Croats, and Serbs in the Balkan Peninsula is a scary one. No one wants American society disintegrating into a collectivity of groups hostile to one another. Nor do they want the "snuffing out" or "shipwreck" of the American republic by new immigrants that English immigrant Peter Brimelow ironically warns us about with apocalyptic rhetoric in *Alien Nation*.[1]

Complaints and threatened lawsuits against the federal government by the governors of California, Florida, and Texas in 1994 struck a responsive chord with many native-born Americans. The governors contended that the government had lost control of the nation's borders, resulting in large concentrations of illegal aliens in their states, thereby placing a severe strain on their state's financial resources in increased education, health, and welfare costs.

Minority actions also reinforce nativist perceptions. The rhetoric of leaders from the National Council of La Raza and the League of United Latin American Citizens (LULAC) for the maintenance of Spanish language and culture at the public's expense, both in the schools and the workplace, demonstrates to native-born Americans an unwillingness to assimilate.[2] The insistence of some African American leaders for slavery reparation payments to all Blacks enrages many Whites as an unreasonable demand. The "clannish" retail shopping patterns of Asian Americans and their noninvolvement in community activities annoy many local residents and merchants. News reports about militant actions, public mayhem, street crimes, and mob violence all trigger other negative reactions against minorities.

Once we talked about the United States as a melting pot of immigrants becoming Americans. Now there is something called multiculturalism, which Schlesinger, Brimelow, and others fear is undermining the cohesiveness of American society.

What is happening? Are such instances illustrations of a different pattern emerging than in previous generations? Are we witnessing a new social phenomenon? Are we being overwhelmed by a flood of immigrants who do not wish to integrate? Are they and the people of color born in the United States pursuing separatist paths that will lead to the disuniting of our society? Is the land of *e pluribus unum* (from the many, one) therefore disintegrating into *e pluribus plures* (from the many, many) right before our very eyes, as Diane Ravitch warns?[3]

What This Book Is All About

These questions and issues reflect real concerns of many Americans. They require responses that are more than subjective impressions of the current scene, for what people may think is happening is not necessarily what is actually occurring. This book attempts to provide those responses and it will do so, but later, in the last third of the book. First, we need to cover some other very important material.

The famed Roman orator Cicero once remarked, "Not to know what happened before we were born is to remain perpetually a child." Just as children usually gaze with wonderment on things they see for the first time, so too can adults react to social phenomena as new and different unless they recognize them as variations of past patterns.

I contend that the perceptions of many Americans are tainted because (1) they lack an accurate understanding of past American diversity, and (2) they fail to view contemporary events in a larger context. Part of the problem lies in something I call the Dillingham Flaw, an erroneous way of thinking that I shall explain shortly.

A central thesis of this book is that multiculturalism has always been part of the American scene and is no more a threat to the cohesiveness of society today than at any time in the past. Rejecting claims that modern circumstances create a very different situation than in the past, this book will show parallels, similarities, and continuities. It will also show instances when American society was actually *more* multicultural than it is today.

Another central tenet of the book is that assimilation and pluralism are not mutually exclusive entities, nor are they necessarily enemies of one another. They have always existed simultaneously among different groups, at different levels. Whether they are persistent subcultures or convergent ones that gradually merge into the dominant culture over several generations, culturally distinct groups have always existed. Even when their numbers have been great, they have never threatened the core culture. Assimilation remains a powerful force affecting most ethnic groups even though it has been relatively ineffective with racial minorities.

Although proponents of one position may decry the other, both pluralism and assimilation have always been dual realities within American society.

The idea behind this book, then, is to place the current debate on immigration and multiculturalism in a proper sociohistorical perspective. Within a sociological context of social patterns and social change, the historical record of America's past and present cultural diversity will be presented. Included will be the factors of economic conditions, elitism, nativism, racism, social class biases, and the struggle for power that mitigate against harmonious intergroup relations.

The first two-thirds of this book contain a brief portrait of American diversity through five eras: Colonial, Early National, Growth and Change, Industrial, and High Technology. These chapters will outline how cultural diversity has always been characteristic of American society. They will also show the continuity of various social patterns from one era to the next, down to the present.

Women, of course, have constantly been an integral part of the American experience, although their efforts have often received little public attention until recently. Partly to compensate for that neglect, the period portraits in the following chapters will include information about women during those times. Our intent is to emphasize their gender experiences of status, power, and influence within a sociohistorical framework as a prelude to understanding today's feminism.

In these discussions on women, you will learn how their experiences varied greatly depending on their locale, social class, and length of residency in the United States. Indicators of how they fared compared to men will delineate gender diversity in terms of rights and power. Explanations about their social activism will also show a parallel to the militancy of other minority groups seeking equal treatment.

Seeing Is Believing, But Is It Knowing?

Some people believe what they see, but appearances can be deceptive, as are optical illusions or mirages. Magicians are human illusionists and the good ones can stupefy us with their artful tricks on a grand scale. We know they tricked us, but we don't know how.

In everyday life we think we know what we see, but here too we may be deceived. As Peter Berger observes, "The first wisdom of sociology is this—things are not what they seem."[4] He suggests that social reality has many layers of meaning and, as you discover one layer, your perspective of the whole changes. So perceptions, about diversity or anything else, change with increased knowledge. Seeing is not enough. You need to know what it is that you are seeing.

Complementary to Berger's statement is the aphorism "You can't see the forest for the trees." Its message is clear. When you are too close to the situation, you can't see the entire picture. You can't get a sense of the whole because you are caught up in small details. It is necessary to find a detached viewpoint if you are to comprehend what you see.

That viewpoint can be found in the sociological perspective, which provides, says Berger, "a special form of consciousness" (p. 23). It enables us to focus objectively on aspects of our social environment that may previously have escaped our notice, allowing us to interpret them in a different, meaningful way. If we add a historical frame of reference along with a sociological analysis to our study of diversity, we gain a valuable dimension to observe what continuities and changes are occurring.

The Cultural Homogeneity Myth

Let's use this sociohistorical approach to establish an overview of the book. Diversity in America has been an ongoing social reality in the United States, not just since its inception as a nation, but even in its primeval colonial cradle.

This viewpoint is not the prevalent one. The prevailing belief that this nation was essentially a culturally homogeneous launching pad for the new nation is steeped in the historical myth that the thirteen colonies were almost entirely populated by English immigrants and their descendants. Such was not quite the case. As we shall see shortly, this "historic reality"—this fallacy of cultural homogeneity—changes under careful sociohistorical analysis.

That we are a nation of immigrants is an undeniable fact, but this fact is often not connected to the current multicultural picture. Contemporary public views on multiculturalism are often based on the erroneous assumption that what occurred in the past were fleeting moments of heterogeneity that yielded to fairly rapid assimilation. The cultural diversity that exists in America today is misperceived as different, more widespread, and resistant to assimilation—which should be celebrated, respected, and maintained, say its proponents—thus making diversity, in the eyes of alarmed others, not only a new construction but somehow also a threat to the cohesiveness of American society.

Only an objective analysis that peels away layers of myths, assumptions, presumptions, and misconceptions can provide an accurate assessment. To do so, we must take a sociohistorical perspective, moving beyond only present-day realities and noting instead long-term patterns throughout the nation's history. In this way we can put the current scene in a wider context and determine more precisely how unique or not our situation is. Before we embark on this examination of our past and present, however, we must first address three areas that affect judgments about diversity in America. The first of these is the changing views about minority adaptation to American society. Second is the melting pot concept and its limitations of application. Last, but extremely important, is the Dillingham Flaw, in which perceptions about immigrants can be misdirected through faulty comparisons.

The Rise, Fall, and Rise of Pluralism

Because this term is of recent vintage, many incorrectly conclude that multiculturalism is a fairly new social phenomenon, the product of a changing world and changing government policies. Yet, as Nathan Glazer (1993) and Peter Rose (1993) correctly assert, multiculturalism is actually a refashioning of an older concept of cultural pluralism that includes differences in language, religion, and value orientations.[5]

Early Advocates

In the early twentieth century, educator John Dewey and social worker Jane Addams both spoke against assimilation destroying the cultural values of immigrants. In 1915, their advocacy was formally advanced as an ideology in an essay in the *Nation* by Horace Kallen, an immigrant from Eastern Europe.[6] Citing the persistence of cultural identity among the Irish in Massachusetts, Norwegians in Minnesota, and Germans in Wisconsin, he promoted a multicultural society, a confederation of national cultures. As Peter Rose puts it:

> To Kallen . . . the United States was not a fondue of amalgamation but a symphony of accommodation. Pushing his own metaphor,

Kallen saw the orchestra—that is, the society—as consisting of groups of instruments—nationalities—playing their separate parts while together making beautiful music resonant with harmony and good feeling.[7]

Kallen's ideas, expanded in his seminal work on cultural pluralism, *Culture and Democracy in the United States* (1924), contained only incidental references to racial groups.[8] Foreshadowing today's opponents to multiculturalism, part of Kallen's focus was on public concern that the recent arrivals of his time might not integrate fully into society.

Assimilationists Prevail

Despite the pluralist advocates, a chain of events encouraged assimilation over ethnic persistence. Patriotic hysteria following the U.S. entrance into World War I effectively ended the German subculture. Restrictive immigration laws in the 1920s, a world depression in the 1930s, and World War II dramatically reduced immigration. With little new blood to keep everyday ethnicity viable, with the second generation growing up as Americans, and with the housing and education entitlements offered to GIs, White ethnics by mid-century had moved closer to the center, loosening their ethnic ties as they did.

As the old idea of America as a melting pot seemed to reaffirm itself, major books by sociologists Robert E. Park[9] and Milton M. Gordon [10] influenced social scientists to think more about assimilation than pluralism.

In *Race and Culture* (1950), Park offered a universal cycle theory suggesting all groups go through a progressive, irreversible process of contact, competition, accommodation, and eventual assimilation. Park acknowledged the process might take centuries and might even include a semipermanent racial caste system, but ultimately even racially subordinate groups would assimilate.

Gordon delineated, in *Assimilation in American Life* (1964), seven processes of group adaptation to the host society. Most important was his distinction between cultural and structural assimilation, showing how a group can change its cultural patterns but not yet mainstream into primary relationships in the cliques and associations of the society.

The Reassertion of Pluralism

Just as a series of social changes enabled the assimilationists to prevail over the pluralists, a new set of circumstances reversed the situation. The civil rights movement of the 1960s and the White ethnic revival of the 1970s were precipitating factors. However, a major element was the third wave of immigration that began after the 1965 immigration law removed national quota restrictions, opening the door to millions of Third World immigrants.

Pluralism had flourished earlier at a time of peak immigration to the United States and ebbed when immigration declined. With a new influx of culturally distinct immigrants, it has flowered again. Renamed multiculturalism, its advocacy of the preservation and appreciation of ethnic cultures and identities, as well as peaceful coexistence between groups, echo the sentiments of Kallen, Addams, Dewey, and other cultural pluralists.

This time, however, the movement includes people of color, not just White ethnics. Some arrive with a strong background that empowers them economically, allowing them to organize more effectively and assert themselves more so than past immigrants. Their ranks include educated, articulate spokespersons who can use television and computerized direct mailings to reach millions of people their predecessors could not.

Yet even though pluralism has been gaining new advocates, another influential sociological voice has reaffirmed assimilationist patterns. In *The Ethnic Myth* (1981), Stephen Steinberg argues that pluralism only appeals to groups who stand to benefit from maintaining ethnic boundaries.[11] Disadvantaged groups, he maintains, willingly compromise their ethnicity to gain economic security and social acceptance. Moreover, he claims, the United States is closer than ever before to welding a national identity out of its melange of ethnic groups.

The Multiculturalist Challenge

Nevertheless, with minority group assertiveness, massive Third World immigration, and bilingual/pluralist government policies, the change in popular usage from "cultural pluralism" to "multiculturalism" helped suggest to some that a new era for social consciousness of diversity had arrived. To others it signaled that the disuniting of America through "ethnic tribalism" was upon us. The battle was joined and still continues.

Multiculturalism is especially strong on college campuses, where the ranks of multiculturalists include many college professors whose advocacy in their teaching and publications have spread the doctrine far and wide to millions of others. They have challenged the once-prevailing idea of the United States as a melting pot, a concept many social scientists now regard as an idealized myth.

The Melting Pot

In an oft-quoted passage from *Letters from an American Farmer,* which was published in London in 1782, Michel Guillaume Jean de Crèvecoeur, an immigrant to the United States from France, defined an American and popularized the concept of America as a melting pot:

> What is an American? He is either a European, or the descendant of a European; hence that strange mixture of blood which you will find in no other country. I could point out to you a man whose grandfather was an Englishman, whose wife was Dutch, whose son married a French woman, and whose present four sons have now four wives of different nations. . . . Here individuals of all nations are melted into a new race of men, whose labors and posterity will one day cause great changes in the world.[12]

Overstating Ethnic Intermarriages

Even if Crèvecoeur actually knew of such an exogamous family and did not invent it to illustrate his idealized concept of a melting pot, he was not accurately portraying the reality of his times. This would have been an atypical family in the late eighteenth century, because most White ethnics then did not intermarry. Ingroup solidarity—based on nationality, clustering, geographic separatism, and most especially religion—mitigated against personal social interaction among the distinct groups, let alone intermarriage.

When Crèvecoeur spoke of English, Dutch, and French intermarriages, he was covering a considerable span of the eighteenth century and most likely including several religious faiths in a time when religious ecumenicism was unknown. Religious tolerance may have slowly evolved out of a period of bigotry, close-mindedness, and intolerance just a few generations before, but that hardly meant the ethnocentric barriers had vanished and amalgamation was flourishing.

No Racial Minorities

The greatest problem with Crèvecoeur's melting pot model is his omission of African and Native Americans.[13] Was this a reflection of his ethnocentrism or a deliberate choice to augment his concept? Surely he was aware of their presence in significant numbers throughout the colonies. Perhaps he thought they were not relevant to the destiny of a nation struggling to be born.

Such an attitude was shared by many. The framers of the Constitution, in Article I, Section 2, excluded "Indians" and counted each slave as three-fifths of a person to determine a state's representatives. In 1790, the First Congress passed the Naturalization Law, which limited citizenship only to free White aliens. Until passage of the Fourteenth Amendment in 1868, people of color born in the United States were not citizens.

Crèvecoeur's melting pot model was thus not accurate for several reasons. By restricting its application only to those with political power (the Whites), it excluded a sizable segment of the population (people of color). In doing so, it did not describe a society that had "melted." Moreover, even in its narrow focus on Whites, the model ignored the cultural diversity and social distance existing among the diverse White groups.

Emerson's Vision

Crèvecoeur influenced others who helped popularize the image of the United States as a melting pot. Ralph Waldo Emerson, for example, struck a similar theme in 1845:

> Well, as in the old burning of the Temple at Corinth, by the melting and intermixture of silver and gold and other metals, a new compound more precious than any, called Corinthian brass, was formed; so in this continent—asylum of all nations—the energy of Irish, Swedes, Poles, and Cossacks, and all the European tribes—of the Africans, and of the Polynesians, will construct a new race, a new religion, a new state, a new literature, which will be as vigorous as the new Europe which came out of the smelting-pot of the Dark Ages, or that which earlier emerged from Pelasgic and Etruscan barbarism.[14]

Emerson's private journal entry is interesting for several reasons. He "hated" the "narrowness" of nativist reactions against immigrants as "precisely the opposite of true wisdom." Significantly, he included people of color (but not Native Americans) in his vision of an amalgamated society, but it was a vision of the future, not a pretense about his times or of Crèvecoeur's time sixty-three years earlier. For Emerson, America as a melting or smelting pot was a tomorrow to come, not a reality that was.

Turner's Frontier

On the other hand, Frederick Jackson Turner saw the American frontier as the catalyst that had already fused the immigrants into a composite new national stock. His frontier thesis of 1893 followed the 1890 declaration of the Census Bureau that the "unsettled area has been so broken into . . . that there can hardly be said to be a frontier line."[15] Unlike Emerson's private musings known only to a few, Turner's update of Crèvecoeur's melting pot greatly influenced historical scholarship for more than forty years:

> Thus the Middle West was teaching the lesson of national cross-fertilization instead of national enmities, the possibility of a newer and richer civilization, not by preserving unmodified or isolated the old component elements, but by breaking down the line-fences, by merging the individual life in the common product—a new product, which held the promise of world brotherhood.[16]

The above quotation is taken from Turner's 1920 book, *The Frontier in American History*, in which he expands on his 1893 essay. He argues that because pioneers confronted many problems and harsh conditions, their adaptation necessitated innovative solutions that they shared with others. Out of this mutual assistance evolved a new and distinct culture, a blend of shared cultural contributions, but noticeably different from any of their source cultures.

Turner's argument popularized further the romanticized notion of a melting pot, but it also did not accurately reflect frontier reality any more than Crèvecoeur had depicted his times. The pioneers did adapt to their new environment but the culture remained Anglo American in form and content. Furthermore, in many areas of the Middle West Turner speaks about, culturally homogeneous settlements of Germans or Scandinavians often maintained distinct ethnic subcultures for generations.

Zangwill's White Fusion

Another voice raised in support of the melting pot was Israel Zangwill's 1908 play, appropriately called *The Melting Pot*. Some of its oft-quoted lines are these:

> Ah, what a stirring and a seething—Celt and Latin, Slav and Teuton, Greek and Syrian. America is God's Crucible, the Great Melting Pot where all the races of Europe are melting and reforming!

... Germans and Frenchmen, Irishmen and English, Jews and Russians, into the Crucible with you all! God is making the American!

... the Real American has not yet arrived. ... He will be the fusion of all races, perhaps the coming superman.[17]

The term *race* was once used more loosely to refer to either racial or ethnic groups. Although we cannot be certain that Zangwill meant only White ethnic groups when he spoke of the melting or fusion of all races, his speaking of the "races of Europe" and exclusion of any specific example of people of color suggest that is the case. His curious inclusion of Syrians as Europeans does not alter Zangwill's words echoing those of Crèvecoeur in describing the melting pot as a White ethnic phenomenon, thereby implying that an "American" is a White person.

Recent Studies on Intermarriage

The White ethnic intermarriage that Crèvecoeur prematurely asserted as evidence of his melting pot now appears to be a reality. Richard D. Alba (1991) reported only half as many third-generation Italians of unmixed ancestry born after 1949 had spouses of unmixed Italian ancestry compared to third-generation Italian males born before 1920.[18] Stanley Lieberson and Mary C. Waters (1988) found significant declines in endogamous marriages among virtually all White groups.[19]

Although such intermarriage patterns provide support for melting pot proponents, they do not necessarily indicate assimilation. As Lisa Neidert and Reynolds Farley (1985) reported, third-generation members of second-wave ethnic groups are not yet indistinguishable from the core English group, although they have been successful in their occupational achievements.[20] Furthermore, within-group marriages are still fairly common among people of unmixed ethnic ancestry.

When race and culture are similar, marital assimilation is more likely. Given the past patterns of eighteenth- and nineteenth-century White Americans, however, this process is likely to require about a six-generation period.

The Dillingham Flaw

The continuing debate between assimilationists and pluralists revolves around the issue of cultural homogeneity. Part of those polemics often contain what I shall identify and define as the *Dillingham Flaw,* an erroneous way of comparing people from one time period with people living in the present. As a consequence, one group usually suffers in the comparison and is judged negatively.

The Dillingham Commission

Senator William P. Dillingham of Vermont chaired the House-Senate Commission on Immigration, which conducted extensive hearings between 1907 and 1911. The Commission listened to the testimony of civic leaders, educators, social scientists, and social workers. Committee members even made on-site visits to Ellis Island and New York's lower eastside where hundreds of thousands of impoverished immigrants lived. After completing the investigation, the Commission issued a forty-one-volume report, part of which was based on social science research and statistics.

Unfortunately, the report was flawed in its application and interpretation of the data. It was more than the fact that the Commission members, however well intentioned they may have been, reflected the perceptions and biases of their times. The Dillingham Commission members committed several errors of judgment that led them to conclude that immigration from southern, central, and eastern Europe was detrimental to American society. Their conclusion led them to recommend the enactment of immigration restrictions.

The Commission first erred in using simplistic categories and unfair comparisons of the "old" and "new" immigrants, thus ignoring differences of technological evolution in their countries of origin. They also erred in overlooking the longer time interval that immigrants from northern and western Europe had in which to adjust, in addition to the changed structural conditions in America wrought by industrialization and urbanization.

Intelligence testing was another element used to draw contrasts. By 1908, Alfred Binet and Thomas Simon had developed the intelligence quotient (IQ) measurement scale. Using an alpha test (for those literate in English) and a beta test (for those illiterate or non-English speaking), the low scores of newly arriving southern, central, and eastern Europeans, in contrast to higher scores by native-born Black and White Americans, seemingly gave scientific evidence that mentally deficient ethnic groups were entering the United States.

Although many social scientists today recognize cultural biases affected those outcomes, controversy continues about whether intelligence measures reveal genetic or environmental differences. This "nature versus nurture" issue boiled over in the 1960s with the writings of Arthur Jensen and William Shockley and again in 1994 with the publication of *The Bell Curve* by Richard Herrnstein and Charles Murray. Each of these writers has argued genetic differences between Black and White Americans, a point fiercely contested by others.

Back in 1911, the test results were unquestioned and were just one more aspect to convince the Dillingham Commission members about the rightness of their views. The social conditions in 1911 help explain how such flawed conclusions were accepted so easily. President Theodore Roosevelt had called for the Commission to address the "immigrant problem," thereby creating a mindset about the situation in the first place. Both he and the Commission reflected the biases and perceptions of most native-born Americans witnessing the unprecedented influx of immigrants who were culturally and often physically different. The Commission's findings reinforced public opinion and were therefore readily accepted.

The Concept of the Dillingham Flaw

In our society, similar errors of thinking also influence people's perceptions of outgroup members. An outgroup is any group with which an individual does not identify or belong. In our discussion, we are referring to the foreign born as the outgroup to native-born Americans of different backgrounds.

Because some of today's negative judgments flow from the same faulty logic as that of the Dillingham Commission, I call this weakness the Dillingham Flaw. Here is a quick definition: the Dillingham Flaw is any inaccurate comparison based on simplistic categorizations and anachronistic observations. This occurs whenever we apply modern classifications or sensibilities to an earlier time when they either did not exist or, if they did, had a different form or meaning. To avoid the Dillingham Flaw, we must overcome the temptation to use modern perceptions to explain a past that its contemporaries viewed quite differently.

Examples of the Dillingham Flaw

One example of an inappropriate modern classification would be the word "British" to describe colonial Americans from the British Isles. Today, dictionaries define this word as referring collectively to the people of Great Britain, which includes the English, Welsh, Scots, and Scots-Irish. However, in the eighteenth century, "British" had the much narrower meaning of only the English, and for good reason. The English, Scots, and Scots-Irish may have been English-speaking, but significant cultural and religious differences existed among them. Moreover, the geographic segregation, social distance, and even hostility that existed between English Anglicans and Scots-Irish Presbyterians created a wide cultural gulf between them. They did not view each other as "similar."

Even among the English themselves, divergent religious beliefs created numerous subcultures whose shared sense of identity, social insulation, and endogamy resulted in limited outgroup social interaction. Ecumenicism, the tendency toward greater Christian unity that is occurring in our times, is a far cry from the antipathy among the Protestant sects and denominations of colonial America. Because religion was a far more meaningful component of everyday life in the eighteenth century and cause for outgroup prejudice and avoidance, its impact on intergroup relations must not be overlooked. It would therefore be a mistake to presume the English were a single, cohesive entity.

It is also misleading to speak broadly either of African slaves or Native Americans as single entities. In a period of White dominance and racial exploitation, ethnocentric generalizations such as these failed to pay heed to the fact that these groups consisted of diverse peoples with distinctive cultures. In the chapters to follow, we shall discuss how tribal diversity among Africans and Native Americans set these respective racially similar peoples apart from one another linguistically and culturally.

The Dillingham Flaw Chain Reaction

Once someone falls victim to the Dillingham Flaw, other misconceptions usually follow about one's own time. This is to be expected. Such victims falsely believe they understand their nation's past and so confidently assess their own world in what they presume is a wider context. Certain they have a knowledgeable and objective frame of reference, they tend to be highly critical of the present scene because they perceive it as different from the past.

However, because their observations and reactions are predicated on a reference point rendered inaccurate by the Dillingham Flaw, they will be more likely to reach incorrect conclusions. Like that old congressional commission, they will be susceptible to mistaken impressions about a "threat" posed by recent immigrants whose presence and behavior they view as different from past immigrants.

For instance, many people suggest that today's steadily increasing ranks of Asians, Hispanics, and Muslims present an unprecedented challenge to an integrative American society. The undercurrent of this thinking includes the continuing large numbers of new arrivals, their racial group membership and/or non-Judeo-Christian background, and their alleged nonassimilationist patterns.

Such concerns and fears echo those raised about earlier groups, such as the racist responses to the physical appearance of southern Europeans or the anti-Semitic reactions to East European Jews. Or consider the petition to Congress by nineteenth-century Germans in the Northwest Territory to create a German state with German as the official language; it easily matches the fear of some nativists that Florida may become "America's Quebec."

Understanding Today
by Knowing About Yesterday

Understanding the sociohistorical reality of the diversity of America's past allows for a more accurate comparison with today's multicultural society without falling victim to the Dillingham Flaw. In this way we can avoid that flaw and debunk the cultural homogeneity myth. It is essential to know truly what we were if we are to comprehend what we are and what we are becoming.

Today, telecommunications enable each of us to bear witness to our multicultural society, but our knowledge about our nation's past comes to us chiefly through the words of others whose ethnocentric perceptions often hide from us what truly was that reality. Although never before presented in this comprehensive form, enough data exist to peel away the layers of nationalist myth-building to expose the sociocultural actualities about our multicultural past.

What follows is not an exercise in revisionist thought, but a sociohistorical analysis of that past and of our present. It is to be hoped that this book will provide the perspective that diversity is America's strength, not its weakness.

2

Diversity in Aboriginal America

Multiculturalism flourished in the land for centuries before Europeans ever set foot on its soil. Although students in an anthropology course on Native Americans learn that fact quickly, most Americans are typically caught in the Dillingham Flaw when thinking about these diverse peoples. For many, the image of Native Americans is a stereotypical generalization of tipis, buffalo, warriors on horseback, war paint, feathers, moccasins, and either brutish savages depicted in countless westerns or romanticized noble primitives as recently depicted in *Dances with Wolves.*

Such a simplistic misconception is easy to understand. Those early explorers, missionaries, traders, soldiers, colonial officials, and settlers were untrained observers who generalized about the various tribes as if they were a single entity. Reflecting both ethnocentric judgments and racial prejudice, most Whites saw little value in learning about the cultural differences among the tribes. Their concerns rested primarily on conquest, expansion, profit, survival, and their own welfare. Whites tended to view "Indians" more as an obstacle to their own goals than as a people of equal importance worthy of understanding, not exploitation.

Most modern films have also offered simplistic portrayals, stamping in the average American mind a picture of the nomadic Plains Indians on horseback as representative of all tribes. However, the indigenous peoples have always been far more diversified than these simplistic portrayals.

To offer a detailed account of the many aspects of Native American diversity would require an entire book much larger than this one.[1] This

AUTHOR'S NOTE: Much of the material about Native American cultural attributes in this chapter is drawn from James A. Maxwell, ed., *America's Fascinating Indian Heritage* (Pleasantville, NY: Reader's Digest, 1978); Alvin M. Josephy Jr., *The Indian Heritage of America* (New York: Knopf, 1968); Harold E. Driver, *Indians of North America,* 2d ed. (Chicago: University of Chicago Press, 1969).

chapter, then, is only a brief overview to provide the reader with at least some sense of the multiculturalism present in precolonial America.

Language

Before European colonization, somewhere between two to possibly ten million aboriginals, divided into about two hundred or more distinct societies, spoke approximately two hundred languages unintelligible to each other, along with hundreds of dialects. These languages were so incomprehensible among the tribes because of the many variances in phonetics, speech sounds, and grammatical structure.

In their expedition to chart the northern section of the Louisiana Territory (1804-1806), Capt. Meriwether Lewis and Lt. William Clark repeatedly commented in their journals about the phonetic differences among the languages of the various Native American peoples they met. As the explorers traveled from tribe to tribe across the North American continent, they observed how some of the tongues sounded harsh and guttural, but others sounded liquid and melodious.[2]

The Interdependence of Language and Culture

The significance of these many Native American languages is the mutual interdependence of language and culture. Although a culture's language expresses how that society perceives and understands the world, the language itself influences that society's perceptions and understandings. This concept was effectively argued two generations ago by Edward Sapir and Benjamin Whorf, pioneers in American linguistics. They contended that human beings live in a social reality that is at the mercy of their language. The so-called real world is, to a large extent, subconsciously built from the group's language habits. Because no two languages are ever sufficiently similar to represent the same social reality, they reasoned, the worlds in which different societies live are distinct worlds and not merely the same world with different labels attached.

For example, in 1929 Sapir explained that the Hopi in the Southwest use verbs that have no tense—no past, present, or future.[3] Instead, their verbs differ depending on such factors as the relative length of time an event lasts, its completion or expected occurrence, and its regularity or predictability of occurrence. The Hopi focus on the recurring cycles of life, rather than viewing their reality as a segmented series of events locked into a time frame.

Another example would be the Yana of California who have both masculine and feminine forms of most words, the former used only in all-male conversations and the latter in male-female or all-female conversations. The language of another tribe, the Navajo, does not distinguish among such third-person pronouns as *his, her, its,* or *their,* and instead uses a compound word of adjectives and nouns such as "one-wife-of-one-man" to indicate "his wife."

Without getting too involved in linguistic details, these examples are just small indicators of the significant differences in grammatical structures among the Native American languages. The many languages of the indigenous people are not a single entity with two hundred minor variations. Their differences are far too complex and reflect the different worlds of the many diverse tribes.

Major Language and Culture Areas

Despite the complexities and distinctions among Native American languages, they can nonetheless be classified according to their broad resemblances to one another. When similarities exist, it is usually among tribes clustered in adjacent areas. Linguists have classified North American Indian languages into nine genetic categories (phylum), within which there are 42 language group families containing 190 languages. Also, 31 language isolates are not part of any language group family, which brings the total number of different North American native languages to 221.

There is a fairly close, though not exact, match between the major language areas and the culture areas. For the latter, anthropologists commonly identify the North American regions as the Arctic, Subarctic, Northwest Coast, California, Plateau, Great Basin, Southwest, Plains, Southeast, and Eastern Woodland (see Figure 2.1). The anthropological definition of culture refers to the entire way of life of a people. Delineation of these culture areas, then, marks the geographic area where the diverse peoples within it share a significant degree of cultural similarity with each other but a significant degree of dissimilarity with the cultures of the peoples outside that area.

Language and Diversity

The prevalence of two hundred distinct languages is one dimension of the multicultural reality of pre-Columbian America. Just as we view

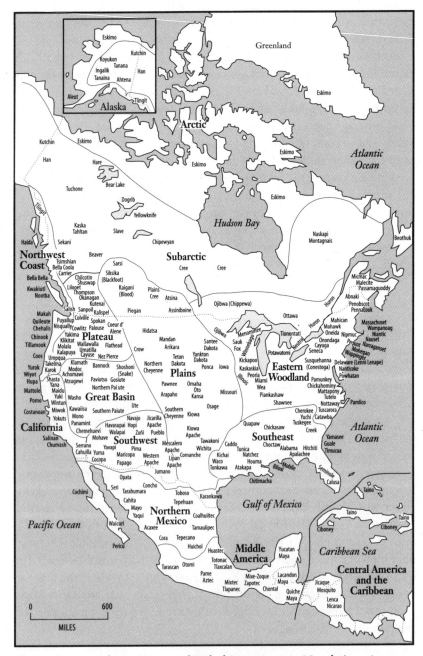

Figure 2.1.   *Culture Areas and Tribal Locations in North America*
Source: Alvin M. Josephy Jr., *The Indian Heritage of America* (New York: Knopf, 1968).

White ethnic groups speaking different languages as distinct from one another, so too must we look upon the many Native American tribes as diverse entities. Speaking in different tongues, they constituted a mosaic of separate worlds each aware of neighboring tribes but nonetheless dissimilar in language.

We begin to overcome any simplistic Dillingham Flaw judgments by recognizing further that the interdependent relationship of language with culture results in a social reality for tribal members that sets them culturally apart from another tribe that is linguistically different. Although it may take a skilled linguist to understand the diversity among these two-hundred-plus languages, social observers can distinguish other cultural attributes more easily, as we shall now discuss.

Kinship, Lineage, and Gender Roles

Native Americans established primary relationships either through a clan system (descent from a common ancestor) or through a friendship system, much like tribal societies in other parts of the world. These relationships were the basic building blocks of Native American society, from nuclear families up to vast empires.[4]

Most of the Great Lakes tribes were divided into two groups, or moieties, with one moiety composed of clans named after birds and the other after land and water animals. Most of the tribes approved and even encouraged marriage between cross-cousins: a girl might marry the son of her father's (but not her mother's) sister, and a boy, the daughter of his mother's brother. But all marriages had to be with members of the opposite moiety.

Matrilineal Societies

In matrilineal and matrilocal societies, women had considerable power because property (housing, land, and tools) belonged to them. Because property usually passed from mother to daughter, and the husband joined his wife's family, he was more of a stranger and yielded authority to his wife's eldest brother. As a result, the husband was unlikely to become an authoritative, domineering figure. Moreover, among such peoples as the Cherokee, Iroquois, Pueblo, and Navajo, a disgruntled wife, secure in her possessions, could simply divorce her husband by tossing his belongings out of their residence.

Women's role in tribal governance was often influential in matrilineal societies, as among the Iroquois, in which the principal civil and religious offices were kept within maternal lineages. The tribal matriarch or a group of tribal matrons nominated each delegate, briefed him before each session, monitored his legislative record, and removed him from office if his conduct displeased the women. Despite the feminine checks and balances, the actual business of government was a masculine affair.

Division of Labor

In the Northeastern Woodlands and on the Plains, where hunting and warfare demanded strenuous activity away from home, the men often returned exhausted and required a few days to recover. Wearied by both these arduous actions and the religious fasting that usually accompanied them, the men relaxed in the village while the women went about their many tasks. Seeing only female busyness in these native encampments, White observers misinterpreted what they saw and wrote inaccurate stereotypical portrayals of lazy braves and industrious squaws. Such was not the case.

In the Southeast and Southwest, men and women performed their daily labors with observable equality because the men did not go out on grueling expeditions as did the men in the Northeast and Plains. In California, the Great Basin, and Northwest Coast, the sexual division of labor fell somewhere between these two variations.

Women had certain common tasks in each of the U.S. culture areas: cleaning and maintaining the living quarters, tending to children, gathering edible plants, pounding corn into meal, extracting oil from acorns and nuts, cooking, sewing, packing, and unpacking. Certain crafts were also usually their responsibility: brewing dyes, making pottery, and weaving such items as cloth, baskets, and mats. In the Southwest, however, men sometimes made baskets and pottery, and even weaved cloth.

In regions where hunting provided the main food supply, the women were also responsible for house building, processing carcasses of game, preparing hides or furs, and whatever food gathering or farming that could be done. In the mostly agricultural societies in the Eastern Woodlands, the women primarily worked in the fields and the men built the frame houses and both shared duties for preparing hides or furs. Similarly, in the fishing communities of the Northwest, the men built the plank houses and helped with the processing of animal skins. In California and in the Great Basin, most aspects of labor, except the defined female tasks of weaving and basket and pottery making, were shared fairly evenly. In the Southwest, the men did most of the field work, house building, weaving, cloth manufacturing, and animal skin processing.

Status and Influence

Female prestige among the Iroquois grew greater after the Revolutionary War, and male prestige ebbed due to continual losses and defeats and the inability to do much hunting due to scarcity of game. By the nineteenth century, mothers played a greater role in approving marriage partners for their children and more consistently got custody of their children in a divorce, unlike the uncertainty of custody in earlier times.

Among many Southeast tribes the women were influential in tribal councils, and in some places they cast the deciding vote for war or peace. The Cherokee designated a female as "Beloved Woman," through whom they believed the Great Spirit spoke. Consequently, her words were always heard but not necessarily heeded. However, she headed the influential Woman's Council (made up of a representative from each clan), sat as a voting member of the Council of Chiefs, and exercised considerable influence. She also unhesitantly used her absolute authority over prisoners. When she died, a successor would be chosen.

The Cheyenne held women in particularly high regard. They played an influential role in determining warfare and sometimes even fought alongside the men. A woman's display of grief over a slain son was a very effective arousal for a punitive expedition. Upon a war party's successful return, the women danced about while waving the scalps, exhibited their men's shields and weapons, and derived honors from their husbands' deeds.

Status, Role, and Diversity

The statuses and roles for men and women varied considerably among Native Americans, depending on each tribe's cultural orientations. Property possession, inheritance, power, and influence rested on whether a tribe's structure was matrilineal or patrilineal. Although a few universal female-designated work tasks existed (cleaning, nurturing, edible plant gathering, food preparation, cooking, packing, and unpacking), others varied by region, means of food production, and social organization. Such variances in gender roles further exemplify the diversity that existed among Native Americans.

Clothing and
Bodily Adornment

If one knew nothing else about them, the varying physical appearances of indigenous peoples before European influence proclaimed their diversity. The apparel worn, in large measure, depended on geographical environment and the materials available from which to make them. Although all tribes fashioned clothing from hides and fur, these were less available to those tribes primarily dependent on agricultural or seafood products, so they tended to make more clothing from plant materials, unlike the tribes who mainly hunted. Yet even among tribes using similar materials, a wide variety of styles could be found.

Generally speaking, the men plucked their facial and body hair, typically using shells as tweezers. Both women and men wore necklaces and earrings made of shells, claws, teeth, beads, or precious stones. Otherwise, great variance in clothing and bodily adornment could be found.

Northwestern Native Americans

Because cedar trees abound along the Pacific Northwest coast, tribes there twisted strips of inner bark into string and then wove them into clothing. In summer, the men usually went naked but sometimes wore tunics; in winter and on ceremonial occasions they wore knee-length robes, made either of animal skins (especially otter) or woven plant fibers. If traveling to the interior, they wore leggings and moccasins.

Women were always clothed, usually with a plant fiber skirt and a woven robe over both shoulders covering the upper body. Frequent rainy weather occasioned the wearing of conical hats of woven plant fibers and waterproof ponchos of the same material. Both men and women wore tattooed family crests and other designs on their face, chest, back of arms, or front of legs. On festive occasions both sexes applied red, white, and black paints to their bodies.

Southwestern Native Americans

The Pueblo of Arizona and New Mexico and their Anasazi ancestors were unique in wearing mostly cotton garments. Women's dresses were rectangular cloths worn under the left arm and tied above the right shoulder, the open right side of the dress kept fastened by a belt of the same material. Buckskin leggings were wrapped around the lower legs and the tops of buckskin moccasins, which had buffalo hide soles.

Men wore a cotton loincloth, its ends held in place by a belt. Over this they wore a kilt that came to midthigh, set off by a sash of braided cotton cords around the top of the kilt and hanging down one side. Sometimes they wore shirts tied at the sides, with flaps for sleeves. Moccasins also had the stiff buffalo hide for soles sewn to buckskin that covered the ankle or else went halfway to the knee. Cold weather prompted the wearing of woven rabbit fur blankets or a cape of feathers fastened to a netted base. Interestingly, men wore more jewelry than women. Both sexes styled their hair the same: bangs just above the eyes, below the ears on the sides, and full length in back.

Northern Plains Native Americans

As in most other areas, the women of the Northern Plains wore more clothing than the men. Their dresses, midcalf in length and fringed at the bottom, were made of two deer or elk hides sewn together. Below-knee leggings and moccasins completed their outfit. The men often wore only moccasins and a breechcloth, adding leggings tied to a belt when they traveled.

A buckskin shirt with sleeve flaps was worn only on special occasions or in cold weather, as was a buffalo robe. Women sometimes wore such robes also, and it could be pulled over the head in bitter weather. Otherwise, a fur cap might have been worn.

Plains natives often made their clothing more elaborate by ornamenting the material with quills and/or beads. They seldom tattooed their bodies. They wore their hair in two braids hanging in front, and the men typically wore one or more feathers in their hair, depending on tribal custom.

Southeastern Native Americans

In the Southeast, men and women only covered the upper part of their bodies in cold weather or on special occasions, at which time they wore robes made of animal hide or of feathers thatched on a netted base. Otherwise the men wore a buckskin breechcloth and the women a wraparound skirt from the waist to the knees. These skirts could be made of buckskin or woven from such materials as grass, inner bark, or bison hair. When traveling, the men wore moccasins and full-length leggings fastened at the belt; women seldom wore moccasins and only half-length leggings, fastened with a garter just below the knee.

Both men and women had tattoos of elaborate design on their face, trunk, arms, and legs. Women grew their hair full length, sometimes wearing

it upswept and other times parted and braided. Men grew a scalp lock
from the crown of their heads, the remainder of the scalp either
completely shaved or else partially shaved except for a crewcut-style
border running from front to back around the scalp lock.[5]

Northeastern Native Americans

Native Americans living in the Northeast Woodlands wore little clothing
in the summer. Children were usually naked; the men wore only deerskin breechcloths and the women knee-length skirts and wampum head-
bands. In southern New England, both men and women might have
worn light capes or shawls of woven textiles. Colder weather throughout the Northeast required robes of fur or woven downy, waterproof
turkey feathers, and leather leggings and moccasins made of moose- or
deerskin.

Boys kept their hair short until they turned sixteen, but girls and
women had full-length hair. Hairstyles, some very elaborate and deco-
rated with porcupine quills, varied from tribe to tribe. Males from the
Lenni Lenape and several Algonquian tribes plucked their hair with mussel
shell tweezers, leaving only a central cock's crest, but other tribes did
not follow this practice. Among all Northeast tribes, ornamental jewelry
included necklaces of beads or pearls with copper tubing, jeweled earrings,
bracelets, pendants, and belts of brightly colored or shining stones,
shells, and beads.[6]

Clothing and bodily adornment, varying so greatly both among and
within the ten culture areas were cultural attributes that attested to Native
American diversity. As the tribes made cultural contact with one another,
style fashions spread from one to the other. European contact also brought
changes in materials and styles as the gun and trade goods brought in
more furs, hides, and needles to sew better garments, often in imitation
of European full-length sleeves and trouser legs.[7] When game became
scarce, the cloth and clothing of the Whites became more common
among Native Americans.

Housing

Climate, terrain, and available building materials all influence housing
construction, of course, but so too does the culture of a people. And
because extensive cultural diversity existed among the Native Americans, their housing styles varied significantly.

John White's exquisite sixteenth-century watercolor of a typical Algonquian village of the Secotan tribe in North Carolina depicts the complexity of a permanent Native American settlement: along a thoroughfare stand a series of barrel-roofed, multifamily houses made of arched saplings covered with bark and woven mats that are easily removable to let in light. Nearby are newly planted and ripening corn fields, an open ceremonial center with a circle of elaborately carved posts, a place of solemn prayer, and a tomb for departed chiefs.

Large Communal Structures

Although all tribes lived within a tribal enclave, some did so within larger communal structures. Perhaps the greatest of these was in Chaco Canyon, New Mexico. There the ruins of the Pueblo Bonito reveal a gigantic, crescent-shaped, single-structure housing project covering more than three acres. The entire complex rose to a height of four or five stories around its outer rim and was enclosed along the front by a long wall. In the central plaza, around which the Pueblo Bonito built arches, were two great kivas—enormous subterranean ceremonial chambers, each able to accommodate hundreds of people for the sacred rites performed there.

This edifice housed one thousand people and thrived for four hundred years until a sustained drought ended its existence in the late thirteenth century. At its peak, this monolithic dwelling place contained 660 rooms, the adjoining units interconnected by doorways and built on a series of graduated terraces that served as streets. Built of stone set in mud mortar, the ceilings were supported by wooden beams and made of sticks, grass, and several inches of mud.

In upper New York state the five nations of the Iroquois Confederation—the Cayuga, Mohawk, Oneida, Onondaga, and Seneca (later a sixth nation, the remnants of the Tuscarora were admitted in 1722)—lived in rectangular-shaped longhouses, ranging in size from 50 to 150 feet in length and 18 to 25 feet in width, depending on the number of families living inside. Average size was 60 by 18 feet, with an 18-foot, barrel-shaped roof. Seasoned elm bark was sewn in overlapping layers, like shingles, over a framework of elm wood poles lashed together. Smaller versions of this house type existed throughout the East.

Within the Iroquois longhouse, on both sides of a central corridor 6 to 10 feet wide, numerous families from a single matrilineal clan each occupied a booth about 6 feet wide and 6 to 12 feet long. The booths were on platforms about 18 inches high, piled with furs for sleeping warmth.

On the exterior wall and rafters hung dried fruits and vegetables, roots, and tobacco. Another platform about 7 feet above was a storage area for weapons, pots, kettles, and other possessions. About every 12 feet down the main corridor a fire burned, its smoke escaping through an open smoke hole directly above, which was partially or completely closed with a sliding panel when there was heavy rain or snow, thereby filling the longhouse with smoke.

A similar multifamily concept can be found in the rectangular plank houses in the Pacific Northwest. Built of wide planks, including the floor, they measured anywhere from 30 by 45 feet to 50 by 60 feet. Roofs were two-pitched with a gable end facing the sea. Inside families each had their own allocated sleeping quarters that, like those of the Iroquois, had drop screens for privacy. These areas were either on platforms or the center of the house was excavated to achieve the same effect. Fire smoke went out of an opening in the roof with a sliding panel that was closed during inclement weather. Outside the house, a totem pole—native only to the Northwest peoples—bearing accumulated family crests and honors indicated a clan's history and rank.

The Pueblo peoples lived in rectangular, flat-roofed rooms directly adjoining one another in multistoried complexes that are comparable to modern low-rise apartment buildings. The Hopi and Navajo lived in mud and stone dwellings with heavy wooden roof beams, the scarcity of wood in the Southwest prompting them to salvage beams from old housing for any new construction. The Mojave-type multifamily structure of the Colorado River Yumans was almost square shaped, its side dimensions about 20 or 25 feet, and covered outside on three sides by sand. The dwelling had a low, four-pitched roof without a smoke hole, requiring the fire to be placed near the door.

Single-Family Dwellings

Elsewhere throughout America most housing units held single families, although adjacent extended family clusters within the tribal village were common. Southeast tribes lived in small houses almost square shaped, the mud-plastered-over-wooden-pole walls about 15 feet long on each side, covered by a 6-foot high, two-pitched thatched roof. In contrast, the Seminole in Florida lived in an open-sided, thatched-roof *chickee*.

The Lenni Lenape mostly lived in round, domed bark wigwams, but the same style of housing among the tribes around the western Great Lakes was made of other materials. The Menominee typically covered theirs with mats of reeds and cattails, but other tribes used pieces of bark and hide in addition to woven or sewn mats. Nearby, the Kickapoo lived in picturesque reed-woven lodges.

Among the nomadic tribes of the Plains in pursuit of food, their portable housing was a well-constructed conical tipi made of long wooden poles covered with tailored buffalo hides. It was often 10 to 12 feet high and 12 to 15 feet in diameter. As in most Native American structures, the fire was in the center and the beds around the sides. In the Southwest, the Apache resided in a *wickiup,* a small, domed hut made of slender poles, brush, and grass that stood about 6 feet high. In the same region, the impoverished Ute lived in primitive lean-tos.

These differences in housing style were much more than architectural variations. They were another cultural "mark" that reflected the diversity among the tribes. Their differing value orientations about family life, communal living, social hierarchy, and tribal welfare influenced their housing designs.

Social Organization

Most Native American tribes maintained a more democratic structure than found among the indigenous peoples in Africa and Oceania. In America, they usually had a tribal structure of equal clans, although some societies were organized into small bands. These bands could be either a loosely organized number of extended families with no central tribal government, such as the Apache, or they could be like the Plains natives who remained in separate groups most of the year but came together as a composite tribe for the annual summer encampment. In doing so, they paralleled the bison—their primary subsistence and cultural base—that merged from small herds into a large mass during the rutting season. At this time, the Plains natives united for a communal hunt, tribal ceremonies, and a renewal of their tribal identity.

Social Status Variations

Among the tribes in the Great Basin culture area (Nevada, Utah, parts of California, Oregon, Idaho, Wyoming, and Colorado), differences in social class, status, and rank—other than those based on age and sex—were minimal. This arid region—home to the Paiute, Shoshoni, and Ute—offered only a meager, harsh livelihood to the sparse native population. Leadership was not hereditary; it rested in the most competent man until he proved otherwise in his skills and judgment and was then replaced by someone better.

Most other indigenous peoples had some ranking system to determine social standing, usually determined by an office held, wealth, or war deeds. After the introduction of the horse and trade with the Whites, Plains culture changed. Accumulation of wealth—such as medicine bundles, horses, guns, and kitchenware—became important, and a class structure based on wealth arose out of previously egalitarian societies.

Northwestern Slavery

A notable exception to democratic structure was the peoples of the Northwest Coast, where two distinct social classes—freemen and slaves—existed. Slaves were usually obtained as prisoners in raids and could thereafter be bought or sold in an institutionalized slave trade. Slaves normally could marry one another, but their children then typically became slaves also. Captive slaves could be ransomed by relatives, but the stigma of a slave status was so great that some refused to do so.

Slaves could be freed on such occasions as the death of the slave's owner, or when the owner's child had ears pierced for earrings, or at a potlatch to demonstrate the owner's wealth in giving up such property. However, "freed" often meant killing slaves at these occasions and was in fact mandatory for foundation sacrifices upon building a new home. At this time, the slaves' bodies were thrown into the holes dug by the front door to hold the carved totems.

Slaves performed only menial tasks and served primarily as prestige items, offering visible evidence of their owners' wealth and high rank. Rather than having a social class order among the freemen, a precise rank order existed, with every man ranked from highest to lowest; no two persons ranked evenly. Birth order, inheritance, or accident determined these rankings and opportunities for social mobility were rare.

Southeastern Caste Systems

Quite possibly a caste system existed among the Chitimacha in Louisiana where endogamous marriages maintained a dichotomy between nobles and commoners. However, the most stratified social order was found among the Natchez people of Mississippi, headed by a chief known as the Great Sun, who claimed descent from the sun. Natchez society consisted of three levels of nobility: Suns, Nobles, and Honored People, and a single group of commoners called Stinkards. The Great Sun held unlimited power over his subjects but a council of elders limited his authority on matters of general concern to the entire society. Curiously, the three upper ranks could only marry Stinkards, although the latter group could also marry within their own social group. The potential depletion of the Stinkards through their upward mobility marriages was offset through replenishment by peoples from nearby conquered tribes.

Both the Chitimacha and Natchez are thought to be remnants of the Mississippian Culture that peaked from about A.D. 1200 to 1500. From Ohio to Louisiana, from Arkansas to Tennessee, these mound builders constructed pyramidal or conical mounds as foundations for temples or chiefs' houses. These earthworks, still standing today, were built by tens of thousands of people who, without benefit of wheeled vehicles or beasts of burden, carried all the dirt in baskets to the sites. Most impressive is Monk's Mound at Cahokia, Illinois, across the Mississippi River from St. Louis. It is a massive earthwork 1,000 feet long, 700 feet wide, 100 feet high, upon which stood either a temple or the residence of Cahokia's ruler.

Iroquois Consensus Building

Much has been written about the Iroquois confederacy, or the League of the Five Nations.[8] This alliance—apparently formed to end warfare among the Cayuga, Mohawk, Oneida, Onondaga, and Seneca—permitted each tribe to govern itself, with larger issues such as relations with other tribes decided at the annual meeting of the Great Council. At this meeting, the forty-nine councilors, with apportioned representation from the five tribes, only acted after unanimous agreement was reached on an issue.

Oratorical skills were important in persuading other members and resulted in some historians identifying this primitive democracy form as a prototype for such provisions of the United States Constitution as reconciliation of differing House-Senate legislation, impeachment, and expansion of new partners. Just as the Iroquois admitted the Tuscarora in 1722 as a Sixth Nation, so did the new U.S. government admit new states.

This Iroquois model of a collective political institution resembled the form of authority within almost all North American tribes. The chief held an honorary status and he primarily played ceremonial and religious roles. Real authority rested not in an individual but in a group, the tribal council.

Diversity in Social Organization

In this section we have discussed social structures that ranged from the southeastern caste system and northwestern slave system to mostly democratic structures elsewhere. Leadership could be hereditary or not, and social class could be nonexistent (Great Basin) or significant (Plains). There could be loose bands with no central tribal government (Apache), tribes who merged once a year (Sioux), or a formal confederacy (Iroquois). The plurality of tribal organizations offers yet another instance of Native American diversity and further ammunition against the Dillingham Flaw of simplistic categorizations of the past based on present-day sensibilities.

Values

Earlier, I mentioned how Plains culture changed to view accumulated wealth as a mark of social status. Among all tribes throughout the land, however, value orientations about wealth varied. The Hupa, Karok, and Yurok of northern California were obsessed by personal wealth; it was to be accumulated, ostentatiously displayed, guarded, and bestowed intact to one's children. In contrast, the people of the Northwest Coast accumulated quality possessions only to have enough to give away at a potlatch. They did so to gain honor among their people, humiliate enemies, or legitimize hereditary claims. In contrast, the Shoshoni measured wealth by the kin whose aid one could depend on, and the Zuni considered wealth as determined by the time and resources one had to participate in religious ceremonies and host the ceremonial dancers.

Religion

Religious beliefs permeated every aspect of Native American life in thought, word, and deed but, once again, differences existed among the tribes. Their religiosity ranged from the simple social organization of the Iroquois, who believed in the Great Spirit as a supreme being, to the complexity of interrelated religious groupings among the Zuni, who were possibly the most religious indigenous people on the continent. The Pueblo acknowledged numerous spiritual entities as equally ranked gods, and the peoples of the Plateau and Great Basin culture areas also believed in large numbers of spirits.

Full-time priests existed within the Mississippian Culture and the derivative cultures such as the Natchez, but part-time priests who also earned their livelihood in some economic activity functioned among the Pueblo.

Only shamans operated in the Plateau and Great Basin regions, but religious leaders in most of the East and Southwest, on the Plains, in California, and on the Northwest Coast displayed attributes of both priests and shamans. For example, Northwest Coast shamans typically came from certain families specializing in shamanism, virtually creating a permanent priesthood. They performed ceremonial rites that also had strong social functions, unlike the Sanpoil in the Plateau area of eastern Washington. The Sanpoil had no standardized rituals and drew their shamans—who held little distinction from others—from anyone in the tribe whose vision quests resulted in unusual good fortune.

Humans and Nature

Perhaps the most important aspect of Native American culture was the absolutely ubiquitous idea that humans were "embedded" in nature. This concept was very different from the Europeans' view of nature as something meant to serve them. These contrasting values would generate controversies with Whites virtually from first contact to the present.

Beyond the Horizon

As culturally distinct as the hundreds of tribes were from one another, the arrival of Whites would have a single effect on all of them: catastrophe. All the tribes would find their self-reliant way of life changed forever by disease, conquest, and loss of their ancestral lands.

Far more deadly than all warfare would be the European diseases, against which the Native Americans had no immunity because they had been isolated from that continent's sicknesses for thousands of years. Carried by European explorers, fishermen, and fur traders, these diseases would spread like wildfire among the indigenous tribes. Smallpox, measles, typhus, tuberculosis, chicken pox, influenza, cholera, and diphtheria would weaken and kill them by the thousands, wiping out whole villages, even decimating entire tribes.

Tribal disintegration would further result from other causes. In return for axes, blankets, cloth, kettles, knives, and rum, many tribes would deplete their environment of beaver and deer to meet European demand for their hides or else raid neighboring communities to procure slaves for local colonists or slave traders. Westward expansion would lead to

continual land thefts, warfare, further decimation, subjugation, segregation on reservations, and dependency.

The rich, vibrant multiculturalism that predated European contact
would yield to this relentless onslaught of settlement and expansion.
Any violent resistance would reaffirm the European and Euro-American
stereotype of Native Americans as "cruel, bloodthirsty savages." They
would lose their lands and independence and become a colonized, exploited people.

Although their conquerors would continue to view them as a single
entity, the Native Americans never were that. Some tribes would internalize
others' views of themselves and try to act "White." Other tribes would
attempt to negotiate a path of marginality, taking what they considered
to be the best of both worlds. Many others would struggle, as best they
could, to preserve both their culture and identity.

3

Diversity in Colonial Times

What most of us remember about our early national history is information about the thirteen English colonies that fought for their independence from the "Mother Country" of England. Because the English achieved cultural and political preeminence in the colonial and early national periods, a myth of cultural homogeneity about those times gradually came into being. The myth was furthered by the actions and/or writings of preeminent English American leaders, historians, and literary figures of those times, whose dominance and influence cast a long shadow across subsequent generations.

Pervading all colonists' lives were cultural norms that reflected the patriarchal values of Europe and, once the colonies were brought under English control, those cultural norms were embedded in English law. As in England, for example, when a White colonist woman married, her personal property—money, land, household goods, clothing—was automatically transferred to her husband. If he died, the property went to the children, not to her, with male heirs receiving larger inheritances than their sisters. Even their children could become the wards of the father's male relatives and not of his widow. In the rare instance of a divorce, the father indisputably retained custody of the children.

As to the composition of the colonial population under English rule, the presence of non-English colonial Americans at first was not a significant factor. In commenting about the population composition of the seventeenth century, historian Mildred Campbell remarks,

For despite the Dutch on the Hudson, and small groups of Swiss, Swedes, Finns, and French Huguenots pocketed along the coast, the small vessels which set out on the American voyage were chiefly English built and English manned. Their cargoes, moreover, consisted largely of Englishmen and, later and in smaller numbers, Englishwomen. Even the Scots and Irish, who in the next

century would crowd the harbors of the New World, were a minority in the first century.[1]

By the early eighteenth century, however, an important change in immigration dramatically altered the population mix. As Stephen Steinberg
observes,

> The simple truth is that [the] English were not coming in sufficient
> numbers to populate the colonies. . . . If there were no compelling
> "pull" factors luring Englishmen to America, neither were there
> potent "push" factors. In fact, after 1718 labor shortages at home
> induced the British government to place restrictions on emigration,
> especially of skilled artisans and other laborers needed in Britain's
> nascent industries. It was this scarcity of emigrants from Britain
> that induced colonial authorities to permit the immigration of
> non-English nationalities.[2]

Historians Bruce Catton and William B. Catton describe the new
colonial immigration as continually increasing:

> Homogeneity was altered in a different way by the increasing infu-
> sion of non-English elements into the colonial bloodstream. This
> did not become noticeable until late in the seventeenth century and
> assumed its largest proportions in the eighteenth, when the sea-
> board colonies entered upon their great period of sustained
> growth. Of greatest significance was the large-scale influx of men
> and women of African descent. Next in importance were those
> from the Rhine Valley and the north of Ireland. (p. 165)[3]

The Cattons also provide some insight into differences among the
so-called British immigrants, a theme I introduced in Chapter 1 with
reference to the Dillingham Flaw and to be further elaborated on later
in this chapter:

> The Scotch-Irish added something special to the colonial brew. They
> tended to be hard cases, politically-unyielding Presbyterians,
> schooled and scarred by generations of turmoil in Ireland, caught in
> the middle between oppressed Irish Catholics and the Anglican
> establishment, hated from both sides, returning the hatred at
> compound interest. (p. 166)

One of their other observations relates to the social distance the ethnic groups deliberately set between themselves:

> These people did not all want the same things, beyond the elemental notions of escape and a fresh start. If, for a determined handful, this meant social engineering and creating communities, for untold larger numbers it meant simply a vague but compelling desire to go where they could be left alone. "Get off my back" is a piece of twentieth-century slang, distinctively American, which well summarized the prime motivation and prevailing mood among immigrants to Britain's mainland colonies. (p. 168)

Some social scientists, although admitting the continued presence of cultural pluralism up to the Revolutionary War, suggest it was minimal and that assimilation was virtually complete even among non-English-speaking ethnic groups. Lawrence Fuchs, for example, asserts,

> By the time of the Revolution, most of the children and grandchildren of Dutch, French, German, and Swedish immigrants in the colonies spoke English and were otherwise indistinguishable from the children and grandchildren of English settlers, although in Albany, where the Dutch predominated, it was difficult to assemble an English-speaking jury, and several counties in Pennsylvania were overwhelmingly German-speaking. Hostility toward speakers of Dutch and German and toward the English-speaking Scotch-Irish, the newest large immigrant group, was widespread. . . .[4]

Fuchs's claim of indistinguishable characteristics among these four groups is questionable for reasons beyond his own inclusion of contradictory examples illustrating both cultural pluralism and intergroup tensions. Many Dutch, French, and Germans—as will be detailed shortly—continued to live in social, sometimes even geographic isolation within culturally distinct ethnic communities apart from the English American society.

Moreover, Fuchs cites the source of his Dutch and German "exceptions" as *To Seek America* (1977) by Maxine Sellers. Yet in the very chapter Fuchs draws from, Sellers argues that although by the outbreak of the Revolution

> the Swedes . . . had become indistinguishable in language and life style from the dominant English . . . others—including some Jews,

some French Huguenots, many Dutch, and many more Germans—
had not.[5]

This minimization of ethnic diversity that overstresses English American cultural and political hegemony is an example of the Dillingham
Flaw. It is also manifested by claims that English numerical superiority
shows cultural homogeneity. Stephen Steinberg, for example, presets this
view by stating, "Three-fourths of the white population in 1790 had
their origins in the English-speaking states of the British Isles" (p. 8).
(This statement ignores the different cultures, religions, and Gaelic and
Scotch languages.) Then, after saying the other immigrants were mostly
from northern or western Europe with "important cultural affinities to
the English majority" (a claim many Scandinavians, Germans, and French
might question), he adds,

> At its inception, the United States had a population that was re-
> markably homogeneous in terms of both ethnicity and religion
> [Protestant]. Devoid of its invidious implications, the claim that
> the nation was founded by white Anglo-Saxon Protestants is rea-
> sonably accurate.
>   To be sure, there was some ethnic differentiation in terms of
> both population and patterns of settlement. New York still re-
> flected its Dutch origins, and had a far greater ethnic mix than did
> New England. Pennsylvania had sizable concentrations of Germans
> and Scotch-Irish, and the Southern states, which a century later
> would become the last bastion of "ethnic purity," were characterized
> by a high degree of ethnic heterogeneity, at least in comparison
> to New England. But it would be a mistake to construe this as
> evidence of a rudimentary pluralism, at least in a political sense.
> Not only were the English predominant numerically, but they en-
> joyed a political and cultural hegemony over the life of the fledgling
> nation. Non-English colonials were typically regarded as aliens
> who were obliged to adapt to English rule in terms of both poli-
> tics and culture.[6]

The 1790 statistics that Steinberg cites require further elaboration,
which will come shortly, but he is correct in saying that political pluralism
did not exist. However, cultural pluralism did exist in a very real sense.
Non-English colonials, often clustered in their own ethnic communities,
did not necessarily feel any compulsion to forego their language and

culture, nor did officials force them. Furthermore, the English were not as cohesive a group as one might think, as this chapter will show.

English cultural and political preeminence do not negate the pluralism of those times, just as Euro-American dominance does not negate today's pluralism. We need to overcome belief in this historic myth about our past that the thirteen colonies were almost entirely populated by immigrants and their descendants from England or that everyone else had mostly blended into that Anglo American society. The colonies were not a culturally homogeneous launching pad for the new nation, which only later received several waves of "different" immigrants. Colonial America was a rich mixture of racial and ethnic heterogeneity right up to the Revolutionary War. As Gary B. Nash states, "Any attempt to portray the colonies as unified and homogeneous would be misguided."[7]

Colonial Beginnings

Coming in the seventeenth century to a land already populated by indigenous people of many cultures was a steady stream of adventurers, debtors, opportunists, social outcasts, and desperate people, all risking a perilous three-month journey across an often stormy ocean to forge a better life for themselves in the New World. Sickness, disease, and death were common traveling companions on those voyages and many never completed their journey, their lives ending with burial at sea.

A Patchwork Quilt
of Ethnic Settlements

Those who successfully completed the journey came from many parts of the European continent, speaking different tongues and varying in their religious beliefs, customs, skills, and talents. And when they settled in this new land, they sometimes intermingled but more often clustered together with their own kind, creating a mosaic of subcultural enclaves, at first on or near the coast and later inland.

The names given to land masses by the early explorers and settlers reflected this ethnic mix: New Belgium, New England, New France, New Netherland, New Spain, New Sweden. Settlement names also reflected new versions of homeland origins, as typified by New Amsterdam (Holland), New Orleans (France), and New Smyrna, Florida (Greece). Others simply named their communities the same as in their native land, such as Cambridge (England and Massachusetts), Guttenberg (Germany and New Jersey), Haarlem (Holland and New York), Hamburg (Germany and New Jersey), and Plymouth (England and Massachusetts).

For a while these settlements in the New World remained fairly self-contained and separate from one another. Most were culturally homogeneous within their boundaries, but together they constituted a patchwork quilt of ethnic diversity. Two early settlements, however, attracted a variety of peoples almost from their inception.

Diversity in the Early Settlements

Philadelphia and its adjoining area offered one example of cultural pluralism. Still a small village in 1700, its population was mostly English and Welsh, but this area also included Danes, Dutch, Finns, French, Germans, Irish, Scots, and Swedes. Even within these individual groups further diversity could be found.[8] The three hundred or so Germans, for example, were a mixture of Lutherans, Mennonites, and Quakers, each remaining separate from the others.

The greatest concentration of cultural diversity, however, was in New Amsterdam, where eighteen languages were spoken on Manhattan Island as early as 1646. Dutch, Flemings, Walloons, French, Danes, Norwegians, Swedes, English, Scots, Irish, Germans, Poles, Bohemians, Portuguese, and Italians were among the settlement's early inhabitants. After the English takeover in 1664, New York's slave population increased to become the largest north of the Chesapeake region. In 1720, the city's Black population numbered 20,000, one-third of the total; by 1741, slaves were still a substantial proportion, one-sixth of the population.

Elsewhere in the colonies some European ethnic mix could be found in most small cities. For the most part, however, the various groups clustered together, at first on the outskirts of the municipality and then more and more to the west along the edge of the frontier.

By the last quarter of the seventeenth century, the English dominated all thirteen colonies. By 1689, the population of colonial America had reached an estimated 210,000 Europeans, about 80 percent of them "transplanted Englishmen." After that, however, the proportion of English Americans declined. Between 1689 and 1775 the population increased twelvefold to about 2.6 million, with only a small portion due to natural increase. Rather, the rapid growth of African slavery and the influx of hundreds of thousands of non-English immigrants in the mid-eighteenth century significantly changed the character of the colonial population.

Geographic Variances in Diversity

Those changes had different impacts on three geographic regions, thereby causing each to develop distinct population mixtures and cultures. All the data that follow are based on colonial population data and estimates from the U.S. Bureau of the Census, as well as 1790 census data extrapolations and anthropological estimates about the Native American population at that time.[9]

The New England Colonies

In the New England Colonies, the greatest degree of cultural homogeneity could be found. As Figure 3.1 shows, about 70 percent of all inhabitants in the region were English. In Massachusetts, home to two out of every five New Englanders, lived the greatest concentration of English Americans of all thirteen colonies. There, 82 percent of the more than 250,000 people were English. The lowest proportion of English was in Maine with 60 percent, but its population was only about 31,000.

Scots accounted for about 4 percent and the Scots-Irish for about 3 percent. Interestingly, the 16,000 Africans in New England represented slightly more than 2 percent of the total. This was more than the combined numbers of Irish, Dutch, and Germans also living in New England at that time.

One problem with the New England statistics is the high percentage of inhabitants in the unassigned ethnic category. About 17 percent had no national origins identification, with most of these people residing in Connecticut, Maine, and New Hampshire. We can only speculate as to their backgrounds. We might assume they were not of English origin or it would have been reported. Perhaps they were of mixed origins or of unknown parentage.

As I'll discuss a bit later, religious prejudice and social distance were significant in colonial America among the different sects, including the English. Despite a common ancestry among so many New Englanders, religious diversity was a divisive factor in daily interactions. Nevertheless, this region by 1775 contained a greater share of fifth- and sixth-generation Americans than the Middle or Southern Colonies. Most of these New England inhabitants had coalesced into reasonably unified

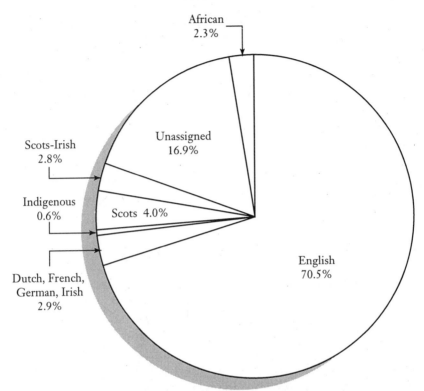

Figure 3.1. *New England Colonies, Approximate Population in 1776*
Source: U.S. Bureau of the Census, *Historical Statistics of the United States, Part II,* Series
Z 20-132 (Washington, DC: Government Printing Office, 1976).

communities, shaped in part by their consensus-driven town meetings that
allowed widespread public participation in the discussion of local issues.

The Middle Colonies

The Middle Colonies were the most diverse of the three regions (see
Figure 3.2). Here the English, totaling almost 41 percent, did not constitute a numerical majority. About 15 percent were German and more
than 12 percent African. The Dutch, Scots, and Scots-Irish were each
slightly more than 6 percent of the total. What is significant about these
groups is that their ethnic clannishness prevented any cohesive cultural
evolution as occurred in New England. Here diversity flourished in a
very real sense with the coexistence of groups side by side.

Throughout the New York-New Jersey region, the Dutch remained
socially insulated and maintained ethnic solidarity up through the Revolutionary period. Buoyed by their numbers (one in six residents in New

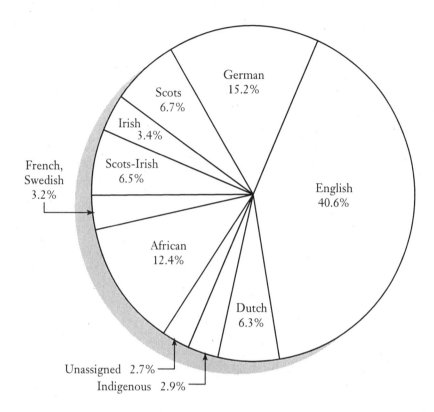

Figure 3.2. *Middle Colonies, Approximate Population in 1776*

Source: U.S. Bureau of the Census, *Historical Statistics of the United States, Part II,* Series Z 20-132 (Washington, DC: Government Printing Office, 1976).

York and New Jersey was Dutch), their culture flourished. Amid the steep-roofed houses—with double doors, blue-tiled fireplaces, and built-in cupboards—stood the Dutch Reformed churches and parochial schools. Endogamy was the norm, and Dutch endured as an everyday language, with English not even introduced into Dutch schools until 1774.

Martin Van Buren illustrated Dutch endogamy and social isolation during the colonial and federal periods when he wrote in his autobiography that his family was

> without a single intermarriage with one of different extraction from the time of the arrival of the first emigrant to that of the marriage of my eldest son, embracing a period of over two centuries and including six generations.[10]

Van Buren's comment could have applied to most of the Dutch families and other ethnics of his time. Fluent in Dutch, Van Buren was chided, rather unfairly, by critics such as John Randolph for his inability to "speak, or write, the English language correctly," a complaint often made today about newcomers.[11]

It was in Pennsylvania, the most heavily populated of the Middle Colonies with almost 300,000 residents, where the most ethnic and religious diversity existed on the eve of the Revolution. Pennsylvania colony, its Quaker-inspired religious tolerance and liberal land policies serving as important lures, superseded all others in attracting a mixed group of non-English immigrants. In 1766, Benjamin Franklin reported to the House of Commons that the Germans and Scots-Irish each comprised one-third of Pennsylvania's population.

The Germans were splintered into numerous religious groupings: they were Lutherans, Reformed, and Pietists: Quakers, Moravians, Mennonites, and Dunkers. Like the Dutch, the different German groups lived in community clusters, persevering as vibrant, distinct subcultures. Countering German pacifist sentiments were Scots-Irish Presbyterians, whose fierce anti-Anglican feelings and swift alignment with the rebel cause were key elements in tipping Pennsylvania colony into a revolutionary posture.

Although some, such as the French Huguenots and Welsh, were quickly absorbed into the dominant Anglo American mainstream, others, such as the Germans and Scots-Irish, created separate and distinct communities for themselves where they maintained cultural cohesiveness, despite their close proximity to other ethnic groups nearby. United by their strong ethnic ties, they practiced a voluntary allegiance to their own distinct social groups. The Scots-Irish eventually assimilated more quickly than the Germans, who remained clustered within a persistent subculture for several more generations.

In Delaware, the lowest-populated colony with just over 41,000, the Swedes were the second largest ethnic group, comprising about 9 percent of the total population. Delaware was where the short-lived colony of New Sweden (1638-1655) had existed before the Dutch takeover. The English were clearly dominant, however, with 60 percent of the total, and the Scots were a close third at 8 percent.

The Southern Colonies

In the Southern Colonies, the English, at 37 percent of the total, were also in the numerical minority but, as in the Middle Colonies, they were the largest single White ethnic group. From a sociological viewpoint,

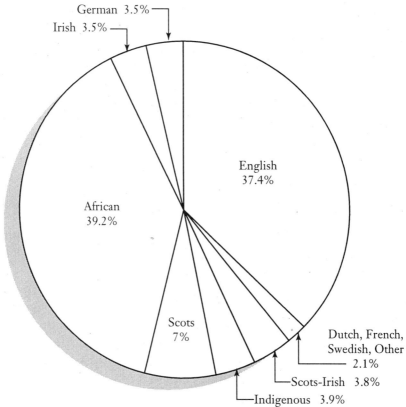

German 3.5%
Irish 3.5%
English 37.4%
African 39.2%
Scots 7%
Dutch, French, Swedish, Other 2.1%
Scots-Irish 3.8%
Indigenous 3.9%

Figure 3.3. *Southern Colonies, Approximate Population in 1776*

Source: U.S. Bureau of the Census, *Historical Statistics of the United States, Part II,* Series Z 20-132 (Washington, DC: Government Printing Office, 1976).

they were the dominant group in terms of power and control in both regions.

Slavery made the Africans the largest group, at 39 percent (see Figure 3.3). Virginia, the most populated colony with more than a half million inhabitants, had about two-fifths of all slaves in the region, but in South Carolina the Africans outnumbered the Europeans.

If we include the approximately 40,000 Native Americans estimated to be living in the Southern Colonies at the time, this makes the Southern Colonies the most racially diverse of the three geocultural regions. Here the non-White population was about 42 percent, or two out of five inhabitants.

The remaining 21 percent of the inhabitants were non-English Whites. Numbering more than 300,000, they were mostly Scots, Scots-Irish, Germans, Irish, and French Huguenots.

African Diversity on the Plantations

Cultural diversity also existed among the African slaves, who came from different tribal backgrounds from all parts of western Africa—particularly Angola, the Gold Coast, Nigeria, and Senegambia. Because of this cultural mixing, no one tribe or language group predominated, with the newly transported slaves speaking about a hundred languages or dialects. The colonists, however, did not look upon the Africans as a diverse group, instead viewing them as a single racial collectivity as well as less than human.

It was not simply the slave system that caused the colonists to ignore African diversity and generalize, because they did the same thing with Native Americans. And it was not simply a racist response or a premodern lack of sophistication. The fact is that ingroup members typically generalize about outgroups, failing to note the diversity that is there. Early twentieth-century Americans lumping together the many diverse peoples from central, southern, and eastern Europe into a single entity, or late twentieth-century Americans generalizing about all Asians or Hispanics are also examples of unnoticed diversity.

In colonial times, the Africans adapted to their harsh new reality and, by interacting with one another, soon overcame their tribal barriers through the process of ethnogenesis.[12] Ethnogenesis is an acculturation process whereby a group retains some of its cultural attributes, modifies or drops others, and adopts some of those of the host society.

The Africans became bilingual, even trilingual, conversing in their native tongue to members of their tribe or language group and in broken English to their owners. To converse with other slaves in the Carolinas, the Africans created *Gullah,* a dialect amalgamating some English and many African words into an African grammatical structure.[13]

By the 1730s, an African American culture began to evolve that became more cohesive after the end of the legal slave trade in 1808. In a harsh, arbitrary world separated along racial lines, enslaved Blacks developed a peasant-like culture. Like European peasants, they too formed close-knit communities based on family and kinship, with religion as an important center of their lives.

Although *Gullah* gradually faded away, many elements of African origin remained in music, dance, marriage rituals, and housing floor plans (front-to-back rooms instead of two rooms side by side in front). Africans held on to their incest taboo as well. Rarely did marriage occur between cousins, unlike such common practice among the slaveowners, who usually did so to maintain inherited property and power.

Three Regional Cultures

By 1725, regional differences in the New England, Middle, and Southern Colonies led to distinct cultures evolving in each of those areas.[14] New England, with its unified farming societies, maintained a strong religious orientation. Its high educational standards, even in rural areas, resulted in a literacy rate of about 90 percent for men and 50 percent for women in 1790. Here a more integrated society functioned and shared, for the most part, a common ancestry. As we shall discuss shortly, religious diversity and intolerance were a counterforce to social cohesion.

In the Southern Colonies a different culture emerged. Most of the adult White women and more than one-third of the White men could not read or write, not even their own names. Illiteracy occurred mostly because a large number of White people, mostly tenant and small independent farmers, lived in poverty and had little or no formal schooling. This socially stratified and racially divided region, with its ethnically distinct backcountry inhabitants, was ruled by a small, aristocratic elite over others for whom education was a low priority.

Within the Middle Colonies, the ethnic clannishness of the diverse groups prevented any cohesive regional culture from developing. Thus, eighteenth-century colonial America was literally a multicultural place, a fact frequently commented on by European visitors and congressional representatives in the 1790s who noted the significant cultural differences among the three regions.

Throughout the three regions, regional residence and social class greatly affected the quality of women's lives. Most spun thread and made clothing, candles, and soap, but rural women had to be even more self-sufficient in a variety of productive tasks. These might include milking goats or cows, churning butter, working in the fields, or doing other farm tasks.[15]

Women in affluent families had servants to do menial tasks while they could devote their free time to such activities as playing the harpsichord or another musical instrument, creating fine embroidery, or perhaps reading good books, particularly Scripture. Working-class women would be more likely either to produce goods for sale (cheese, cloth, shoes, yarn) or to render services (working as cooks or domestics or possibly as servers at inns, restaurants, or taverns).

Ethnic background was another important variable in determining women's place in the social order. Those of English descent were most likely to be found indoors, either engaged in duties in and about the house or, if working class, in such public establishments as mentioned in the last paragraph. Those ethnic groups living even just a short distance away from these English-dominated settlements—especially the Germans, Scots-Irish, and French Canadians—would normally have their women performing a variety of agricultural tasks, working in barns, fields, meadows, and stables or wherever they were needed.[16]

Religious Diversity

Religious diversity was another significant component of cultural pluralism throughout colonial America. Religion played a major role in colonial life, from its importance as a force for initial colonization by many different Christian groups to its influence on the everyday life of the settlers. Clergy were highly honored members of the community and their advice extended beyond spiritual matters to include economic and political concerns as well as gender relations.

Religious values, echoing such teachings as Paul's assertion that "wives should submit to their husbands in everything" (Ephesians, 5:24), greatly influenced social norms in most colonial communities. When Anne Hutchinson, a middle-aged midwife and wife of a merchant, challenged both her subordinate status and the traditional teachings of Puritan clergymen by holding weekly prayer meetings in her house, she was banished in 1637 for heresy. Afterward, Governor John Winthrop declared that she could have lived "usefully and honorably in the place God had set her . . . if she had attended her household affairs, and such things as belong to women."[17]

Most women were the social products of their times and did not challenge the pervasive male authority promulgated by the clergy. Representative of this religious influence is *The Well-Ordered Family* (1712), in which the author, Rev. Benjamin Wadsworth, counsels his female readers, "Tho possibly thou has greater abilities of mind than he has, are of some high birth, and he of a more mean extract, or didst bring more Estate to Marriage than he did; yet since he is thy Husband, God has made him the head and set him above thee."[18] What such a woman could only do, he admonished, was to fulfill her "duty to love and reverence him."

Religious Intolerance

In the seventeenth century, religion was an all-encompassing force that helped people endure the hardships and sacrifices of daily life in settlements they often established as virtual theocracies. Even if their community governance was not based on interpretation of laws by clergy, colonial religiosity instilled a narrow, intolerant view of other faiths. The expulsion of Roger Williams and Anne Hutchinson from Massachusetts colony as religious dissidents is well known. Less known is the fact that many colonies at this time enacted discriminatory legislation against Catholics and Jews, usually by banning their immigration or their right to vote.

Seventeenth-century English settlers were mostly Puritan in New England, Anglican in the South, and a variety of religious sects in the Middle Colonies, reflecting the population diversity and liberal stance of the governments, particularly in Pennsylvania. The American beginnings of the Baptist Church commenced in 1639 in Rhode Island with Roger Williams. After that, Baptists became the most persecuted sect in New England for the rest of the century. Fines, beatings, and whippings were not uncommon, and not until 1708 could Baptists legally have a house of worship in Connecticut. In contrast, Baptists thrived in the more tolerant Middle Colonies, establishing in Philadelphia by 1700 the strongest Baptist center in the colonies. But when the 1691 Massachusetts charter extended "liberty of conscience" to all Christians, including Baptists, it specifically excluded "Papists" (Catholics).

Dislike of Catholics was the one common ground on which all the Protestants could agree. The Presbyterians, Baptists, Quakers, German Reformed, and Lutherans of the back country were intolerant of one another yet shared an intense hatred of Anglicans. The Anglicans, strongest in Virginia but prevalent throughout the South, disdainfully looked upon the New England Puritans, and the New Englanders equally loathed the Anglicans and jealously guarded their communities against them achieving any inroads in their region.

By the eighteenth century secular forces lessened the force of religion somewhat, although it remained an important social influence. A lessening of religious devotion and church attendance, the advance of humanitarianism and rationalism in this Age of Enlightenment, and economic pressures combined to make this so. As a consequence, religious tolerance increased, but only slightly. There were still conflicts to come.

The Great Awakening

A momentous, far-reaching religious revival movement in the 1740s, known as the Great Awakening, brought even more conflict and diversity to the American religious scene.[19] It was initiated by Massachusetts preacher Jonathan Edwards (1703-1758), who proclaimed that an individual's "born again" spiritual awakening was strong evidence of a predestined life of heavenly bliss. Other clergy picked up this theme but the most influential was George Whitefield (1714-1770), an eloquent English evangelist who tirelessly and effectively spread this message of revivalism from Maine to Georgia.

The new movement generated much bitterness between "Old Light" traditionalists and "New Light" evangelists. The emotional preaching and the theme of individual salvation through the Bible appealed to the common folk and challenged the formal services and conservatism of the churches dominated by the elite. The movement spread rapidly, with memberships increasing dramatically among the evangelical sects. Baptists benefited the most from these gains, often at the expense of Anglicans and Congregationalists. The Great Awakening also caused schisms in the Congregationalist, Dutch Reformed, and Presbyterian churches, which further increased the bitterness of the established churches against the dissenting sects. Significantly, the Great Awakening brought democratization to religion because the general public gained a larger voice in the church. In doing so, it strengthened the trend toward liberty of conscience because it raised fundamental questions about the nature of God and human behavior, about moral and political authority, and about economic comportment.

Another interesting consequence was that revivalists boldly went into any hospitable church regardless of creed. Thus, they helped break down provincial barriers to create a more unified evangelical Protestantism that became part of the American character. Furthermore, the Great Awakening reinforced strong community values held by Americans outside the coastal towns and cities.

During this tumultuous religious period, every major Christian sect, concerned about preserving its faith and transmitting its values and beliefs to future generations, took steps to ensure its survival. Each established its own college to educate new clergy and, as noted historian Daniel J. Boorstin states, "to save more Americans from the untruths of its competitors."[20]

In the thirteen decades of colonial life prior to the Great Awakening, only three colleges had operated: Harvard (Congregational), William and Mary (Anglican), and Yale (Congregational). Twice that number were founded between 1746 and 1769: Princeton (Presbyterian), University of Pennsylvania (Anglican- and Presbyterian-sponsored but not under specific church auspices), Columbia (Anglican), Brown (Baptist), Rutgers

(Dutch Reformed), and Dartmouth (Congregational). Several of these institutions began under different names, and two—Dartmouth and William and Mary—originated as places to educate Native Americans and train missionaries to work among them.

Estimates of the number of denominational places of worship in 1775 include the following: Anglican, 480; Baptist, 498; Catholic, 50; Congregational, 658; German and Dutch Reformed, 251; German Pietist, 250; Jewish, 2; Lutheran, 151; Presbyterian, 543; and Quaker, 295.[21] Deep religious loyalties among the members of these variegated faiths induced social distance gulfs that extended beyond avoidance and social isolation.

The Legacy of Religious Pluralism

No single religion dominated, and the proliferation of sects and the growth of religious enthusiasm in eighteenth-century America produced an unplanned, often undesired, religious tolerance. Religious pluralism slowly, sometimes painfully, led to tolerance because no one group was powerful enough to coerce the others. One example is the early creation of interdenominational boards of trustees at the previously mentioned denominational colleges, partially in response to the reality that no single sect could supply its entire student body from the limited population base in its area.

United by their nationalism after winning their war for independence, the colonists put aside their prejudices by institutionalizing tolerance and establishing a bedrock principle of American culture: separation of church and state. Freedom of religion was more an act of practical necessity than of democratic ideals. It is one legacy from America's multicultural past.

Intergroup Conflicts

Not all intergroup tensions led to violence. The earliest recorded instance of an interethnic challenge to the existing social order occurred in Jamestown, Virginia. In 1619, a small band of Armenian, German, and Polish workers went on the first-ever strike in the new land to gain political rights denied to them as "inferiors." Their militant action brought a peaceful resolution to this issue, preserving ethnic relations in this mostly English settlement of about one thousand inhabitants.[22]

Interracial Clashes

Diversity may have existed both racially and culturally, but in a White-dominated society, peaceful interracial relations were contingent on the passivity of non-White groups in accepting the will of the dominant group. This was not an age of egalitarian pluralism. Whenever any form of resistance by the subordinate groups manifested itself, reaction was usually swift and furious.

Early settlers may have looked upon Native Americans as savages but they respected their power. Consequently, they usually attempted to secure land through negotiation. But later, buoyed by their increasing numbers and superior weaponry along with havoc wreaked on Native American populations by the White man's diseases, the settlers gained the upper hand in power. No longer dependent on Native Americans, the settlers became openly contemptuous of land rights. They violated past treaties, recklessly encroaching on tribal lands whenever and wherever they wanted. When the tribes resisted, brutal warfare broke out, beginning a sad pattern of fierce battles and massacres that would continue until 1890.

African Americans also felt the wrath of offended Whites. In 1712, two dozen slaves set fire to a building in New York, killing nine Whites. Authorities quickly retaliated by hanging thirteen Blacks, starving another to death in chains, and burning to death four others, including one over a slow fire so "that he may continue in torment for eight or ten hours."

A 1739 slave uprising near the Stono River, South Carolina, that killed several Whites spread a fear of slave revolts throughout the colonies. Then, when a series of unexplained fires and robberies occurred in New York City in 1741, hysteria mounted about a "Negroe conspiracy" to take control and kill all White inhabitants. It was instigated by sixteen-year-old Mary Burton, an indentured servant, who gave false testimony to claim a £100 reward for information about the unknown arsonists.

Even though her charges contained absurdities and rash contradictions countered by the accused slaves' owners, they triggered hysteria about a large-scale Black conspiracy aided and abetted by the duplicity of Whites. Threatening torture and execution, authorities obtained sixty-seven confessions from the terrified slaves. Before the reactionary frenzy ended, eighteen slaves and four Whites, including a Catholic priest named John Urey accused as the ringleader, were hanged. Thirteen slaves were burned at the stake, 150 slaves and 25 Whites were imprisoned, and 70 other slaves were banished to the West Indies.

These were but a few instances of the interracial conflicts and violent episodes that occurred. Resistance, rebellion, and repression were the commonplace realities of interracial relations in the colonial period.

Clashes Between the Denominations

Religious clashes were another manifestation of intergroup conflict. Just prior to the American Revolution, clashes in the Chesapeake colonies between Anglicans and Baptists were frequent, the result of class antagonism between the planter elite and poor Whites and Blacks. Armed bands of planters and law officials forcibly broke up Baptist meetings, in which preachers condemned the planters' lifestyle of horse racing, gambling, whoring, and cock fighting. Animosity between England-loyalist Anglicans and England-hating Scots-Irish Presbyterians was common. The latter group, living along the western frontier from Maine to Georgia, where they frequently fought the Native Americans, also came into dispute often with the pacifist Quakers and German sectarian groups who advocated peaceful coexistence with the Native Americans.

A Kaleidoscope Society

Some historians have found colorful expressions to describe the diversity of colonial America on the eve of the American Revolution. Michael Kammen calls it an "invertebrate" society composed of disconnected religious, ethnic, and racial groups lacking a "figurative spinal column."[23] James Stuart Olson describes the colonies in 1776 as "a cultural kaleidoscope of three races and dozens of ethnic and religious groups."[24]

English Americans may have held political power in the thirteen colonies, but they constituted less than half the total population. In the Middle and Southern Colonies, they were decisively outnumbered by the combined racial and ethnic groups and in South Carolina by African slaves alone. However, the Anglo Americans were the dominant group, holding political and economic power, backed by the English military. Their language and culture constituted the mainstream, but the English did not force other White ethnics to assimilate, allowing them instead to retain their own schools to teach their children in their native languages.

Minority Separatism

Ethnic colonials thus lived under this tolerant English rule, typically residing apart in culturally distinct ethnic communities. If geographically isolated, they also remained culturally insulated as well. If they lived within the English American cities, they adapted as urban ethnics always have, but they also retained many vestiges of their ethnicity and maintained an ingroup solidarity among their own kind.

Native Americans also desired to live among their own kind and maintain their way of life but, unlike White ethnics, they were not left alone to do so. African Americans, mostly enslaved, had no voice in their own welfare, but within the slave communities, they developed their own subculture. Though relegated to a subjugated existence, racial diversity remained a reality in colonial America.

The separate White groups gave at least grudging tolerance to one another in the early years, united as they were in their fear and defense against the native peoples and the French. Later, with the threat from England, they put aside their differences to fight for their freedom and to maintain their rights through local politics.

The Multicultural Revolutionary Army

The success of Washington's troops in defeating the English came partly from the multicultural elite who played key roles in military training, strategy, and leadership. Baron Friedrich Wilhelm von Steuben (Prussia), General Casimer Pulaski and General Thaddeus Kosciuszko (Poland), Marquis de Lafayette and Baron de Kalb (France) were the most prominent volunteers from Europe who were of great value to the American cause, although de Kalb's death in 1780 at the Battle of Camden, South Carolina, was a major blow to American efforts to recapture the South at the time.

Just as the military leadership consisted of non-English individuals, so too did the ranks of fighting men. Over five thousand Blacks served in the colonial forces, fighting in every major battle from Lexington in 1775 to Yorktown in 1781. Some distinguished themselves in combat, such as Peter Salem and Salem Poore at the Battle of Bunker Hill, and Lemuel Haynes at the Battle of Fort Ticonderoga. James Lafayette, a Virginia slave, was so effective in gaining strategic intelligence about the English for Lafayette's troops that the Virginia Assembly purchased his freedom as a reward.

Patriotic groups formed within ethnic communities, often cooperating or even merging with similar nonethnic groups out of necessity. Numerous ethnic communities recruited their own companies or regiments, staffed with their own officers. Soon they mixed with other ethnic groups or those of English ancestry as they united against a common enemy. Soon the cultural barriers and suspicions between groups faded as they shared common dangers, common hardships, and ultimately common victories.

The Dillingham Flaw Revisited

Understanding the widespread diversity in the thirteen colonies, even among English Americans, helps one to avoid the Dillingham Flaw. To assume that either cultural homogeneity or a common heritage existed is incorrect. To assume that a single entity called "British" shared a common identity and close, meaningful interactions is also incorrect. To understand the cultural diversity of our beginnings helps place in proper perspective the diversity of our present.

As the colonial period drew to a close, 53 percent of the population in the thirteen colonies belonged to racially and ethnically distinct non-mainstream groups. That is more than twice the proportion in 1990. The 1990 census tabulations showed Asians at 3 percent, Blacks at 12 percent, Hispanics at 9 percent, and Native Americans at 1 percent—a total of 25 percent. In 1776, racial minorities alone equaled that figure. Clearly a larger proportion of racial and ethnic groups existed in 1776 than in the 1990s.

Knowing these data helps us avoid the Dillingham Flaw of looking upon our colonial past as a time of cultural homogeneity. By comparing the population compositions of that time and the present, we can begin to understand our own times within a larger context. One could even make the argument that colonial America, proportionately, was a greater multicultural society than ours is today.

Beyond the Horizon

The American Revolution would have both obvious and subtle consequences. Most obvious would be the birth of a nation, but one of the subtle outcomes would be the gradual acculturation of the ethnic minorities of that time. Scots-Irish and French Huguenots, both Calvinists who adapted easily to the individualistic, success-oriented society developing in the English colonies, would assimilate quickly. They did not maintain the ethnic isolation of the Dutch and Germans, whose cultural pluralism endured, but even for these ethnics the cultural barriers and social distance would be reduced.

A process of cultural homogenization among the Whites would begin, bolstered by the attempt to build a national identity, but it would be short-lived. The catalyst was the new nation's audacious declaration that leaders ruled only by the consent of the governed, that all men were created equal and entitled to life, liberty, and the pursuit of happiness.

Those rights and privileges were not yet to be fully extended to women and racial minorities, but the promise of freedom and opportunity would soon attract thousands of hopeful others. Ethnic communities would be revitalized and new ones would form, rejuvenating diversity in a land where it had always flourished.

4

Diversity in the
Early National Period

Cultural differences had been put aside in the fight for independence, bringing previously isolated groups together in the common cause. This interaction reduced the social distance between groups and initiated a lessening of cultural barriers. Another effect most keenly felt throughout society was the disruption in the traditional division of labor and status between the sexes. Military service caused the absence of husbands, older brothers, or fathers, thereby requiring thousands of women to assume major responsibilities for managing the shops or farms. Thrust into such unexpected roles, the women grew in decision-making skills and increased self-confidence in their leadership abilities. After the war, traditional gender role relationships reasserted themselves once more, but the brief emancipation of women in some aspects of daily life did not fade completely.

That newfound autonomy was perhaps best expressed in an oft-quoted letter dated March 31, 1776, from Abigail Adams to her husband John while he and other political leaders gathered in Philadelphia to draft what became the Declaration of Independence. Referring to the subordinate position of women, she wrote, half joking, half serious:

> I long to hear that you have declared an independency—and by the way in the new Code of Laws which I suppose it will be necessary for you to make, I desire you would Remember the Ladies, and be more generous and favourable to them than your ancestors. Do not put such unlimited power into the hands of the Husbands. Remember all men would be tyrants if they could. If particular care and attention is not paid to the Ladies we are determined to foment a Rebellion, and will not hold ourselves bound by any Laws in which we have no voice, or Representation.[1]

Abigail's entreaty did not bring about the changes in law she desired in her lifetime, but her words were prophetic about a time when the "ladies" would organize and challenge laws that were biased against them. Essentially, though, the social and political inferiority of women remained intact during the early national period. Still, the struggle for independence had also sown some seeds in women's minds. Many women, for example, freely discussed political issues in letters and social conversations, much to the dismay of the men. Complaining that the men thought women had no business talking about politics, Eliza Wilkinson wrote in 1783,

> I won't have it thought that because we are the weaker sex as to bodily strength we are capable of nothing more than domestic concerns. They won't even allow us liberty of thought, and that is all I want.[2]

Although gender relations did not advance much, another social process was evolving. Cultural homogenization, begun with the intermingling of ethnic soldiers and support groups during the American Revolution, continued at a rapid pace between 1783 and 1820. These were crucial years in the development of the American political tradition and of a common culture. Strong efforts were made on many fronts to establish a civic culture and socialize the population into following common tenets.

Building a National Identity

Throughout the new nation, a surge of patriotic pride prompted the severing of Old World ties in ways other than political. For example, in such areas as arts and letters, language usage, and religious authority, a distinctly American form emerged. National myth-building, glorifying revolutionary heroes, and shaping the public mind into a shared value orientation became part of building the nation.

Arts and Letters

Literature, art, and music reflect the life and times of a people, revealing much about their values and orientations. So it was in the early national period. For example, as Federalists and Republicans (Jeffersonians) fought with each other to control the political destiny of the United States, political writings were bountiful. They ranged from the thoughtful arguments in the *Federalist Papers* prior to adoption of the Constitution to the scurrilous, vindictive diatribes of political opponents against one another.

In the creative arts, the first American play written and successfully performed in the new nation was a 1787 comedy dealing with American life. In *The Contrast,* playwright Royall Tyler's contrast was between American worth and the affectation of foreign manners. Of significance is the introduction of the character Jonathan, the shrewd, yet uncultivated type of New England farmer who has since become known as the "Stage Yankee" and who served as a model for many editorial cartoonists of the eighteenth and nineteenth centuries for depicting the "real" American.[3]

Songs, poems, and essays appeared in the early federal years, but one of the first pieces of imaginative prose was written by Washington Irving in 1809. Interestingly, it was about an ethnic group, the Dutch. Called *A History of New York, by Diedrich Knickerbocker,* it is a delightful parody, now a classic of American humor and an early example of creative writing distinctly American in form and content.

After the English surrender at Yorktown, painters, sculptors, and writers lionized the new national heroes and practically deified George Washington. The fame of such painters as Gilbert Stuart, John Vanderlyn, Edward Savage, John Trumbull, and John Wesley Davis rests largely on their portraits of statesmen. Books about American, not English, history and other books containing American essays began to appear. The Fourth of July became a national holiday, both as a cause for celebration and part of the concerted effort for Americans to build a national identity.

In Jefferson's inaugural address on March 1, 1801, he asserted that common identity. The first political opponent in world history to replace a rival power as a national leader through a peaceful election process, Jefferson affirmed the mutual sharing of political principles by all. In their Bancroft Prize-winning work, *The Age of Federalism* (1993), Stanley Elkins and Eric McKitrick suggest the eight words of this passage constitute "probably the most famous single sentence Jefferson ever uttered." The third president's words were, "We are all republicans—we are all federalists."[4]

Linguistic Independence

In 1783, a native-born Connecticut Yankee named Noah Webster became a major influence in giving American English a dignity and vitality of its own. In that year he published the *American Spelling Book,* which became commonly known as the "Blue-Backed Speller." The book served to legitimize American English and provided Webster with most of his income for the rest of his life. Never out of print, its total sales exceed 100 million copies.

Webster quickly followed with a grammar book (1784) and a reader (1785). The selections in his anthology were mostly American writings about democratic ideals and dutiful moral and political conduct. In 1828, at the age of seventy, Webster published his two-volume *An American Dictionary of the English Language,* and all 2,500 American copies sold out within a year. Advocating the superiority of language usage by the American commoner over the so-called artificiality of the London tongue, Webster successfully worked to have American language declare its independence from England as well.[5]

Religious Independence

Another manifestation of evolution into a distinctly American culture in the post-Revolutionary years was in religion. One by one the ethnic Protestant churches created local governing bodies to replace previous overseas authorities. Anglican churches, for example, renouncing allegiance to the Church of England, reorganized as the Protestant Episcopalian Church of America.

Even conservative churches took this path. Dutch Reformed churches insisted on approving ministers ordained in Europe before they could preach from American pulpits. The German Lutheran Ministerium of Pennsylvania—a region previously mentioned as the home of the largest German population—required a three-year probationary period for European-trained ministers before they could be accredited for permanent assignment.[6]

In colonial times, there had only been about 25,000 Catholics, most of them living in Maryland, ostracized and out of the mainstream. After independence, Catholics established a special American liaison to the Vatican, headed by Bishop John Carroll in Baltimore. He pioneered in exploring positive relations between Catholics and their Protestant fellow citizens, seeking to overcome the exclusion of Catholics so common in many colonies where Congregational or Episcopal churches were supported by law. This exclusion is an indicator of past friction between diverse groups and a precursor of some of today's problems involving other religious minorities.

The actions of various Protestant denominations to sever Old World ties and of Catholics to seek a dialogue with Protestants contributed toward a further lessening of religious separatism. It was short-lived, however. Beginning in 1820, the first wave of immigration to the new nation revived the ebbing ethnoreligious differences. The influx of millions of Catholic immigrants launched the Protestant Crusade, and nativist suspicion and hostility effectively countered these early ecumenical efforts.

Social Structure and Social Class

The wealth and social status of eighteenth-century Americans varied in part according to which of the four social structures they lived in: the frontier, small farm communities, commercial farm communities, or urban societies. Only a few individuals of considerable means might be found in the frontier or small farm communities, but the commercial farm communities contained larger concentrations of wealthy people who owned large properties. Cities, whether small or major centers, typically contained a larger and richer class who controlled a greater proportion of the property than in the other three communities.

Jackson T. Main reports that, on average, about one-third of the White population living in the North in the revolutionary era were poor. Substantial property owners comprised about 30 percent and small property owners almost as much. The wealthy elite comprised about 10 percent, a large proportion of them merchants benefiting from the growth and commercialization of port towns and their investments in city real estate.[7]

Lines of economic division and marks of social status, already evident prior to the American Revolution, crystallized further afterward. As Gary B. Nash observes,

> This social transformation is statistically measurable, though we can never obtain mathematical precision in these matters, given the selective survival of documents. In the inventories of estate and tax lists lie the silent record of the redefinition of class categories. Most notable is the parallel emergence of the fabulously wealthy and the desperately poor.[8]

Examining two Boston tax lists from the years 1687 and 1771, James A. Henretta detailed the ongoing process of the top echelon amassing greater wealth and the lower class getting a smaller share of the community's assets.[9] By 1771, the top quarter of the city's population controlled 78 percent of Boston's assessed wealth, a gain of 12 percent. In contrast, the next highest 25 percent of the population—artisans, small shopkeepers, traders—saw its share of wealth drop from a 21 percent share to 12 percent. The bottom half of the population dropped from 12 to 10 percent.

Within the cities this growing void between the elite and the laboring class became more evident with the increase in urban mansions and four-wheeled carriages. The cities were less the repositories of ethnic Americans than they were of an economically stratified order of English Americans. Cultural pluralism was to be found in distinct subcommunities outside the cities, more often in rural and frontier communities.

Among the working-class, rural, and frontier families, the women continued working at many tasks that the genteel ladies of the mercantile and upper classes did not. However, one commonality almost all women shared, regardless of social class or residence—they married at a young age, had many children, and were usually grandmothers by the time they were forty.

By 1820, the number of children under age 5, per 1,000 women between the ages of 20 and 44, was 1,295, about triple of what it is in the 1990s. Child-rearing, keeping of home and hearth, and working in the fields, if she was a farmer's wife, were the areas of responsibility for most women. Only 6.2 percent of the women were in paid employment outside the home. For most women, the house or perhaps the farm was their world, their reality, their fate.[10]

Religion, Power,
and Group Consciousness

Classic sociological theorists Max Weber and Karl Marx offered contrasting analyses about the interrelationship between religion and those in power. Weber saw Calvinist beliefs as an important influence on the emergence of capitalism and reinvestment of profits as a foundation for power and affluence.[11] In contrast, two common theses permeate the writings of Marx and other conflict theorists. First, the dominant religion is typically the religion of the economically and politically dominant class. Second, its religious leaders strive to legitimize the interests of the ruling class by providing justification for existing inequalities and injustices.

The United States offered examples of both viewpoints. Illustrating Weber's provocative thesis, New England Calvinists led the way in establishing both trade and manufacturing centers in the new nation but also exemplified the Marxian view because the New England power elite gave financial support from public funds to the dominant Congregationalist Church. Also, as Meredith McGuire suggests, Christianity may have pacified some of the slaves and dulled the anger that often fuels rebellion.[12]

Conflict theorists also find religion to be an intense form of human alienation in its creation of a hostile social environment for those of other faiths. In the heavily Protestant United States, American Catholics indeed found themselves in a frequently hostile environment and subject to differential treatment. Many states, for example, passed laws denying them the right to hold elected office.

Eventually, the ongoing diversity of American society and its political system allowing for freedom of choice brought about many changes involving religion. As more non-English Americans gained political power, they supported dominant group politicians promoting religious equality and sought to punish those who did not.

Religion and Politics

In the last chapter, I mentioned that the doctrine of separation of church and state was a consequence of religious diversity. In all of New England except Rhode Island, however, the Congregational Church maintained its privileged position and public support from tax revenues. This close church-state relationship, made possible because of the predominance of English Americans, remained until the 1830s.

Complete separation of church and state was not exactly the case in most other states when it came to qualifications to run for office. Full political rights were only bestowed on Protestant Christians. Some states were even more specific. Delaware required belief in the Trinity; North Carolina and Pennsylvania stipulated belief in the divine inspiration of both Testaments; New Jersey allowed only Protestants conforming to certain religious beliefs; New York mandated only Christians who renounced all foreign rulers, whether civil or ecclesiastical, thereby eliminating Catholics and Jews.

In Virginia, the planter elite, as members of the Anglican/Episcopalian Church, had long dominated the political scene, although conflict with Baptists and Presbyterians had been commonplace. Therefore, when Virginians Thomas Jefferson and James Madison successfully led the struggle to secure separation of church and state, their efforts brought these men the enduring support of ethnic Americans throughout their political careers.

In a second Virginia action with national consequences, the state legislature rejected a bill supported by George Washington and Patrick Henry for a "general assessment" tax to provide funds for all religious groups. Jefferson then successfully sponsored a state bill in 1786 that endorsed the principle of individual liberty of conscience in religious matters, made all churches equal before the law, and stipulated no direct financial support to any religion. Jefferson considered passage of this religious liberty statute (which became the national principle as well) to be one of his three major achievements and had it so inscribed on his tombstone.

In Pennsylvania that old critic of the Germans, Benjamin Franklin, joined with Robert Morris and Dr. Benjamin Rush to rally German support for the new constitution by endorsing the establishment of a German-sponsored college in the state. Appreciative Germans named the institution Franklin College. Franklin further endeared himself to the various German denominations when he successfully led the opposition in overturning the "Test Act," which had required several religious oaths as a prerequisite to holding any office.

In contrast, Rufus King, the American minister to London, was one of the more vocal opponents of Irish Catholic emigration to the United States. His protests that the country wanted no more "hordes of wild Irishmen" because they would "disfigure our true national character" were printed in the Irish American press.[13] Offended ethnics can have long memories. When King ran for the presidency against James Monroe in 1816, the Irish voted against him en masse and reveled in his defeat.

Parallel Religious Institutions

In the late eighteenth century, two groups of northern African Americans illustrated the conflicting view of a rising group consciousness that promoted social change from a previously accepted subordinate status. No doubt the new national doctrine of equality and the subsequent assertiveness of American churches from European dominance influenced two different Black groups, fed up with subtle and overt forms of racism within the integrated churches they attended, to split from these churches.

In 1787, a group of African Americans withdrew from St. George's Methodist Episcopal Church in Philadelphia and formed their own congregation. They built their own church (Bethel) in Philadelphia, had their first ordained minister by 1799, and formally organized as the African Methodist Episcopalian Church in 1816. Today, their membership exceeds 2.2 million members.

The origins of the African Methodist Episcopal Zion Church, a different entity, trace back to 1796, when the African American members of the John Street Methodist Church in New York City terminated their membership. They too formed their own congregation, built their first church (Zion) in 1800, and formally organized in 1821. Today, their church membership exceeds 1.2 million members.

Creation of these separate churches was by no means the first nor last instance of minority groups establishing parallel social institutions. However, racial discrimination is more likely to be a multigenerational reality than ethnic discrimination. Therefore, these Black churches became part of a larger pattern of racial segregation and isolation that would continue for generations, unlike ethnic churches that often ceased to exist after a few generations. Both Black churches, as their memberships attest, remain viable today.

The Nation's First Census

The 1790 census, with the exceptions of the survey of England conducted in 1086 during the reign of William the Conqueror and the registering of people in Sweden in 1749, was the first national counting of a population.[14]

The first U.S. census revealed a decidedly rural society. Only 3 percent lived in cities of 8,000 or more residents, and only 200,000 lived in towns of 2,500 or more. Most Americans lived in much smaller communities, sometimes in ethnic enclaves where language and Old World customs still prevailed.

The nationality data from this first census have long been cited in history books as a teaching device for what the United States was like as a new nation. Its importance for this purpose is perhaps revealed by its inclusion in the *Historical Statistics of the United States,* a two-volume publication issued in 1976 by the Census Bureau in conjunction with the bicentennial celebration.

The population portrait provided by the 1790 census offers some striking revelations about diversity if we look past the obvious. Before we do so, however, let's take a look at the obvious, because that is the basis for belief in the cultural homogeneity myth about our past and sets the trap for the Dillingham Flaw.

If we rely only on the commonly reported data shown in Figure 4.1, we can fall into that trap. From these data, the usual emphasis has been on the fact that the English, Scots and Scots-Irish comprised 75.2 percent

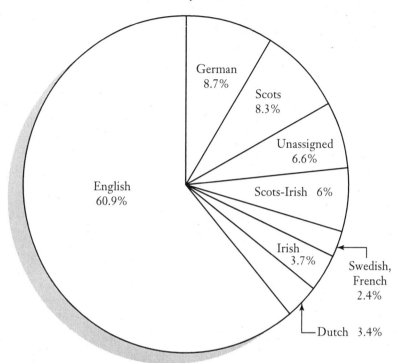

Figure 4.1. *White Population Distribution in 1790*

Source: U.S. Bureau of the Census, *Historical Statistics of the United States, Part II,* Series Z 20-132 (Washington, DC: Government Printing Office, 1976).

of the White ethnic population in 1790. This grouping makes some sense, for by then these previously distinct cultural groups had begun to coalesce into a White Anglo Saxon Protestant (WASP) collectivity. Moreover, as the culturally dominant group, they became the essence of the new national identity and remain to this day as the reference group for comparison with subsequent demographic changes.

This Eurocentric view is misleading, however, because it ignores the actual diversity that prevailed. Herein lies the trap for the Dillingham Flaw. It is one thing to speak of the culturally dominant group but quite another to generalize about the entire population to argue cultural homogeneity.

The Other Side of the Coin

If about 75 percent of the White population were White Anglo Saxon Protestant, then 25 percent were not. This is one in four individuals, approximately 793,000 people out of 3.1 million. Think about that fact for a moment: one in four White Americans in 1790 was not a WASP!

To appreciate the significance of that figure, consider this: if we combine together all the African Americans, Asian Americans, Hispanic Americans, and Native Americans identified in the 1990 census as living in the United States, we would get 25 percent of the total population. This equals the percentage of White Americans in 1790, most of whom were not fully integrated into the dominant culture. They may not have been a subjugated, exploited, colonized people as some racial minorities, but they did constitute culturally distinct peoples who did not possess much power or influence outside their subcommunities.[15]

Who were these non-Anglo Saxon 25 percent in 1790? They were Dutch, French, German, Irish, and Swedish mostly and, except for the Swedes, they remained distinguishable in language and/or lifestyle from Anglo Americans. In smaller numbers they were also Belgian, Danish, Flemish, Italian, Norwegian, Polish, and Swiss, plus scatterings from many other locales. Together, they were the ethnically diverse population segment who did not fit into the WASP category and contradict the false portrait of a new nation peopled almost entirely by Anglo Americans.

With such a significant proportion of 1790 Americans living outside the mainstream among ethnoreligious and linguistically diverse groups, any discussion of late eighteenth- and early nineteenth-century Americans as alike becomes an application of the Dillingham Flaw. Too much cultural heterogeneity existing within socially isolated subcultural groups prevailed at this time. Too many differences—in economic and political power, in social status and stratification, in lifestyle and outlook—comprised this period to mitigate against erroneous generalizations about cultural consistency within a homogeneous population.

Yet it is not just that too many people forget about the many White ethnic Americans living in this era. These commonly reported data distort the past even more because they, do not include racial minorities!

Eurocentric Use of Census Data

When we move past the Eurocentric presentation of the 1790 census data to include the non-White population, we can acquire a more complete understanding of the extensive diversity in America at that time.[16] By doing so, we shall not only find a smaller proportion of society belonging to the dominant Anglo Saxon group, but also further dispel mistaken assumptions about our past that enable the Dillingham Flaw to affect past-present comparisons.

Census tabulations in 1790 counted 757,208 African Americans, about 60,000 of whom were not slaves and living primarily in the North.

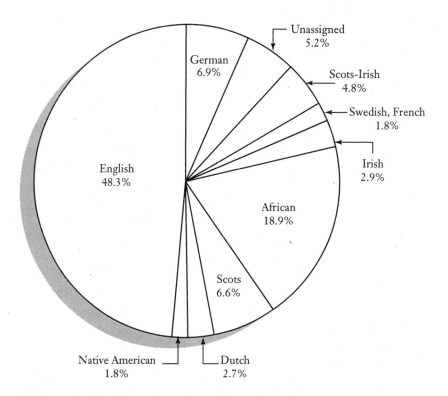

Figure 4.2. *Total Population Distribution in 1790*

Source: U.S. Bureau of the Census, *Historical Statistics of the United States, Part II,* Series Z 20-132 (Washington, DC: Government Printing Office, 1976).

Added to the White population, this increases the total population to 3.9 million, of whom 1.5 million are not WASPs. This means that instead of the 25 percent of American society previously identified as not fitting the mold of an Anglo Saxon populace, the figure becomes 38 percent.

We can go higher if we include Native Americans. They may not have been included in the census, nor protected by the Constitution, nor even then considered part of "American" society, but they were nonetheless part of the total population. Most may have lived apart from the Whites, but they still lived within the states' boundaries and were a factor in trade, land disputes, and warfare.

Exact numbers on Native Americans in 1790 are not available. According to many anthropologists, a conservative estimate of those living east of the Mississippi River at this time is about 70,000. Adding that number to our previous Black/White numbers, we reach a total U.S. population of approximately four million people in 1790.

When we include all the people living in what was the United States in 1790—African, European, and Native Americans—we find that roughly 40 percent were not Anglo Americans (see Figure 4.2). This is hardly the picture in the minds of many Americans today about America back then. In 1790, two out of five Americans were outgroup members whose race and/or culture set them apart from the dominant group of Anglo American Protestants.

Expanding Territory and Diversity

Between 1783 and 1820, the United States doubled its size. Each expanse, the result of diplomatic treaties, brought even greater cultural diversity within the nation's changing borders.

Tens of thousands of farmers moved into the Northwest Territory (later Ohio, Indiana, Illinois, Michigan, and Wisconsin), where 57 percent of the White population in 1790 were French, reflecting that nation's prior control of this region. Only 30 percent were English, the smallest proportion anywhere in land claimed by the United States. Germans and Scots each accounted for about 4 percent, the Scots-Irish for 3 percent, and the Irish for about 2 percent. Clearly this region possessed significant White ethnic diversity.

Native American Resistance

This westward migration—into lands inhabited by the Shawnee, Chippewa, Ottawa, and Potawatomi—brought frequent conflict into the Northwest Territory in the 1790s. The warfare ended with federal troops led by General "Mad Anthony" Wayne defeating the Western Indian Confederacy at the Battle of Fallen Timber in 1794. Another effort by a new confederacy leader, Tecumseh, to stop White encroachment of Native American lands was stopped at the Battle of Tippecanoe Creek in 1811, thereby sealing the fate of Native Americans with their eviction from their ancestral lands.

New Territory Acquisitions

In 1803, when Jefferson purchased the Louisiana Territory, 865,000 square miles of dazzling country, he incorporated more of the French community into the United States. French influence in architecture, language, and culture, including Catholicism, remained vibrant in the Mississippi

Delta, its presence still felt today. Also absorbed into American jurisdiction were many new Native American tribes, many of them encountered by Meriwether Lewis and William Clark in their expedition to chart the new American region.

Another acquisition was the forced ceding of Florida to the United States in 1819. The Seminole now came under U.S. authority, as did the small number of Spanish inhabitants.

By 1820, the United States was very different from its 1783 beginnings. It was twice as large as before, and the inhabitants of its newest additions were mostly French, Spanish, and Native Americans. In fact, some of the new regions had no Anglo American presence at all.

The Drop in Immigration

About 250,000 new immigrants came to the United States between 1790 and 1820. Because no records were kept then, we can assume that these newcomers were in reasonable proportion to the nationalities of those already living in the United States. This would mean that about three-fourths of the new arrivals were British.

Two other nationalities came in significant numbers. About 25,000 were French-speaking immigrants, the majority not refugees from the French Revolution but from the French islands in the Caribbean where slave uprisings caused an exodus of almost the entire White population. Thousands of others were Irish revolutionaries fleeing the failure of a major rebellion against English rule that had broken out in 1798.

Despite the arrival of these French and Irish political refugees, U.S. immigration was low at this time, averaging only 8,300 annually. Immigration always depends on the interplay of "push" and "pull" factors. Normal immigration is usually predicated on economic motives, but which homeland conditions "push" people out and which societal conditions of the host country "pull" immigrants to that land? In this instance, which elements slowed immigration?

One factor in the drop in immigration was an English law passed in 1788 prohibiting the emigration of skilled artisans from Ireland and England. Then in 1803 England drastically lowered the maximum number of passengers permitted in a ship, thereby reducing the profit margin for shipping companies. The resulting higher fares lessened the demand for indentured servants, because increased costs were passed on to purchasers of the indentured contracts. Consequently this form of migration decreased.

Other European countries also tried to restrict the emigration of skilled artisans and men of military age. Furthermore, the French Revolution and Napoleonic Wars (1802-1815), eventually embroiling the United States in the War of 1812, disrupted European travel. Uncertainties and political turmoil in the United States between Federalists and Republicans also reduced the attraction of emigration.

The Significance of Natural Population Growth

Although immigration lessened between 1790 and 1820, the nation's population increased significantly from 3.9 million to 9.6 million in that same period. Only a small fraction was due to the territorial expansion previously mentioned; it was in the older territories and states where population growth primarily occurred. Natural increases from high birth rates and the tendency to have large families were the main reasons for this rise in population.

This growth spurt of mostly "American stock," itself a composite of many ethnic groups, enabled cultural homogeneity to evolve within American society to a degree never before attained and never again realized after 1820. Without a significant additional admixture of new ethnics either to reinvigorate the ethnic communities or to commingle with other groups, a new generation came forth in a society emphasizing its new identity. Reared by parents who lived through the Revolution, taught in schools where all things American were emphasized, and attending churches where clergy preached about God's blessings on America, these children were the first to be socialized into the newly developing American culture.

Emergence of a Common Culture

Before children could be taught a common culture, however, adults needed to find for themselves that mutual framework of life before passing it on to them. Besides the initial bonding begun by the comradery that the Revolution engendered, two other factors helped break down the walls of ethnic isolationism. First, fewer new arrivals meant no renewal of ethnic subcultures, thereby allowing acculturation of ethnic Americans to proceed unimpeded. Second, as western expansion continued, helped in part by lands given to Revolutionary soldiers in lieu of cash, many ethnic enclaves broke up as individuals and families left their old communities for the frontier.

The emerging American culture contained three major beliefs or value orientations. Political democracy had been at the core of the nation's founding, and it was indelibly reaffirmed with the peaceful transfer of power from Federalists to Republicans after the presidential election of 1800. Individual enterprise, the second hallmark, inspired both immigrant and native born and became the basis for countless private economic initiatives. Third was a strong commitment to the institutionalization of a Protestant culture, quite understandable in a society comprised almost entirely of Whites sharing that religious orientation, along with some converted African and Native Americans. Soon the influx of millions of Catholic immigrants would challenge this cultural attribute.

Even as a common culture emerged, French influence was evident in cooking, fashions, and manners. French ads in American newspapers advertised "restauranteurs" who had previously been conventional American cooks and bakers. French chefs and recipes were popular. Inns and taverns renamed themselves "hotels." Americans became eager to learn from French dancing and fencing masters or have their children become ladies and gentlemen by learning French manners and grace. French books, customs, dress, and music all were fashionable in the early nineteenth century.

As Americans sought to establish their own national identity, the prevalence of French influence on the public alarmed some, particularly the Federalists. "Medusa's snakes are not more venomous," declared one Federalist writer, "than the wretches who are seeking to bend us to the views of France."[17]

Decline of Foreign Languages

Foreign language usage in a host country usually retains its vitality only under certain conditions. A continual inflow of compatriots will preserve the vitality of the alien language. Geographic isolation will prevent the typical pattern of children learning the host country's language. Social isolation may allow a persistent subculture to retain its language as part of its outgroup norms.[18]

In the United States during the early national period, none of these conditions prevailed to any large degree. On the frontier, pockets of ethnic isolation still existed and, in those regions, foreign language remained a vigorous, everyday reality. Elsewhere, though, without an influx of new arrivals to sustain its resiliency, foreign language went into decline.

A good example is the Germans, who comprised the largest non-British population segment. Prior to the Revolution, Baltimore, New York, and Philadelphia each had two or three German-language newspapers, but by 1815, none were left. Other languages declined in use as well, because by then the Dutch schools, the Scandinavian schools, and others had introduced English into the classrooms.

This is not to say that the old languages died out completely, for that was not the case. Many of the older adults, unable to master the English language to any appreciable degree, held on to their native tongues. Some churches held duplicate services in both languages, enabling worshipers a choice.

Anti-Foreign Responses

Even though immigration was lighter than in earlier years and the populace was coalescing into a common culture, a visible foreign segment remained. It was comprised mostly of the French and Irish, whose numbers and buoyant ethnicity alarmed some of the native born.

The Federalists, sensing the weakening of their power, were alarmed by the excesses of the French Revolution and the growing support for the Jeffersonians among Irish and French foreign born. In fiery speeches and newspaper editorials, they argued these immigrants would "contaminate the purity and simplicity of the American character." One Federalist wrote, "Generally speaking, none but the most vile and worthless, none but the idle and discontented, the disorderly and the wicked, have inundated upon us from Europe."

Noah Webster admitted that some immigrants were industrious, peaceable, and even voted the Federalist ticket, but, he warned, "For for one such 'good' European, we receive three or four discontented, factious men—the convicts, fugitives of justice, hirelings of France, and disaffected offscourings of other nations."[19]

Controlling the three branches of the federal government, the Federalists used their power to eliminate what they viewed as a threat to American society and to their own privileged position. Their actions were the first of several instances in the nation's history in which the dominant group successfully legislated against an "undesirable" foreign-born element.

In 1798, President John Adams signed three bills passed by Congress. The Naturalization Act extended the residency requirement for citizenship from five to fourteen years, in the hope of curtailing this new voter base of the Republicans. The Alien Act gave the president the power to arrest and deport undesirable aliens at his discretion. The Sedition Act prescribed fines and imprisonment for anyone criticizing the government.

Although Adams never used the Alien Act, his administration did implement the Sedition Act—a serious invasion of individual rights and liberties. Several foreign-born newspaper editors were arrested for seditious writings. Despite this law's blatant violation of the First Amendment provision for freedom of the press, a principle originating with the celebrated court victory of Peter Zenger in 1734, the Federalists enforced it.

The Alien and Sedition Acts expired after two years and faded away forever. As president, Jefferson succeeded in revising the Naturalization Act back to its five-year residency requirement, where it has remained ever since.

The False Horizon

No one living in an era really knows when it is drawing to a close. Only when it is past can we look back and mark the moment when the change occurred. So it was in 1820.

That year saw James Monroe re-elected, surely one sign of continuity. However, it was the first presidential election in which the Federalists did not field a candidate, for they had virtually disappeared as a political force by then. New, still unfelt political winds were blowing. Even though the Democratic-Republican party seemed invincible, before the decade ended it too would be gone, replaced by others taking parts of its name.

A whole generation had grown up, knowing nothing but independence. Older adults could look back on the far-reaching changes since their youth. Three states had been added to the first thirteen by the turn of the century, and by 1820 that number had grown to twenty-three.

Commerce flourished in the Northeast, agriculture under an entrenched slave system prospered in the South, and westward expansion at the expense of Native Americans continued unabated. Canals, railroads, highways, and steamboats—plus such inventions as the reaper, the cotton gin, and the telegraph—would soon create an enormous economic empire rich in natural resources.

Probably many White Americans envisioned a tomorrow that would be better and essentially a continuation of what they knew. It would not be so, however. In 1820, a new era was dawning, some of it to be influenced by babies born that year, such as the daughter of Massachusetts Quakers Daniel and Lucy Anthony, whom they named Susan.

More immediately, American literature at last began to flower. Washington Irving's second work, *The Sketch Book,* appeared in 1820. The following year would see publication of James Fenimore Cooper's first novel, *The Spy,* and William Cullen Bryant's first volume of poems. These "Knickerbockers," as they were called, would contribute to the rise of a national literature of stature and scope.

Thanks to low immigration and high natural population growth, together with the pervasive acculturation process, the American society had become more culturally homogeneous. Assimilation and societal cohesiveness were far more prevalent than White ethnic pluralism. And because religious intolerance and conflict between the different Protestant denominations had virtually ended, many Americans deceived themselves into thinking that their society had evolved into its final synthesis.

This too was an illusion, for beyond the horizon that Americans could see was the first great wave of immigrants to come since the nation began. The sheer numbers of these culturally distinct newcomers would pose enormous challenges to American institutions, embroil many in violent conflicts, and change forever the America these Americans of 1820 knew.

5

Diversity in the Age of Expansion

At first glance, the total 8,385 immigrants entering the United States in 1820 may have seemed but a continuation of the 8,300 annual average of the preceding thirty years. Few paid much attention, judging by the lack of commentary in that year's publications. Perhaps some might have commented to friends that they detected a few more Irish in their midst but, if they did, they probably attributed it to the 3,000-strong Irish labor crew building the Erie Canal.

We now know it was more than just a case of a few more Irish arriving. In 1820, 47 percent of the emigrants from Europe were Irish Catholics. That proportion, almost one out of two, was significantly larger than the fairly small Irish presence of about 4 percent among the American population at that time.

In hindsight, we recognize that this ratio in 1820 was a clear signal of something new happening. That Irish group of newcomers in 1820 became the vanguard of almost two million Irish who followed them in the next forty years.

A then-record influx of over five million immigrants entered the country between 1820 and 1860. Their numbers and births contributed greatly to the total population increasing by one-third each decade. From 9.6 million inhabitants in 1820, the nation grew to 31.4 million by 1860. In the 1820s, immigration totals represented less than 2 percent of the total population, but by the 1850s that decade's immigration totals constituted over 11 percent of the total population.

Statistics such as these help to show the dramatic increases in immigration and foreign-born residents. They may hint at the ethnic diversity of the times, but we need to get a much clearer portrait of the American people in this era if we are to understand its relationship to our times.

AUTHOR'S NOTE: Immigration statistics given throughout this chapter are from the U.S. Immigration and Naturalization Service, *1993 Statistical Yearbook* (Washington, DC: Government Printing Office, 1994), Table 2: 26.

In this era, as in all others, the dual patterns of assimilation and pluralism could be found. For the new arrivals in cities and in self-contained communities elsewhere, ethnicity was an everyday reality. As Joshua Fishman has observed, the persistence over generations of Dutch, French, German, Navajo, and other languages became a normal part of American life.[1] It is also true, as Calvin Veltman has shown, that with some exceptions, a language shift to English was usually a two-to-three-generation phenomenon.[2]

Settlement patterns from colonial times manifested themselves again now, as they would in future generations. Brought by various push-pull factors through a chain migration process to a particular locale, immigrants clustered together in culturally distinct communities. There they established parallel social institutions, with most immigrants living in relative social isolation from outgroup members. Unless replenished by new foreign stock, ethnic vitality would gradually fade over successive generations, usually due to a combination of factors, such as the initial process of ethnogenesis, the Americanization of youngsters, and a local population increase of outgroup members who might outnumber the nationality group.

Travelers Discover the Ethnic Mosaic

Intrigued by the dynamics of a new nation and the diversity of its people and landscape, Europeans came to visit and record their impressions. Most notable among these were Charles Dickens, Harriet Martineau, and Alexis de Tocqueville. Although the focus of their written perceptions was not specifically on ethnic diversity, their works contain references to the ethnicity they found. We shall save Charles Dickens, the last of these three to arrive, for a little later.

Tocqueville's Dismay at Racial Suffering

Tocqueville spent nine months during 1831 to 1832 in the United States with his friend Gustave de Beaumont, studying American prison reforms. They coauthored a book on the subject; later, Beaumont wrote another book on slavery and Tocqueville produced *Democracy in America* (1835), a masterpiece in political sociology for its analysis of the vitality, excesses, and potential future of American democracy. His observations about American associational life, collective pressures, individualism, competition, and materialism remain the bedrock for modern analyses of the American character.

Tocqueville's comments on diversity centered on racial prejudice and oppression. Personally witnessing in December 1831 a band of Choctaw crossing the Mississippi at Memphis as part of the government's Indian removal policy and also seeing the effects of slavery, Tocqueville observed, "I saw with my own eyes many . . . miseries . . . and was the witness of sufferings that I have not the power to portray" (p. 359). He envisioned a bleak American future with Native Americans perishing in isolation and African Americans, if freed from the slavery he condemned, continuing to experience racial prejudice. As Tocqueville explained,

> The prejudice of race appears to be stronger in the states that have abolished slavery than in those states where servitude has never been known. . . . Thus it is in the United States that the prejudice which repels the Negroes seems to increase in proportion as they are emancipated, and inequality is sanctioned by the manners while it is effaced from the laws of the country.[3]

Martineau's Defense of Immigrants

Harriet Martineau was a remarkable Englishwoman whose fine analytical writings on social, economic, historical, philosophical, and religious topics were widely read. After her visit to the United States (1834-1836) while in her early thirties, she wrote *Society in America* (1837), in which she offered many of her observations about the American people, including the immigrants. To those critics of the immigrants, she countered,

> It would certainly be better if the immigrants should be well-clothed, educated, respectable people (except that, in that case, they would probably never arrive). But the blame of their bad condition rests elsewhere, while their arrival is, generally speaking, a pure benefit.

She went on to illustrate the value of immigrants to America:

> Every American can acknowledge that few or no canals or railroads would be in existence now in the United States, but for the Irish labor by which they have been completed; and the best cultivation that is to be seen in the land is owing to the Dutch and Germans it contains.[4]

Bremer's Portrait
of Ethnic Diversity

A lesser-known European visitor, Frederika Bremer, offered some warm and astute commentary about the ethnicity in midwestern cities in *The Homes of the New World* (1853). One city that appealed to her was St. Louis, where she found such an "interesting mixture" of French, German, Irish, and Spanish characteristics, as illustrated in the diversity of books and magazines sold, the variety of retail stores, and languages spoken on the street.[5]

Olmsted's Discovery of
Isolated Ethnic Communities

American travelers sometimes surprised themselves by unexpectedly stumbling on isolated American communities that maintained an ethnic solidarity. Frederick Law Olmsted, later to become the famed landscape architect of many city parks, was one such person.

Traveling throughout the South in the 1850s, Olmsted described in *A Journey Through Texas* (1860) encountering a one-year-old farming community of Silesian Poles as well as numerous German farming settlements throughout West Texas, where their homes, work, and leisure activities reflected to Olmsted their native origins.[6] He was especially impressed with New Braunfels, a German town named after Braunfels, Germany, located to the southeast of Bonn.

Olmsted also came upon the village of Castroville, founded in 1844 by Alsatian French. Its population of six hundred still spoke French and read French newspapers and maintained two churches with worship services conducted in—what else?—French.

The French

French cultural influence, so popular among the public in the early national period, diminished by the 1820s but retained its vitality in the many areas where the French were concentrated. In the Mississippi Valley region, for example, elements of French influence from colonial times continued throughout the nineteenth century. Many rivers and towns bore names indicating their French origin, as did the names of the largest cities: Detroit, New Orleans, and St. Louis.

America's "Flanders"

Flanders, an area along the North Sea extending along northern France and western Belgium, still retains its medieval appearance. When Charles Dickens visited St. Louis in 1842, he went into the older section of the city long ago built by French settlers. It was there he would write in *American Notes* that the place reminded him of Flanders:

> The thorough-fares are narrow and crooked, and some of the houses are very quaint and picturesque; being built of wood, with tumble-down galleries before the windows, approachable by stairs, or rather ladders, from the street. There are queer little barbers' shops, and drinking-houses too, in this quarter; and abundance of crazy old tenements with blinking casements, such as may be seen in Flanders. Some of these ancient habitations, with high garret gable windows perking into the roofs, have a kind of French shrug about them; and, being lop-sided with age, appear to hold their heads askew besides, as if they were grimacing in astonishment at the American Improvements.[7]

The large presence of French Catholics in St. Louis prompted the Vatican to create a new diocese for them in 1823. Mathias Loras, a native of Lyons, France, became their first bishop. Here, as in many other American cities, French priests dominated the American Catholic hierarchy until midcentury, when massive Irish immigration ended their power.

America's "Little Paris"

New Orleans, of course, remains foremost today in its preservation of French architecture, language, and culture. A picturesque reminder of Old World cities, it did not yield to "blue laws," which prohibited commercial activity or paid entertainment on Sundays, as Boston, New York, and Philadelphia did in the early nineteenth century. On Sundays the New Orleans stores remained open, street musicians continued to play and sing, the markets were busy, and the theatrical performances drew large audiences.[8]

The richness of French culture in the city is partly revealed through the abundance of productivity. Between 1806 and 1811, the New Orleans Theatre St. Pierre offered seventy operas. French historians, novelists, and poets created a vast outpouring of distinguished French literature between 1820 and 1860.

French Immigration

As with other ethnic groups, the French subculture remained resilient in part because of the steady arrival of new immigrants. More than 316,000 immigrants from France came between 1820 and 1880, almost half of them arriving between 1840 and 1860. Much of this latter immigration resulted from the political disturbances preceding the Second Republic in 1848 and the dictatorship of Louis Napoleon, who became Emperor in 1852. The previous year, 1851, was the single greatest year of French immigration to the United States, when more than twenty thousand arrived.

Typically, the French preferred city life and so most settled in many American cities. Besides those already mentioned, sizable French populations in pre-Civil War cities could be found in Charleston, Chicago, Cincinnati, New York, and Philadelphia. French newspapers and social organizations were commonplace. With the outbreak of the Civil War, French military battalions formed in many cities to join in the cause on both sides.

The Irish

From the first-recorded passenger lists of 1820 until 1860, the Irish dominated U.S. immigration statistics. Almost 2 million came in that period, with 1.2 million of them concentrated in the years between 1847 and 1854. The folklore of both sending and receiving countries is filled with stories of the thousands who did not survive the ocean crossing and the squalor endured by the survivors in the slums of the eastern cities.[9]

America's First Ghetto People

Although the Irish were mostly tenant farmers in their homeland, they were ill equipped for American agriculture. Potato farming in Ireland required only rudimentary skills and equipment, because it involved all manual labor on fairly small plots of land. American farms required capital investment not only in larger tracts of land, but also in axes, saws, seed, horses, mules or oxen to pull the plow, and credit or other means to survive until the harvest.

The impoverished Irish had neither money nor credit standing. Moreover, the low population density of rural America was significantly different from home, where they lived in tight clusters in their villages, about three hundred per square mile. Accustomed to family, friends, neighbors, and church all within short walking distances, the mostly illiterate Irish peasants found the congestion of America's cities more to their liking than the isolation of rural life.

With no capital to become farmers and industrial America offering lots of jobs in the cities, others settled in what became known as "Dublin Districts," living in overcrowded tenements, dirt floor cellars, converted warehouses, or shanties made of wooden crates and tar paper. Conditions were deplorable. Poor ventilation, heating, and lighting were common, and so were the open sewers in the streets and poor sanitation systems that contaminated drinking wells.

Epidemics of cholera, typhoid, diphtheria, smallpox, and tuberculosis caused thousands of deaths among the immigrants. In 1849, for example, five thousand people, mostly Irish immigrants, died from cholera in New York City. In 1860, the mortality rate in Boston, New York, and Philadelphia was thirty-four deaths per thousand, more than twice that in rural regions.

Labor, Religion, and Politics

Some Irish males worked as farmers, miners, or businessmen, but most worked at manual jobs in or near cities. They were in all types of construction: paving roads, laying down railroad tracks, digging out canals, and building dikes, houses, or ships. They loaded or unloaded freight on trains and ships; cleaned streets and other people's houses, laundry, and chimneys; or labored in the factories and mills.

Many Irish were single women taking jobs as domestics or nannies for the native-born urban elite. In 1800, there was one domestic servant for every twenty families, but by 1840 the ratio had dropped to one servant for every ten families. Unmarried Irish (and Scandinavian) young women often came first and worked in American homes. Their daily typical workload was sixteen hours of cooking, cleaning, tending to the children, and nursing the sick, six days a week. With little time to themselves, these women would save their earnings for passage money for other family members. The difficulties women had seeking jobs in a household compared to men finding work in labor gangs was illustrated between 1845 to 1850 by the Boston Society for the Prevention of Pauperism, which received employment applications from 14,000 female foreigners in contrast to 5,034 male applications.

The loss of husbands through accident, desertion, or sickness left many women without means to support large families except, perhaps, by taking in boarders or hiring out to do others' laundry or sewing at home. Among the Irish, female-headed households reached 18 percent by 1855. Although dropping to 16 percent by 1875, this proportion remained significantly higher than the national average for White Americans.

The Irish, far more than the French and Spanish, brought Catholicism to this Protestant country on a large scale. Bringing with them their priests and nuns, building churches, convents, and parochial schools, they established a church hierarchy that would dominate American Catholicism for generations and would later create some occasional interethnic resentment by Catholic immigrants of other nationalities.

Andrew Jackson's election in 1828 opened the political door to the common man, and the Irish rushed through it. Using their political organizational skills, they forged a powerful voting bloc, city political machines, and a spoils system second to none. Graft and corruption may have been an integral part of machine politics, but so too was the proactive aid to the poor with food, fuel, and jobs.

The Germans

By 1820, German Americans were so rapidly assimilating that the Lutheran and Reformed churches not only offered regular worship services in English but also opened their memberships to those of English, Scottish, Welsh, and Scots-Irish descent as well. As the wave of German immigration rose to tidal proportions in the nineteenth century, however, German culture quickly revived and flourished throughout the land.

Driven by hunger, political discontent, and a series of wars, 1.5 million Germans entered the United States between 1820 and 1860, followed by another 1.5 million in the next twenty years. Some came for political reasons, but economic reasons motivated most. By the 1850s, newly arriving German immigrants outnumbered Irish arrivals, a lead they would sustain for the next sixty years.

So massive was the German immigration and so widespread were their settlement patterns that their presence was felt almost everywhere.[10] They entered through almost every eastern or southern port city, some to put down roots in those areas and others to move inland by train or boat along the Erie Canal or Mississippi and Ohio rivers.

The Midwest—particularly Ohio, Indiana, Illinois, and Wisconsin—attracted many. Large concentrations of Germans lived throughout the South before the Civil War, such as in Wheeling, West Virginia; Richmond; Charleston; Mobile, Alabama; Louisville, Kentucky; Nashville; New

Orleans; and Stuttgart, Arkansas. Some Germans went to the West Coast, as did John Sutter, on whose land the discovery of gold touched off the gold rush to California.

The German "Athens"

If New Orleans was the definitive French city of the United States in the 1850s, then Milwaukee was the definitive German city. Two-thirds of the city's 13,000 inhabitants in 1850 were foreign born, and Germans accounted for two-thirds of this number. The city became the distributing center of German settlers throughout the north central states.

In contrast to the coarseness and dullness of most frontier towns, Milwaukee was an oasis of culture in the 1850s. Its musical and literary cultural levels shone so brightly that travelers called it the "German Athens." The city possessed numerous German organizations, including a highly respected German American academy, a freethinkers club, a *sangerbund* (singing society), a theatre, and a *Turnvereine,* which blended physical fitness and German patriotism. Breweries, beer gardens, pork stores, mutual aid societies, and fire and militia companies were other aspects of the German presence.

German Diversity

Nineteenth-century German immigrants defied categorizing because of many differences within their own group, which impeded any sense of pan-German ethnicity. An extreme cultural gap existed between the Catholics, mostly from the southern and southwestern provinces, and the Protestants, who were mostly from the northern provinces.[11]

Yet the Protestants themselves were distinct subcultures. The Calvinists—Baptists, Presbyterians, and Reformed—did not share the cultural nationalism espoused by the German Lutherans, and all of these religious groups were less culturally isolated than the Pietists—Amana, Amish, Hutterites, and Mennonites—who lived in separate but closely-knit (*gemeinschaft*) communities.

Other distinctions among the Germans were occupational and residential patterns. In rural areas throughout the land, Germans turned uncleared or partly cleared wastelands into productive farms with their agricultural aptitude. These industrious and conservative Germans were knowledgeable about livestock, dairying, and crop raising, but they were far less cosmopolitan than their city-dwelling compatriots.

Artisans and merchants settled in Germantown sections in virtually every American city. As their numbers increased, their many social and cultural activities sometimes replaced the preeminence of an earlier group, as in St. Louis where French music and customs yielded to those of the Germans. Not all Germans in the cities were economically secure people enjoying social and cultural activities, however. Others lived in abject poverty, struggling each day just to survive. In New York City, for example, some unemployed Germans became scavengers. Men, women, and children gathered decaying produce discarded by grocers or bones thrown away by slaughter houses. Even rotting vegetables were better than none, and meat fragments on bones could be boiled for a broth. Filthy rags from hospitals and gutters could be boiled too, then dried, bagged, and sold to refuse dealers for a few pennies a bag that would help them persevere.

For most German immigrants, the reunification of Germany in 1871 intensified their sense of German ethnicity. The common German language reinforced that awareness and mitigated against going to a non-German church regardless of faith. A German Reformed Church, not Dutch; a German Lutheran Church, not Norwegian; or a German Catholic Church, not Irish, made one feel more comfortable by practicing the faith in one's native language. A common expression in those times for German Catholics was "language saves the faith," and so German-language masses continued despite the protests of the Irish American-dominated church hierarchy to Rome.

Native Americans

White attitudes toward Native Americans were mixed in the nineteenth century. Although some simply wanted them out of the way, idealists sought to integrate the indigenous peoples through assimilation. Various missionary groups attempted to turn them into individualist Christian farmers who spoke English instead of communal, foreign-speaking "heathens" who depended on hunting and subsistence agriculture.

Assimilation Efforts

Some Native Americans in the old Northwest Territory did convert to Christianity and attempt to assimilate. In doing so, they found themselves to be a dually marginal people, for they were now social outcasts from their own tribes, victims of ridicule and even physical abuse, and also not accepted by the Whites. Confronted by a double dose of discrimination, many chose to return to their old ways rather than suffer a lifetime of social isolation.

By 1820, hundreds of thousands of Whites lived in Georgia, Tennessee, and the brand-new states of Alabama and Mississippi. Their food source and lifestyle endangered by White encroachment, five tribes—the Cherokee, Chickasaw, Choctaw, Creek, and Seminole—tried to keep their lands by adopting the White man's way of life. Greater power comes to those who assimilate into a society than those who live on its fringes, and these tribes thus sought power through integration to control their destinies rather than lose further power through resistance and thus have no voice in their future. Because of the tribes' conversion to their culture and Christianity, White Americans gave them the ethnocentric appellation of the "Five Civilized Tribes."

"As Long as Grass Grows and Water Runs"

Living on rich, fertile land at a time of agricultural growth, particularly in cotton, the tribes stood in the path of further White settlement. President Jackson sent agents to negotiate, offering them lands west of the Mississippi River where "their white brothers will not trouble them" and where they "can live upon it, they and all their children, as long as grass grows and water runs."[12]

As a witness to one small part of this expulsion, Tocqueville offered this poignant commentary:

> It is impossible to conceive the frightful sufferings that attend these forced migrations. They are undertaken by a people already exhausted and reduced; and the countries to which the newcomers betake themselves are inhabited by other tribes, which receive them with jealous hostility. Hunger is in the rear, war awaits them, and misery besets them on all sides. To escape from so many enemies, they separate, and each individual endeavors to procure secretly the means of supporting his existence by isolating himself, living in the immensity of the desert like an outcast in civilized society. The social tie, which distress had long since weakened, is then dissolved; they have no longer a country, and soon they will not be a people; their very families are obliterated; their common name is forgotten; their language perishes; and all traces of their origin disappear. Their nation has ceased to exist except in the

recollection of the antiquaries of America and a few of the learned of Europe.[13]

For those tribes not pressured into agreeing, Jackson ordered the military to expel them from their lands and to force march them into Oklahoma Territory to live.[14] Despite a U.S. Supreme Court ruling in favor of the tribes, Presidents Jackson and Van Buren, the Congress, and the public sided with economic expansion over cultural accommodation. By 1838, Indian removal was complete except for the Seminole who, aided by runaway slaves who had married into the tribe, waged guerilla warfare until 1842, when they too were defeated and removed to Oklahoma.

In the old Northwest Territory, only the Sauk and Fox, led by Chief Black Hawk, fought against removal until their defeat in 1832. Like the Delaware, Kickapoo, Miami, Ottawa, Peoria, Potawatomi, Shawnee, Winnebago, and Wyandot tribes before them, the Sauk and Fox were also moved across the Mississippi.

All that now remained east of the Mississippi were the Iroquois of upstate New York, whose land was not coveted, and remnant bands from the expelled tribes who had escaped detection. Most Native Americans now lived in the western half of the nation on lands that were supposed to be theirs forever.

The End of Forever

"Forever" was less than twenty years. Acquisition of Oregon in 1846 and the Southwest in 1848 extended the U.S. border to the Pacific Ocean. Native Americans found new pressures for their land from a relentless White migration, encouraged by discovery of gold in California in 1848, the Homestead Act of 1862 giving 160 acres of free land in the Great Plains to migratory Whites, and completion of the transcontinental railroad in 1869.

Skirmishes, massacres, and major battles erupted throughout the West. Deliberate, large-scale slaughter of the buffalo made them nearly extinct, devastating the culture and economy of the Plains tribes. In time, the independence of all the tribes ended, and they began a new life as dependent wards of the government, segregated on open-air slums called reservations.

Because ethnic Americans, mostly German and Irish, served in the American army in numbers greater than their proportion in the population, they played a major role in the bloody Indian wars of the nineteenth century. Military service offered them a well-paid job without discrimination and enabled them to assert that they were "real" Americans. Adopting to the cultural biases of their new country, they saw it as their duty to kill the "bloodthirsty savages."

The Africans

In 1820, there were almost 1.8 million African Americans, of whom all but about 230,000 were slaves. By 1860, the slave population had increased to almost 4 million and the number of free Blacks had grown to about 488,000. Virtually all of this growth was due to natural population increase, as international slave trade had been outlawed by Congress in 1808.

Southern Blacks

Three separate cultures evolved in the South among (1) the nonslave-owning Whites primarily living in the back country, (2) the plantation owners, and (3) the slaves. Even among the slaves some diversity existed. Most were field hands working from sunup to sundown, but a small number were domestic servants or skilled workers. Of the tens of thousands of skilled workers, some lived and worked on plantations, but many were artisans hired out in the cities. In some cities, notably New Orleans, these artisans were permitted a remarkable degree of free physical movement and personal behavior, but they were slaves nonetheless.[15]

In 1860, when about four million African Americans lived in the South, Whites totaled only seven million. In South Carolina and Mississippi, Blacks far outnumbered Whites, but in Georgia, Florida, Alabama, and Louisiana, the two races were about evenly divided in numbers. Only in Virginia, Arkansas, and Texas did Whites outnumber Blacks by about a three to one ratio.

Life as a slave was a blend of labor exploitation, sexual exploitation, illiteracy, limited diet, and primitive living conditions. Only in their private times of leisure in the evening or on Sundays and holidays could slaves find respite from the relentless demands of bondage. Then they could hunt, fish, gamble, visit, gossip, sing, dance, picnic, or attend church. Essentially, slave culture revolved around three elements: family, music, and religion.

The family was the primary institution of slave society despite the breakup of families through sale or transfer of ownership or the White sexual exploitation of Black women. The typical slave household had two parents, fulfilling their traditional gender roles with the male as disciplinarian and head of the family and the female in charge of their home and children.

Several clues reveal the strength of Black family norms in the antebellum South. Their sexual mores allowed premarital sex but condemned adultery. This commitment of a man and woman to one another, first legitimized in the "jumping over the broomstick" ceremony, was reinforced by tens of thousands of former slaves legalizing their marriages through an official ceremony after the Civil War. Moreover, many actively searched for children, spouses, and parents after the war to reunite separated families.

African music has a rich history and variety. Beginning with the recorded observations of Hanno the Carthaginian in the fifth century B.C., many have written about the varied African musical instruments, including flutes, lutes, fiddles, lyres, reed pipes, drums, xylophones, and musical bows. African music also differs from Western music in that one cannot separate music from dance or bodily movement; even the playing of an instrument involves a complex combination of body movements.

Music reflects the life and times of a people. In their slave society, African music was an important component of work, leisure, and worship. Using the forms, tones, and rhythms of their heritage, the African Americans expressed their emotions and feelings through songs and spirituals. Frederick Douglass—whose rise from an illiterate slave to an articulate, abolitionist writer and speaker is an inspiration to anyone born into poverty—noted the importance of music to his brothers still in bondage: "Slaves sing most when they are most unhappy. The songs of the slave represent the sorrows of the heart, and he is relieved by them, only as an aching heart by its tears. . . ."[16]

Religion was another important outlet in which slaves could express their deep feelings, bind together, and find hope. Traditional African cultures are rooted in a world view of continuous interaction between spiritual forces and the community. It was thus a logical step for slave religion to blend the spiritual and secular worlds, connecting themselves both to a glorious past and a more rewarding future. Converting mostly to the Baptist and Methodist faiths because they permitted Black clergy, African Americans used their Christian faith to sing the joys of God's love for all and the promise of glory and salvation in heaven.[17]

Northern Blacks

Theoretically, northern Blacks were free but in reality they were not equal. Most states passed laws denying them the right to vote, serve on juries, or migrate from another state into theirs. Segregation was the norm in public facilities and residential areas. Job discrimination was widespread. Confined primarily to menial occupations, the northern Blacks also fought a losing battle in the northeastern cities against the inroads of Irish competition.

Socially ostracized, disfranchised, and economically discriminated against, northern Blacks created their own subsocieties. Parallel social institutions, comparable to those of White ethnics, sprung up. Besides the many Black churches were the fraternal and mutual aid societies. These organizations offered educational programs, medical and burial services, and provided forums to air grievances and enhance self-esteem.

The Chinese

Just as many Americans, both native born and foreign born, went west across land to seek their fortunes, the Chinese came east across the Pacific Ocean to seek theirs. Only 88 Chinese immigrants entered the United States between 1820 and 1853, but in 1854, 13,100 arrived, attracted by the discovery of gold. When the 1850s ended, more than 41,000 Chinese had come, followed by another 64,000 in the 1860s.

Most Chinese came to the United States in the nineteenth century as sojourners, intending to work for a limited time and then return home. Few women came—about one in twenty arrivals from China was a female. The men worked as miners, farm laborers, and fishermen. Many were soon employed as railroad workers and builders of dams, levees, and irrigation systems.

Cultural Distinctions

Obviously the Chinese brought a new element to an already diverse American society. They were a non-Western, non-Christian people whose appearance (race, clothing, hair), belief system, food, language, music, and other cultural attributes clearly set them apart from the rest of society.

Another distinction was the social structure recreated by the Chinese in the United States.[18] Traditional clans were a primary source of identity and emotional ties to family. Settlement patterns depended on clan location, because each tended to take up residence in selected areas. The *hui kuan* associations were mutual aid societies that represented six sending regions of China. With wider influence than the clans and often mediating disputes between clans, the *hui kuan* played a key role in helping Chinese newcomers find work and lodging, lending money, providing health care and burial arrangements, and meeting other social needs as necessary.

The tongs, or secret societies, brought a disruptive element to the Chinatowns. Involved in such organized crime activities as gambling, dealing heroin and operating opium dens, and prostitution, the tongs challenged clan and *hui kuan* leadership, resulting in frequent bloody clashes. Because the tongs were better organized, they more effectively offered life insurance and welfare assistance to the sick, disabled, and unemployed, thus mixing fear and support to gain influence.

These three groupings—the clan, *hui kuan,* and tongs—provided the Chinatowns with an infrastructure that resulted in self-sufficient ethnic communities. Ignored by politicians because they could not become citizens and vote, the Chinese in nineteenth-century America preserved their way of life much as Germans in isolated rural communities, for example, sought to preserve theirs by different means.

The Mexicans

Beginning in the 1820s, thousands of American settlers crossed the Louisiana border into the Mexican land of Texas and started hundreds of cotton plantations in that fertile region. A decade later, more than twenty-five thousand Americans lived in eastern Texas. Their presence set a chain of events in motion that resulted in the U.S. annexation of Texas from Mexico, war with Mexico, and the subsequent acquisition of New Mexico and California territories. With the signing of the Treaty of Guadalupe Hidalgo in 1848, eighty thousand new ethnics became part of the American population.[19]

The new Americans were mostly a blend of a small group of wealthy landowners and a much larger group of artisans, ranch hands, or farmers who lived in an area also occupied by tens of thousands of Native Americans. Soon widespread land fraud, expensive litigation, or forced land sales under violent duress caused almost all the Mexican American elite to lose their land titles by 1880 to squatters or emerging White land barons for little or no money. Federal troops would eventually subdue the tribes as they had others.

Northern California and Texas were the locales of the most violent episodes of interethnic conflict with the Spanish-speaking Catholic residents. Banditry, riots, terrorism, vigilantism, and even open warfare were common throughout the 1850s. In southern California and New Mexico, ethnic relations were more peaceful because arid conditions attracted far fewer White settlers. Completion of the southern transcontinental railroad in the 1870s, however, brought in many new settlers and a repetition of the cycle of ethnic hostility and loss of land titles to the Whites.

Although some *mexicano* landowners managed to keep their property, most did not. Gradually, the Mexican Americans took on the status of a colonized people. School segregation, political disfranchisement, and economic dependence as laborers on the now powerful Whites changed the Mexican Americans into essentially a suppressed minority. One telling statistic about the impact of colonization and poverty on family organization is the increase in Mexican American female-headed households, which numbered one-third the total by 1880.

The Rise of Social Movements

Two movements, temperance and abolitionist, evolved from the late 1820s into major social forces. Prompted by such Congregationalist ministers as Lyman Beecher and Theodore Dwight Weld or the fiery William Lloyd Garrison, publisher of *The Liberator*, both movements attracted hundreds of thousands of male and female supporters who ardently campaigned either against the evils of drunkenness or slavery. Black abolitionists Frederick Douglass and Maria W. Stewart were other powerful voices championing the antislavery cause.

Soon women became deeply involved in other social reforms aimed at improving conditions in almshouses, asylums, hospitals, and prisons.[20] Many woman leaders arose in these various endeavors, including Susan B. Anthony, Amelia Bloomer, Dorothea Dix, Margaret Fuller, Lucretia Mott, Elizabeth Cady Stanton, Lucy Stone, Harriet Beecher Stowe, and Sojourner Truth.

Out of the abolitionist movement arose some radical feminists, such as Angelina and Sarah Grimke, who championed women's rights, fully supported by Angelina's husband, William Lloyd Garrison. At national women's rights conventions, held annually in the 1850s, the speakers advocated women's rights, including the right to vote. Becoming organized and gaining publicity for their feminist causes, they ceaselessly lobbied state legislatures.

Gradually the women's crusade achieved a few small gains. Following New York's lead in 1848 of granting women property rights, fourteen other states followed suit by 1860. Even divorce laws, in a very limited way, were liberalized. Nevertheless, most women still lacked many legal rights, including ownership or control of property, guardianship of children if widowed, the right to vote and to go to college. In almost every state a man could legally beat his wife, provided it was "with a reasonable instrument."

Feminist efforts at women's suffrage were thwarted by amendments enacted during Reconstruction. The Fourteenth Amendment in 1868 brought the word "male" for the first time into the Constitution, as it penalized any state denying its adult male citizens the right to vote. In 1879 the Fifteenth Amendment gave the right to vote to all regardless of race, color, or previous condition of servitude but said nothing of gender. Women's suffrage was still forty-one years away.

Intergroup Conflicts

Numerous interethnic clashes occurred throughout the nineteenth century, such as those previously mentioned that occurred in the West and Southwest between the dominant group and Mexican or Native Americans. Space precludes a full discussion of these and other conflicts, but we must give at least brief attention to what occurred in the Northeast in mid-century.

Greatly upset over the large influx of Chinese, Irish and German Catholics, and other foreigners, a right-wing reactionary group formed, calling itself the Supreme Order of the Star Spangled Banner. Dubbed "Know-Nothings" for their refusal to talk about their secret activities, they lobbied extensively for strict immigration laws and discrimination against Catholics.

Their vicious hate campaign was often accompanied by brutal violence, with mobs raiding Irish and German homes, churches, schools, and businesses. Arson, vandalism, beatings, and murders occurred throughout the 1850s, with virtually every large northeastern city experiencing major disturbances.[21]

Organizing politically into an American party, they elected seventy-five congressmen in 1854. By the next year they had elected six governors and many local officials. In 1856, their presidential candidate, ex-President Millard Fillmore, ran a distant third to James Buchanan and John C. Fremont, although he did receive about 22 percent of the vote. This movement afterwards faded into oblivion as North-South antagonisms mushroomed into civil war. It was not the last time American minorities would face right-wing extremists.

Beyond the Horizon

In this era, the large numbers of Asians, Hispanics, and Europeans, particularly Germans and Irish, who became part of American society, had brought significant cultural diversity into the land. Some assimilated, but the numerous pockets of ethnic pluralism returned an expanded America to another version of its earlier colonial patchwork ethnic quilt. On the negative side, the violence perpetrated by antiforeign or anti-Indian forces and the exploitation of racial minorities scarred the American minority saga. Yet it was also a time when the national conscience was stirred into various social reforms, including the end of slavery, and when feminists organized and launched a campaign for women's rights, though with only limited success. In all these areas, much more was to come.

The Civil War curtailed immigration but did not stop it completely. When the awful carnage had ended and the nation was reunited, immigration resumed even stronger than before. Where it had taken forty years before the war to absorb over 5 million immigrants, that figure was surpassed in just twenty years, with the arrival of 5.1 million between 1861 and 1880.

Irish immigration, however, had peaked and was now about half what it had been in the 1850s. German immigration dropped too, but not as much, and exceeded the Irish by more than 630,000 between 1861 and 1880. Other groups began to make their presence felt more, most notably the Chinese, French Canadians, Russians, Scandinavians, and Swiss.

By 1880, the U.S. population exceeded 50 million, more than five times what it had been in 1820. It was filled now with millions of Irish and German Americans, tens of thousands of Chinese, Mexican, and Native Americans, plus many other White ethnics, none of whom were Anglo Americans, and most of whom were still unassimilated.

Yet even though the process was incomplete, this era was drawing to a close and a new one was beginning. In 1890, the Census Bureau would declare the frontier no longer existed; in urban areas, steel girders and elevators would dramatically alter the cityscapes and population density; and inventions such as the telephone (1876) and incandescent light (1880) were beginning to revolutionize life at home.

An industrializing America would now roar into an industrial age, with new factories opening almost daily. The world would become a smaller place, thanks to advances in transportation and communications. Steamships would soon fill their holds with human freight, as millions of "new immigrants" from Asia, Europe, and the Middle East would seek the American Dream.

The America they would come to would be vastly different from what earlier immigrants had found. And these new immigrants would be vastly different from what Americans had known of immigrants. Physically and culturally distinct, the newcomers would bring even greater diversity, challenges, and progress to the American scene than ever before.

6

Diversity in the Industrial Age

Astounding changes occurred in American society between 1871 and 1920. Railroad track miles tripled from 53,000 in 1870 to 167,000 in 1890, creating an efficient transportation system that welded the nation into an enormous, unified market.[1] The spectacular growth of cities dramatically altered the American way of life. Industrialization brought the majority of the labor force into manufacturing, because it created thousands of jobs and a labor shortage.

Opportunity and Exploitation

The influx of 26.3 million immigrants between 1871 and 1920 filled America's desperate need for labor. Whether they worked in the mines or on railroad construction in remote areas or in the factories and mills of the cities, the immigrants helped the nation come of age industrially. In a pattern comparable to today, they were obliged to take jobs of low status, low pay, long hours, and difficult work that the native born shunned. By their presence, the immigrants represented the paradoxical duality of opportunity and exploitation.

As terrible as the living and working conditions were for the immigrant workers, circumstances in their homelands were even worse. Some may have been deceived by false claims of labor recruiters or steamship companies, but most had realistic expectations from letters sent by friends and relatives already in America. The chain migration launched by these letters gives testimony to the opportunities the immigrants found here, as does the willingness of most to remain.

AUTHOR'S NOTE: All immigration data in this chapter come from the U.S. Immigration and Naturalization Service, *1993 Statistical Yearbook* (Washington, DC: Government Printing Office, 1994), Table 2: 26-27.

Yet whatever economic opportunities the immigrants found, they were often exploited nonetheless. Large-scale immigration enabled industrialists to keep wages low and circumvent labor union organization efforts. This split labor market, as described by Edna Bonacich, was a constant reality because employers hired newcomers as strikebreakers or as lower-paid workers to replace higher-paid ones.[2] The result was ethnic antagonism of native-born or older immigrant workers against the new arrivals for either taking their jobs away or else depressing their wage scale.

Stephen Steinberg asserts that large-scale immigration enabled industrialists to maintain

a cheap and highly mobile labor force for the most exploitative jobs at a time when American capitalism was in its most rapacious phase. . . . The existence of a labor surplus . . . exerted pressure on workers to accept long hours, poor conditions, and low wages. The real function of the liberal immigration policies of the period, therefore, was to flood the labor market in order to keep labor abundant and cheap. Without this contrived surplus of immigrant labor, the costs of economic growth would have been immeasurably greater, thereby shrinking the capital base that was essential for economic growth.[3]

Disparaged for their cultural differences and lower-class status, victims of prejudice and exploitation, immigrant groups eventually rose from the wage-scale bottom to better-paying positions. Those opportunities came about for many reasons, including a drop in immigration, labor union advances, and the Americanization of the immigrants that was promoted in the schools and many companies.

Minority Family Economies

Within the immigrant communities, gender played an important role in the organization of economic activities. Although the men sought employment in a variety of occupations, cultural norms dictated that married women should not work outside the home. Indeed, less than 5 percent did so in 1890, often only because their husbands were disabled, missing, or unemployed. Typically, the wife's role was to maintain the house. If family needs required her income because the children were too young to work, then she would take on work at home (such as laundry or sewing) or else care for boarders (a common practice given the high number of male immigrants).

The world of work for women thus fell mostly to the young and single. More than half of all gainfully employed women at the turn of the century were between sixteen and twenty-four years old. These young women were often employed in factories or mills in "suitable" positions such as machine tenders or seamstresses perhaps, or else as assemblers, inspectors, packers, and the like in various types of plants.[4]

About one-third of all employed female workers at this time were blue-collar workers. Another third were domestic workers: maids, cooks, nannies, and so on. In the North, many single Irish or Scandinavian women had journeyed without family to begin life anew in America. In the South, African American women held similar positions. The final third of female workers were usually not first-generation Americans. Employed women in this category were in such white-collar positions as nurse, teacher, or sales clerk.

Children, usually at about the age of eight or nine, often went to work in the mills and the mines. With no child labor laws yet to protect them, they worked the same long hours under harsh working conditions as did the adults, but usually for one-tenth an adult's wages. Economic necessity dictated their working, however, for without the children's small wages, families could not survive.

In nonurban settings—whether the family be African, Asian, Hispanic, White ethnic, or native-born American—the entire family unit worked everyday, each family member—man, woman, and child—performing necessary farm tasks for the welfare of all. Here, too, the work was hard, although one's labors were at least within a family environment.

An expanding economy and population and the institution of child labor laws (not applicable to agriculture) brought about an increase in jobs for women. Included in this significant rise of female participation in the nonfarm labor force were married women as well. By 1920, one in five paid workers was a woman, and one in ten married women, twice that of 1890, had become a wage earner.

The Growth of Business

As the United States became a land of factories, machines, and railroads, large-scale enterprise also began. Companies discovered the benefits of vertical integration—controlling all aspects of production from its raw material stage to its distribution—and launched national firms capable of handling all aspects of an entire industry.

Through mergers and buyouts, larger companies took advantage of their size to eliminate or control competition. Big business and monopolies emerged as major components of American industry and so did a turbulent labor period, as fledgling unions and strikers fought back against long hours, low pay, and harsh working conditions.

The Growth of Cities

American cities experienced spectacular growth, creating an urban culture previously unknown.[5] By 1900, one in five Americans lived in a city of one hundred thousand people or more; one in ten lived in a city of at least one million people. Workers in 209 principal cities produced two-thirds of the total industrial output.

Although the affluent and the middle class were spared such problems, this dynamic urban expansion created overcrowded tenements, pollution, crime, unsanitary conditions, sickness, disease, and death among the poor. Into this rapidly urbanizing, industrializing society came 26.3 million immigrants between 1871 and 1920. Almost 8.8 million arrived between 1901 and 1910, until now the decade of greatest immigration.

Population Diversity

Considerable attention has been paid to the great influx of southern, central, and eastern Europeans in this period. To be sure, their numbers and distinctive characteristics did create an impact and trigger strong nativist reactions. However, this was also a period of high immigration from northern and western Europe and other parts of the world, including 1.7 million Canadians, 840,000 Asians, 277,000 Mexicans, 307,000 West Indians, and 90,000 Central and South Americans.

America's racial and cultural diversity were distributed throughout the land. Those new Canadian and European Americans settling mostly in the Northeast and Midwest were complemented by African Americans mostly living in the South, Asian Americans on the Pacific Coast, Mexican Americans in the Southwest, Native Americans throughout the West, and West Indians in the northeastern cities.

Racial Occupational Patterning

In cities, towns, and reservations, America's racial minorities lived segregated and socially isolated from White America. Some were former slaves or their descendants. Others were a conquered people. Still others were voluntary immigrants seeking their fortune. All shared, however, a common fate. As Robert Blauner observed, most were relegated to primary occupations that did not provide the same upward mobility opportunities as industrial jobs did for Europeans.

> In an historical sense, people of color provided much of the hard labor (and the technical skills) that built up the agricultural base and the mineral-transport-communication infrastructure necessary for industrialization and modernization, whereas the European worked primarily within the industrialized, modern sectors. The initial position of European ethnics, while low, was therefore strategic for movement up the economic and social pyramid. The placement of nonwhite groups, however, imposed barrier upon barrier on such mobility, freezing them for long periods of time in the least favorable segments of the economy.[6]

Pluralism and Assimilation

The "new" immigration, encouraged by a rapidly expanding economy, brought considerable cultural diversity into the country. Previously little-known nationality groups now flocked to the nation's shores, establishing their ethnoreligious cultural marks. By the turn of the century, most northeastern cities would contain two-thirds or more of a foreign-born population.

Vibrant ethnic communities, albeit mostly impoverished ones, thrived among these diverse transplanted newcomers. From Boston's West End to New York City's Lower East Side to Chicago's Near West Side and many points in between, a mosaic of small worlds sprung up and flourished. A host of parallel social institutions—clubs, organizations, foreign-language newspapers, stores, churches, and synagogues—took form and helped sustain ethnic subcultures over many years.

Yet even as pluralism manifested itself in new or revitalized ethnic communities, ethnicity began to fade among other groups. Second- and third-generation Americans of northern and western European ancestry were less inclined to retain an ethnic identity. Even though they had not yet become fully assimilated, the Irish and Germans moved toward economic equality with older groups and gained political power. The native born of Dutch, French, and Scandinavian ancestry were more likely to have attained structural assimilation, even as new arrivals from those areas replenished the ethnic mosaic.

In short, the dual realities of assimilation and pluralism were once again evident. The rest of this chapter offers a brief look at various groups who comprised that diversity.

African Americans

Freed from slavery, most African Africans remained in the agricultural South after the Civil War. Many worked on farms as sharecroppers, obtaining credit through the year from storekeepers on a crop-lien system, in which proceeds from the crops first paid off debts accrued. Because the storekeeper was also the landowner or collaborated with the land-owner, he charged high prices to assure the farmer was still in debt after the harvest. This practice kept southern Blacks in economic bondage.

Interracial Harmony, Then Dissolution

For a while interracial cooperation offered promise of a new era in race relations in the South. Blacks and Whites worked side by side in coal mines, lumber camps, and on waterfront docks, their efforts encouraged in the mid-1880s by the interracial unionism of the Knights of Labor. White and Black dirt farmers formed separate Farmers' Alliance organizations, but the two worked together for agrarian reform. They united behind the Populist party in 1891, but vicious opposition and voter fraud resulted in defeat almost everywhere. The embittered poor Whites turned against their Black allies as the cause of their losses, strongly encouraged in this direction by the White conservative elite.

Out of this struggle was born a malicious form of White supremacy, determined to establish a rigid color line. As George M. Fredrickson succinctly said,

> In the late nineteenth century, when blatant racism was reaching the extreme point of its development, the resurgent white supremacists of the South put new and more stringent laws on the books. Not only were anti-miscegenation statutes re-enacted or reaffirmed, but more rigorous definitions of whiteness were put into effect. By the beginning of the twentieth century most southern states were operating in accordance with what amounted to a "one-drop rule," meaning in effect that a person with any known degree of black ancestry was legally considered a Negro and subject to the full disabilities associated with segregation and disfranchisement.[7]

Political demagogues throughout the South used race baiting as a means to win votes from southern Whites still resentful over northern economic and political dominance. Race hatred became an acceptable outlet, with violent attacks and lynchings practically a way of life.

Institutionalizing Racial Stratification

Poll taxes, initiated in some districts in 1877 to disfranchise Black voters, now spread. Literacy tests were another effective means enacted to prevent voting, because about 75 percent of Black Americans were illiterate. (Illiterate poor Whites were exempted by "grandfather clauses," if their grandfathers had been eligible to vote in 1860.[8])

Beginning in Florida in 1887, mandatory segregation laws regarding train passengers were passed in several states. When the U.S. Supreme Court upheld such laws in *Plessy v. Ferguson* in 1896, the "separate but equal" doctrine became institutionalized. Between 1901 and 1910, most Southern states passed a wide array of Jim Crow laws, bringing racial segregation into all places of public accommodation.

Racial hatred manifested itself in its ugliest form in violence. Between 1892 and 1921, almost 2,400 Blacks were lynched, most in the South. The growing presence of Blacks in the cities and perceptions of them as an economic threat led to deadly race riots erupting in Georgia, Illinois, Indiana, and Ohio between 1904 and 1908.

Fear of economic competition triggered another deadly, White-dominated race riot in East St. Louis in 1917. When union organizers placed a newspaper ad claiming that local industries were recruiting Blacks to reduce White wages, the workers attacked the Black ghetto. In the aftermath, thirty-nine Blacks and nine Whites had been killed. Two years later, riots exploded in twenty-six cities, leaving thirty-eight killed in Chicago and six dead in Washington, DC.

Life in the North

The promise of better education and work opportunities lured Black migrants to the North. Their numbers were not that noticeable next to the large European inflow, but the 80,000 migrants between 1870 and 1890 increased to 200,000 between 1890 and 1910, bringing the northern Black population to about one-tenth of the total at the turn of the century.[9] Economic hard times and boll weevil destruction of cotton crops prompted many more to head north in the next decade, raising the northern Black population from 850,000 in 1910 to 1.4 million in 1920.

Labor union hostility in the North and *de facto* segregation (unequal and differential treatment of a group or groups entrenched in social customs and traditions) created a dual society there just as *de jure* segregation (unequal and differential treatment of a group or groups established by law) had done in the South. Black churches and other parallel social institutions formed the bedrock of the segregated racial community. A Black middle class, many graduates of Black colleges, emerged and achieved success in business and the professions. Black artists and writers creatively depicted Black life in America, and musicians contributed blues and jazz to the popular culture.

Southern Blacks remained a rural people, struggling within a system designed to keep them subjugated. Northern Blacks were an urban people, some of them poor, others working or middle class. A 1918 Census Bureau analysis showed that 79 percent of all Black males over age 10 were gainfully employed, 49 percent of them in agricultural pursuits.

Economist Robert Higgs reports that, in over a third of a century between 1867 and 1900, Black incomes more than doubled, thus increasing more rapidly than White incomes. He adds, however, that in absolute numbers, the Black income level in 1900 lay far below the White level:[10]

> Even if the Blacks could have steadily raised their income per capita twice as fast as the Whites, about 70 years would have been required to close the gap. Black income per capita probably did not exceed four-tenths of the White level in 1914. (p. 125)

Black exclusion from political influence and public discrimination in education and legal treatment impeded their economic development. Yet even if there had not been racial discrimination, argues Higgs, the years of the industrial age were not sufficient to enable Blacks to acquire the literacy, skills, experience, and capital needed to close the economic gap with Whites. These "swift competitors" had too large a head start.

Asian Americans and Pacific Islanders

Between 1871 and 1920, the Asian American population changed from a fairly small, mostly Chinese one to a significantly large, multi-Asian and Pacific Islander presence.[11] Japanese, Filipinos, Asian Indians, and Koreans came to the U.S. mainland, as tens of thousands of others went to Hawaii, most to work there on the sugar and pineapple plantations.

Each of these non-Western groups brought, and kept fairly intact, a racial and cultural diversity throughout the western states. Despite Asian American differences in nationality, language, and culture, to most Americans they all looked alike, they all were alike, and they all were unassimilable and undesirable. Not surprisingly, fear, resentment, antagonism, and violence soon marked Asian-White relations.

National leaders fanned the flames of racial bigotry. U.S. Senator James G. Blaine, who narrowly lost the presidency to Grover Cleveland in 1884, declared in an 1879 Senate speech, "The Asiatic cannot go on with our population and make a homogeneous element."[12] Pressured by labor unions and newspapers, Congress enacted in 1882 the first national human embargo on a particular race. In 1924, spurred by the efforts of Senator Henry Cabot Lodge and Secretary of State Charles Evans Hughes, Congress specifically denied Japan an immigration quota in the Immigration Act of 1924.

What can we make of these actions? It is too simplistic to attribute them solely to racial bigotry, although it certainly was a factor. From an interactionist perspective, non-Western differences in physical appearance, language, belief systems, customs, stoicism, and observable behavior affected social distance perceptions and resultant interaction patterns. Once removed from any affinity to the dominant group, the Asians were more likely to generate tensions, violent outbreaks, and governmental restrictions.

It would be a mistake, however, to confine interracial problems to racist motivations and/or perceived cultural dissonance only. Economic competition played a major role, as indicated by the rising intensity in demands for Chinese exclusion during the depression of the 1870s, when a lull in railroad construction brought the Chinese back into California. In another example, Roger Daniels describes a "crusade against Japanese contract labor" in the 1890s by the San Francisco *Morning Call*, which claimed Japanese immigrants were taking work away from Americans.[13] Organized labor continually viewed the Asians as a threat to the American worker and lobbied extensively against their immigration.

The Chinese

By 1880, the Chinese presence had tripled in twenty years to more than 105,000, following the Burlingame Treaty of 1868, which guaranteed free Chinese immigration and most-favored-nation treatment. In 1882, Chinese immigration peaked with 40,000 new arrivals, prompting passage of the Chinese Exclusion Act previously mentioned.

Frequent victims of mob violence in most western cities—including murderous riots in Los Angeles and Rock Springs, Wyoming, that left a total of forty-nine dead by hanging or bullets—many Chinese retreated to their Chinatowns. Here they lived in cultural isolation, preserving their language, customs, and traditions in a miniworld within American society.[14] Other Chinese returned to their homeland, and by 1920 their numbers had dropped to about 67,000 from almost 101,000 in 1880.

The Japanese

From a census count of merely 148 Japanese Americans in 1880, their numbers increased to over 24,000 in 1900, and to over 111,000 by 1920, including almost 30,000 "picture brides" who joined husbands they had married by proxy. Concentrated primarily on the Pacific coast, most Japanese earned a living in agriculture. Highly productive and competitive with White farmers, they fell victim to state laws denying land ownership or long-term land leases to them or their minor children. Continuing to work mostly as tenant farmers, the Japanese lived in social isolation in the fertile river valleys where they maintained their cultural diversity.

The Asian Indians

Asian Indian immigrants slightly exceeded 300 between 1881 and 1900. This miniscule number was augmented by almost 7,000 more arrivals in the next twenty years.[15] Most were Sikh males from the northern province of Punjab, distinctive in their traditionally worn beards and turbans. Also settling primarily in the Pacific Coast states, they quickly drew the wrath of nativists who called for their exclusion. Hundreds of Asian Indian workers were forcibly driven from lumber camps and towns in Washington state in 1907, and zealous immigration officials, under pressure from the Asiatic Exclusion League, barred the entry of almost 3,000 new immigrants between 1908 and 1920. Working as contract farm laborers, most lived and worked in the Imperial, San Joaquin, and Sacramento valleys in California.

The Koreans

About seven thousand Koreans migrated to Hawaii as farm laborers in the early twentieth century, and two thousand of these continued on to the mainland. Before the legislation in 1924 ended their immigration, several thousand more Koreans joined their compatriots on the mainland. Their relatively small numbers lessened the extent of labor antagonism they generated in this period.

The Filipinos

Filipinos became U.S. nationals in 1898, but few migrated right away to the United States. Only 160 are listed in the 1910 census, and 5,603 in 1920. Like most early Asian immigrants, most Filipinos were male, worked in agriculture, and were slow to acculturate. Again, their fairly small numbers and work on commercial farms mitigated against much labor antagonism.

Hispanic Americans

In the last two decades of the nineteenth century, approximately 300,000 Mexican Americans living in the Southwest continued to experience serious challenges brought by thousands of Anglo Americans and European immigrants coming to settle in the region. Victims of drought, discriminatory taxes, foreclosures, questionable local judicial rulings, and violent intimidation, many lost their lands. Mexican Americans also fell victim to economic change, because the large commercial farms of agribusiness, with their extensive investments in machinery and irrigation systems priced the small farmers out of business.[16]

Changes in Family Structure and Status

Decline of their rancho system—landed estates that were powerful, independent economic units—played havoc with their traditional values that had long sustained the cohesiveness of a paternalistic extended family system. A nuclear family pattern slowly emerged, accompanied by an increase in common law marriages and consensual unions. In urban areas such as Los Angeles, a startling increase in female-headed families occurred; by 1880, one-third of the Mexican American families were matriarchal, most living in substandard conditions.

Reduced to the status of low-paid laborers for the large growers, Mexican Americans became stereotyped as lazy and backward. Living in the *barrio* of a city or town, or in rural isolation, they were virtually a colonial people lacking in economic or political power.

Elsewhere in the United States, the Hispanic presence was small. About 1,500 Puerto Ricans lived in the continental United States in 1910. Florida was home to most other Hispanics at this time, although a small Cuban community across the Hudson River from New York City continued to thrive since its beginnings in 1850.

Native Americans

This era was a bleak one for the indigenous peoples of the United States. Made dependent wards of the government in 1871, confined to reservations out of the White man's way, they would soon lose even two-thirds of these reservation lands through deceitful and fraudulent real estate transactions. This followed passage of the ill-conceived Dawes Act of 1887, which attempted to divide tribal lands into individual tracts in an effort to "civilize" its inhabitants.[17]

Whites' fears of a resurgence of Native American beliefs and practices, prompted by a Native American spiritual revival known as the Ghost Dance Religion, led to the tragic massacre at Wounded Knee in 1890 in which 150 defenseless Sioux were killed. It was the last violent episode, as the government continued its efforts at Anglo conformity through education and Christian missionary work.

The northern Plains Indians were given the southern section of the Dakota Territory and the southern Plains Indians were placed in the Oklahoma Territory along with the Cherokee, Chickasaw, Choctaw, Creek, and Seminole. The Navajo and Apache were on reservations in the Southwest, whereas other tribes were scattered in the Rockies and beyond.

Change in Social Structure

Reservation life changed the tribes from self-reliant harvesters of nature's bounty to dependent wards of the government, obliged to rely on food shipments for sustenance. With their food-producing, often nomadic lifestyle nullified, Native Americans also found their cultural, familial, and communal well-being subverted as well. Their social structure, built on an active role for all within the tribe, collapsed under an imposed passive role.

Escapist Responses

Loss of their independent male role as leaders, hunters, providers, protectors, and warriors denied the men any means of maintaining self-esteem.

As an escape from their harsh reality and from the hopelessness and despair they felt, many thousands of Native American men turned to drink and drugs.

Despite laws against Native American possession of alcohol, it was readily available, even supplied by government agents to keep the reservations tranquil. Alcoholism became a problem, as did the chronic use of the hallucinogen *peyote,* a derivative of the cactus plant. Its use spreading over several decades from the Mescalero Apache to virtually all tribes, peyotism was institutionalized in the Native American Church. With no control over their lives, Native Americans struggled to maintain their sense of identity and oneness with the universe by any means possible.

As the Native Americans lived their lives in a reduced state of dependency, their population shrank to about 237,000 by 1900 (it had been 600,000 in 1776).[18] During the late nineteenth and early twentieth centuries, they remained pockets of diversity, ignored by most of society, pacified through alcohol by government agents, and encouraged by assimilationist idealists and missionaries to divest themselves of their diversity and embrace "White civilization."[19]

Middle Eastern Americans

About 3,000 Arab immigrants came in the 1880s, followed by more than 30,000 in the 1890s. Another 70,000 followed until the outbreak of World War I in 1914. Most came from what is now Syria and Lebanon, but because they lived in a region under the control of the Ottoman Empire, their passports designated them as "Turks." Not until 1899 did a separate category for "Syrian" appear on immigration rosters. Although about 85 percent came from Lebanon, identification of "Lebanese" did not gain acceptance until the 1930s.

Religious Diversity

About 10 percent were Muslims, a very small number were Jewish, and almost all the rest were Christians fleeing religious persecution from the Turks. The Christians divided into Maronites, Melkites, Orthodox, and Presbyterians.

Their theological differences translated into social and structural separation in their ethnic communities in the United States, as it had in the Middle East. What bonded them together was a conviction that those sharing similar beliefs belonged to a social order qualitatively different from the rest. They looked upon themselves not as Syrians, but as co-religionists from a particular village. Americans lumped them together as the single entity of "Syrian," much as they had combined other provincial groups into single nationality groups. And, as with other ethnic groups, these first-generation immigrants soon saw themselves as Americans perceived them.[20]

Settlement and Occupational Patterns

Most immigrants settled in a "Syrian belt" stretching westward from the textile mills of southern New England and New York-New Jersey through the steel towns in Pennsylvania and Ohio to the automobile factories in Detroit. In each of these regions near the factories where they worked, the Syrians established their ethnic communities.

Some Syrians became itinerant peddlers or salesmen. Once financially secure, they became shopkeepers, wholesalers, and fabric or department store owners. By 1911, Syrians were in almost every branch of commerce, including banking and import-export houses, and the government reported that Syrian American median income was only slightly lower than the $665 annual income of adult native-born White males.

Northern and Western European Americans

For many countries situated in the northwestern part of the European continent, the late nineteenth and early twentieth centuries marked the time of their largest numbers of emigrants leaving for the United States. Belgium, Denmark, England, Holland, Norway, Scotland, and Sweden sent more emigrants at this time than in any other period.[21]

Pronounced Cultural Diversity

Because more than 8.1 million immigrants arrived from this part of the world between 1880 and 1920, northern and western European cultural diversity was as marked a presence as that of other nationality groups.

English immigrants, for example, numbered 1.5 million between 1881 and 1920, and other parts of Great Britain accounted for almost an additional half million. Almost a million Swedes, more than a half million

Norwegians, and almost a quarter million Danes came. Germany sent over 2.4 million immigrants, whereas Ireland supplied over 1.5 million. More than 100,000 Belgians, 170,000 Dutch, and 216,000 French came as well.

Some of these numbers were tightly clustered within only a portion of this forty-year period, making the ethnic community vigor of some groups even more pronounced. In the 1880s, the 5.2 million immigrants included approximately 1.5 million Germans, 655,000 Irish, 645,000 English, 177,000 Norwegians, 392,000 Swedes, 150,000 Scots, 88,000 Danes, 53,000 Dutch, and 50,000 French. Between 1901 and 1910, the 8.8 million immigrants included about 388,000 English, 341,000 Germans, 339,000 Irish, 250,000 Swedes, 190,000 Norwegians, 120,000 Scots, 65,000 Danes, 48,000 Dutch, and 41,000 Belgians.

The Irish

These new arrivals, in a typical chain migration pattern, often settled near family or friends. Consequently, by the turn of the century, almost seven million Irish Catholics were concentrated in the urban Northeast, living in "Paddy's Villages" or shantytowns usually located in older, less desirable residential sections of most cities. Experiencing job and social discrimination because of their religion, their full absorption into the mainstream was at least one generation away.

The Germans

Over nine million Germans, diverse in their religions and backgrounds, lived in both rural and urban clusters. Most major cities throughout the Northeast had Germantown sections, but the greatest concentration remained in the German triangle of the Midwest (the area between Milwaukee, Cincinnati, and St. Louis). Wherever they lived, German Americans, particularly first generation, functioned in a culturally isolated ethnic world where a wide array of parallel social institutions helped maintain their language and customs.

Other Northwestern Europeans

The Midwest—particularly Illinois, Iowa, Michigan, and Wisconsin—also attracted the recent Dutch immigrants because of favorable soil and climate conditions. More than 1.5 million Danes, Finns, Norwegians, and Swedes lived on farms or in towns of the northern Midwest, retaining a vibrant Scandinavian imprint on that region.

The residence in New England of more than a half million French Canadians and in Louisiana of about a quarter million Cajuns generated circumstances that would allow for the establishment of persistent ethnic subcultures lasting into present times. In addition, more than 150,000 French immigrants arriving between 1871 and 1900 were too recent to yet be fully assimilated.

Southern, Central, and Eastern European Americans

Much has been written about these "new" immigrants, and for good reason. Here was a huge inrush in a short span of time of physically, culturally, linguistically, and religiously distinct peoples who generated many reactions.[22]

Whether for economic, political, or religious reasons, they had come to "Golden America" to seek a better life. They were Armenians, Greeks, Italians, Portuguese, and Turks from the southern part of the European continent; Czechs, Hungarians, Poles, and Slovaks from the plains of central Europe; Austrians and Swiss from the high mountain country; Latvians and Lithuanians from the Baltic area; Byelorussians, Ruthenians, Ukrainians, and others from the western regions of Czarist Russia; and Jews from all parts of eastern and central Europe, especially Russia.

Even within these groups, much diversity could be found. Among the Slavic group, for example, were Bohemians (Czechs), Bulgarians, Croatians, Dalmatians, Montenegrins, Serbs, Slovaks, Slovenians, and still others. Each had their own identity and culture, which they attempted to preserve in their adopted country.

No More Farming

Even though most came from agrarian regions in Europe, few went into farming in the United States. Most had little money left when they arrived and could not afford to travel further to the nation's interior where there was cheap land. Only Germans and Scandinavians mostly could continue onward, finding support among countrymen or family already there. Jews, prohibited from owning land in Europe, had not been farmers and so the jobs they took in the United States were in such fields as the mercantile and needle trades.

Most of the southern, central, and eastern European peasants had lived in compact, *gemeinschaft* village communities, and so found little appeal in isolated farms in rural communities. Lacking sufficient funds and motivation to become farmers, most worked in the factories, mills, and mines, where wages were actually better than the income of the average farmer.

Millions upon millions of immigrants settled in densely populated urban neighborhoods, often under the most deplorable living conditions imaginable. Our larger cities in the northeastern quadrant became the repositories of a foreign-born majority speaking a multitude of tongues. Never before in the nation's history had there been so massive an influx of immigrants heavily concentrated in our cities turning entire neighborhoods into foreign entities.

Cultural Dissonance

Arriving in record numbers, these nationality groups were strikingly different in appearance, culture, customs, language, political experiences, and ideology. Physical appearance—whether the darker features of those from the Mediterranean region, or the eastern European women with kerchiefs on their heads, or Jewish men with yarmulkas and full beards—set them apart from native-born Americans. Because most were Catholics, Jews, or Orthodox Christians, Protestant America also reacted with disdain at this large manifestation of diverse groups whose religious buildings and clergy were daily reminders of change in American society.

Native-born Americans, most of northwestern European descent, were aghast at the heavy immigration of dissimilar cultural types and blamed the new arrivals for all existing social discontents. They condemned them for the increase in crime, even though every objective investigation proved the crime rate among first-generation Americans was lower than for the rest of the country. (The increase more typically occurred among the second generation.) Labor disputes and calls for political and economic reform furthered criticism of the "un-American agitators."

The "Birds of Passage"

Hundreds of thousands came as sojourners, or "birds of passage," as some called them. They came not to stay, but to make enough money to return home and realize their goal of buying land, redeeming the family mortgage, or providing dowries for sisters or daughters. They had less interest in learning English, getting involved in the labor movement, or acculturating. Greeks, Poles, and Italians particularly were sojourners. Half of all Italians to arrive in the 1880s and 1890s returned home, creating a "shuttle migration." In some years between 1908 and 1920, the number of Italians returning home reached between 60 and 70 percent of the new immigrants. More than 500,000 Poles returned between 1900 and 1915, as did tens of thousands of Greeks.

Gradually, more who came as sojourners decided to stay. Other sojourners returned to the United States with their wives and children. As these joined other family groups putting down roots, their birth rates—considerably higher than for that of multiple-generation Americans—became a cause for nativist alarm. Some cited population statistics to project the "old" Americans becoming a minority to the "inferior" newcomers. Eugenicists like Madison Grant, president of the New York Zoological Society, argued in *The Passing of the Great Race* (1916) for those of Anglo Saxon, Nordic, and Teutonic origins to marry only among themselves to prevent racial hybridism and reversion to the "lower type" through contamination of their "racial purity."[23]

The Merger of Gender
and Immigrant Issues

Feminists continued efforts begun a generation earlier to secure women's rights. Only Wyoming (1869) and Utah (1870) had given women the right to vote prior to the industrial age. Colorado (1893) and Idaho (1896) then joined their ranks but, with little movement for full voting rights for women anywhere else, the women's movement turned toward social reform.[24]

Women's organizations successfully lobbied in state legislatures for a minimum wage scale and maximum work day, public assistance programs for women with children, and other protective legislation. Middle-class, college-educated women, inspired by Jane Addams and Ellen Gates Starr founding Hull House in Chicago's West Side in 1889, established dozens of other settlement houses in the slum areas of most major cities.[25] In these community centers, the immigrants rescued from abominable slum conditions became residents who benefited from improved living conditions, educational instruction, recreation, and other opportunities for self-realization.

About half of the settlement house female residents went on to find careers in social service, particularly the newly emerging field of social work. As this new generation of feminists, drawn from a different class, continued their efforts at social reform and social service, they bridged the class lines. It was not just affluent, middle-class women who turned anew to women's suffrage, but a sisterhood of immigrants and native born, middle class and working class. The new combination brought added strength and vigor to the feminist cause.

Women's Suffrage

Voting rights for women were soon approved in other western states, beginning with Washington in 1910. Other states followed: Arizona, California, Kansas, and Oregon (1912); Montana and Nevada (1914).

As women grew more militant, staging demonstrations, protest marches, and rallies, they met fierce resistance. They were ridiculed, insulted, and abused—slapped, tripped, and pelted with overripe fruits, vegetables, and burning cigars. Chaining themselves to posts, fences, and grillwork of public buildings, these early feminists were arrested and jailed. In 1913, in Washington, DC, federal troops arrived to quell the unrest, and in 1916, six months of picketing the White House ended with mass arrests and imprisonment when the women refused to pay the "unjust" fines.[26]

After a 1915 New York state referendum failed, voters in 1917 approved a new referendum giving women the right to vote. In 1918, three other states—Michigan, Oklahoma, and South Dakota—also granted women's suffrage. In 1918, the House passed a women's suffrage constitutional amendment but it took eighteen more months for the Senate to approve it. Finally, with ratification by Tennessee in August 1920, the Nineteenth Amendment gave women the right to vote everywhere.

Few women ran for political office, usually only serving as appointees to fill their dead husband's unexpired term. The League of Women Voters came into being, as did numerous women's lobbying groups. After initially fearing women's voting power and passing some "female-friendly" laws, such as health care assistance to reduce infant and maternal mortality, Congressional politicians soon realized that women did not vote as a bloc and became less sensitive to their lobbying efforts.

Intergroup Conflicts

Nativist hostility and violent clashes marked the industrial age as they had the earlier part of the nineteenth century. In addition to the race riots previously mentioned, interethnic conflicts also arose. Organizations such as the American Protective Association (APA) and the Ku Klux Klan drew widespread popular support in their campaigns for a "pure" America.[27]

The APA began in Iowa in 1887, and by 1893 it claimed about one million members in twenty states, primarily in the midwestern "Bible Belt." An anti-Catholic organization, it particularly attracted the Scots-Irish, as well as Germans, Scandinavians, and English. Committed to an English-only school curriculum, removal of Catholic teachers and school board members, longer naturalization periods, restrictive immigration, and election of Protestant officeholders only, the APA claimed 100 members serving in the 54th Congress (1895-1896).

The Ku Klux Klan, reconstituted in 1915 after being sympathetically portrayed in D. W. Griffith's silent film classic *Birth of a Nation,* reached a membership of almost five million by 1926. Their membership, strongest in Indiana and Ohio, drew loyal support from thousands of Pennsylvania Dutch Klansmen, who held intense feelings against Roman Catholics. Dedicating itself to White supremacy, Protestant Christianity, and Americanism, the new Klan used intimidation, violence, and politics to influence employers, voters, schools, and textbook content, seeking moral regulation and a stabilization of the old order.

American neutrality in the first three years of World War I encouraged German Americans to be pro-German and raise relief funds to support their countrymen. American entry into the war in 1917 touched off an anti-German, patriotic hysteria. This ranged from renaming sauerkraut "liberty cabbage," to German Americans losing their jobs, to mob attacks on German establishments and communities. Anything German was to be eradicated: German-language publications, school courses, or church services; concert music; street names; and organizations.

In each instance, these reactionary movements flourished and faded within a few years. Internal struggles, corruption charges, and the free silver issue undermined the APA. Corruption among the leadership of the KKK and restrictive immigration laws lessening public concern hastened its decline. The end of World War I in 1918 soon enabled the German American community to reassert its ethnic marks of organizational activities, although its cultural resilience never sprang back fully to its former vitality.

Beyond the Horizon

A new flurry of immigration after World War I brought calls anew for restrictions. Passage of the National Origins Quota Act of 1921 reduced immigration to 3 percent of any nationality living in the United States in 1910. Amended in 1924 to a temporary limit of 2 percent of those here in 1890, the limit was raised again to 3 percent in 1929 with a ceiling of 150,000 total immigrants.

Designed to favor the northern and western Europeans, this legislation was hailed by its supporters as a way to prevent further dilution of the American population and its cultural composition. In their desire to "keep America American," nativists succeeded in ending the Great Migration.

Yet as William James once observed, "Change begets change." American's labor market still needed workers in good economic times. With few Europeans to fill expanding needs, Mexicans and Puerto Ricans would meet the demand for new labor, setting in motion a greater Hispanic migration than ever before.

Ahead lay the Roaring Twenties, the Great Depression, and World War II, which would bring in about 400,000 Displaced Persons afterwards. It was a paltry number compared to past immigrant totals or the nation's 150.7 million people in 1950.

Even though in 1930 almost one out of three Americans was foreign born or the child of immigrant parents, ethnicity became less visible. With few new immigrants to renew them, ethnic communities would fade, causing a new generation of Americans to forget the great cultural diversity that had been such a dynamic part of American society. Once again, as in the early nineteenth century, low immigration in the late 1920s and throughout the 1930s, together with the pervasive acculturation process, created a culturally homogeneous population. Even though assimilation remained the ongoing process it always had been, the ebb in immigration gave it preeminence over the ever-present reality of pluralism.

This time, though, there would be differences. Some groups—the Armenians, Greeks, and Jews—would quickly enter the middle class. Others—like the Italians, Poles, and Slavic peoples—would mostly remain in working-class occupations for another generation, as would Asian Americans. African Americans, Mexicans, and Native Americans—victims of racial discrimination and internal colonization—would mostly struggle to survive in poverty or near-poverty circumstances.

Further ahead lay suburbanization, the Vietnam War, the civil rights movement, space exploration, the fall of Communism, the end of the cold war, and the high technology age. Significantly, also ahead would be a new immigration law and a third wave of immigration that would once again bring widespread diversity to the land and test once more its people's acceptance of that diversity.

7

Diversity in the Information Age

A s early as 1948, the invention of the transistor signaled the dawn of an electronic revolution. In the 1950s, the discovery of the structure of the genetic material DNA, the first successful transplant of an organ (the kidney), the development of an effective polio vaccine and of an oral contraceptive, the building of atomic energy plants, and the successful orbiting of Sputnik, the first artificial earth satellite, all expanded the limits of human achievement.

The 1960s, an incredible decade of turbulence and reform, also heralded new accomplishments once the sole province of science fiction. We developed the laser beam, transplanted hearts, and launched communication satellites instantly linking the world with images and sound from anywhere. Sending men into space and landing on the moon fired our imaginations even more.

In the 1970s came microprocessors, test tube babies, space shuttles, and the eradication of smallpox. On the heels of those advances arrived VCRs, CDs, personal computers in the home and workplace, Internet, and the information highway. As the electronic revolution unfolds further, we anticipate still other exciting possibilities.

The Human Element

This exciting world of scientific advancement is, of course, only one part of the human dimension and, in many ways, other aspects of life

AUTHOR'S NOTE: The data presented throughout this chapter about group population sizes and residential patterning come from the U.S. Bureau of the Census, *1990 Census Special Tabulations,* 1990 CPH-L-89 and 1990 CPH-L-91 (Washington, DC: Government Printing Office, 1990). The immigration statistics come from the U.S. Immigration and Naturalization Service, *1993 Statistical Yearbook* (Washington, DC: Government Printing Office, 1994), Tables 2 and 3: 26-31.

are unchanged from past generations. People in the world still suffer from hunger, deprivation, persecution, and repression. They still dream of a better life for themselves and their children. And, for many, that dream has a name: America.

In July 1963, when President John F. Kennedy urged an end to national quota restrictions in a special message to Congress, he initiated a change in our immigration policy that culminated with President Lyndon B. Johnson symbolically signing the new bill in 1965 on Liberty Island at the base of the Statue of Liberty. With his signature he ended a discriminatory immigration policy that emphasized place of birth and not individual worth or family reunification.

Unexpected Consequences

Most government officials expected the new legislation to open the doors to increased European migration. After all, there was an extensive waiting list for visas in many European countries severely restricted under the old quota system, yet in a typical year the British Isles, for example, was sending less than 40 percent of its allotted quota.

Immigrants from some countries—namely Greece, Italy, Poland, Portugal, Spain, the Soviet Union, and Yugoslavia—did increase notably. However, the "push" factors to leave were now greater in other parts of the world and soon European migration was quickly eclipsed. By the 1980s, European immigration represented only 10 percent of the total, with countries such as Greece, Italy, and Yugoslavia declining significantly in the number of emigrants leaving for the United States.

In the 1960s, immigrants from the Caribbean and Latin America outnumbered Europe for the first time and have done so in increasing proportion ever since. European immigration was more than two-and-a-half times Asian immigration in the 1960s, but only slightly more than half the Asian total in the 1970s. In 1993, Europe accounted for 18 percent of all immigration, Asia for 38 percent, and the Caribbean and Latin America for 37 percent. Canada, Africa, and Oceania accounted for the remaining 7 percent.

A Different America

The high-tech age dramatically altered American society just as the industrial age had. Previous immigrants from agrarian Europe had to make a triple adjustment to a new culture, an urban environment, and an industrialized society. Many of today's immigrants also make a triple adjustment, but for some the third part is often a bigger leap, from a preindustrial background into a postindustrial society.

Gone are many unskilled and semiskilled jobs enabling the newcomers to gain even a toehold in their new society. Many factory and mill jobs, once plentiful in the cities a short distance from where immigrants clustered in ethnic urban neighborhoods, are now often in industrial parks away from where many of today's immigrants can afford to live. New types of jobs now exist in the service sector, but many are low-paying, dead-end ones.

Some arrive possessing entrepreneurial skills or the education and training needed for better-status, better-paying positions. Their income enables them to settle in residential areas unaccustomed to the presence of first-generation Americans, particularly racially and culturally distinct Asians. Many of our suburbs now have a racial and cultural diversity once mostly confined to our cities.

Today's diversity is visible everywhere, not just in a few geographic locales. Some states receive more immigrants than others, and some have greater numbers of one or more groups than others, but no state is immune to the influx of Third World immigrants. Each of the fifty states now contains an unprecedented mixture of racial and ethnic groups that reflects current immigration patterns.

For Americans lulled by forty years of lower immigration totals, and new arrivals primarily from the sending countries of the past, the presence of so many different groups and languages is strange, but it is *deja vu* for this nation. Some of the groups may be new to the American scene, but the patterns of acculturation and ethnogenesis among them and of negative dominant responses are replays of yesteryear.

However, as this latest version of pluralism manifests itself, some new ingredients have been added. Government policy now supports pluralism instead of forced assimilation. Bilingualism in ballots, driver education manuals, education, and other public aspects are controversial realities. Social legislation from the 1960s ensures minority rights and opportunities as never before. Because diversity is more visible and protected than ever, some Americans fear the loss of an integrative, assimilationist force in the land. Moreover, some Americans question the extent of financial costs that new immigrants place on public budgets of education (including community colleges), health care, and Supplemental Security income for elderly immigrants (many of whom could well be supported by their children). Calls for reform range from tighter controls to total exclusion.

This chapter contains a brief overview of present-day diversity in America. The intent is simply to offer a portrait of contemporary American society to connect it with past diversity as a prelude to examining the concerns and controversial issues of today, which will be discussed in subsequent chapters.

Institutionalizing Minority Rights

Significant legislation passed in the 1960s brought American ideals about equality closer to reality for minorities long denied their rights. The Civil Rights Act of 1964 was the most far-reaching law against racial discrimination ever passed. It dealt with voting rights, employment practices, and any place of public accommodation—eating, lodging, entertainment, recreation, or service. It gave broad powers to the U.S. Attorney General to intervene in private suits regarding violation of civil rights and directed federal agencies to monitor state and local recipients of federal funds and withhold monies whenever noncompliance was found.

In 1965, Congress simplified judicial enforcement of the voting laws and extended them to state and local elections. In 1968, new legislation barred discrimination in housing and gave Native Americans greater rights in their dealings with courts and government agencies. Affirmative action, initiated by an executive order in 1963 by President Kennedy, became a powerful tool toward reducing institutional discrimination in hiring, promotion, and educational opportunities for minority group members or women.

In the decades since, important gains have been made, some of which will be delineated in the following sections on specific groups. For women, whether of the majority or of minority groups, we will note some progress now.

Females have achieved near parity with the males of their race in the level of educational attainment. A greater proportion than ever before are in the labor force, with growing numbers of women entering male-dominated occupations, including such advanced-degree professions as medicine, dentistry, law, and engineering. Whereas only 9 percent of bachelor's degrees in business and management were awarded to women in 1971, almost half now are. Even in the male domains of computer science and the physical sciences, in which women earned 13 percent of the degrees in 1971, they now earn at least 30 percent and are steadily increasing in numbers.[1]

The current Congress has the most female senators and representatives in its history, and the number of women serving in state legislatures is four times greater than twenty years ago. Two women now serve on the

U.S. Supreme Court and thousands of others hold judgeships at the federal, state, county, and local levels.[2]

All of these and many other gains too numerous to mention are very encouraging, yet there are many disquieting signs as well. Gender bias continues in the public schools, even among female teachers, according to a 1992 study by the American Association of University Women Educational Foundation.[3] Many occupational fields remain mostly sex segregated, usually with lower pay levels than comparable male sex-segregated fields. Women face a "glass ceiling" in upward mobility, as illustrated in a 1991 Department of Labor report showing that only 3 percent of the top executive positions of the largest U.S. corporations are held by women, a figure unchanged in ten years.[4] A few women may be U.S. Supreme Court justices, or governors, or in Congress, but their ratio is far lower than their population proportion.

Women of racial minority groups face the double problem of both racism and sexism. As in generations past, women from affluent, mainstream groups enjoy greater advantages and are often social activists in quest of gender equality. That destination has not yet been reached for many women, but their journey is nearer its destination than ever before.

The Europeans

Even though Europe is no longer the principal sending region for immigrants to the United States, it nonetheless continues to send a sizable number. Between 1961 and 1993, over 3.1 million European immigrants arrived. Included are almost 600,000 British, about 465,000 Italians, more than 361,000 Germans, 228,000 Portuguese, 224,000 Greeks, and almost 200,000 immigrants from the former Soviet Union.

California, Texas, and New York, in that order, were the primary places of intended residence for the Germans in 1992. For the Irish, it was New York, Massachusetts, and California. Polish immigrants preferred Illinois, New York, and New Jersey, but Soviet Union immigrants liked better the states of California, New York, and Illinois. British immigrants mostly chose California, New York, and Florida.

According to the 1990 census, the states with the highest density of people with English ancestry were Utah (44 percent), Maine (30 percent), and Idaho (29 percent). Highest German densities were Wisconsin (54 percent), North and South Dakota (51 percent each), Iowa and Nebraska (50 percent each). Highest Irish densities were Massachusetts (26 percent),

Delaware, New Hampshire, and Rhode Island (21 percent each), Arkansas, Missouri, and Oklahoma (20 percent each).

Other significant high ancestry densities were Italian in Rhode Island (20 percent), Connecticut and New Jersey (19 percent each), and New York (16 percent); French in Vermont (24 percent), New Hampshire (19 percent), and Massachusetts (18 percent); Polish in Connecticut, Michigan, and Wisconsin (10 percent each), Illinois and New Jersey (8 percent each).

Asians and Pacific Islanders

Because Asia is such a vast continent containing diverse peoples, we will divide its immigrants into coming from West, Central, or East Asia.[5] From western Asia come the Arabs, Iranians, and Israelis—people also known as Middle Easterners, which can really confuse those who do not know their geography. Central Asians include those from India and Pakistan, and among East Asians are the Chinese, Japanese, Koreans, Vietnamese, and other Indochinese.

As they erroneously did with the Native Americans and the southern, central, and eastern European immigrants, many Americans view Asian Americans as a single cultural entity because they are of the same race. In fact, they are quite different from each other in language, primary religious beliefs, and cultural attributes.

The Chinese

The earliest of the Asian immigrant groups to put down roots in the United States, the Chinese have become a very strong presence. Numbering about 435,000 in 1970, they increased to 806,000 in 1980, then doubled to 1.6 million in 1990. An average of 27,000 new arrivals in recent years suggests continuing growth and vitality in their communities.

Although Chinese Americans live in all fifty states, very few reside in North or South Dakota. Their greatest concentrations are in California and New York, with high aggregates also found in Massachusetts, Illinois, New Jersey, and Texas.

For many Americans, the image of Chinese Americans comes from the residents of Chinatowns in our major cities, but that is only part of the picture. A bipolar occupational distribution exists for Chinese Americans. Their ratio of professional and technical workers is twice that of the White labor force, but they also have twice as many low-skilled service workers.[6]

About one in four works in a low-skilled service job, often for long hours and meager compensation. Many of these workers are, to use a Chinese American expression, "FOB" (fresh off the boat) immigrants living in overcrowded, dilapidated buildings in Chinatown districts. However, with about 30 percent of all Chinese Americans in professional or technical fields, the median family income for Chinese Americans is higher than the national figure.

The Filipinos

Unlike East Asians on the continent, Filipinos have a heritage marked by an extensive Spanish and American influence. Smaller in number than the Japanese at 343,000 in 1970, they surpassed them in 1980, increasing to 775,000 and then to 1.4 million in 1990. In recent years, they have averaged an annual immigration total of 66,000, more than twice the Chinese average.

Other than Mexican Americans, no other foreign-born group is as heavily concentrated in one state as are the 512,000 Filipinos in California. Other states where their numbers are significant include Hawaii, New York, Illinois, New Jersey, Washington, Texas, and Virginia.

Mostly Roman Catholics, American-born Filipinos tend to have less education and occupational skills than newcomers from the Philippines and so work in low-paying, private-sector jobs.[7] Many of the new arrivals find work in professional and technical fields, especially in health care. Because of licensing and hiring problems, many are underemployed, unable to secure jobs comparable to their education, skills, and experience.

Few Filipino Americans operate small businesses, unlike many other groups from Asia. In a reversal of the usual immigration pattern, the women—many of them nurses—often precede the men as immigrants. After saving enough money, they send for their husbands and children.

Filipino Americans are fragmented linguistically, politically, and socially. Although they have strong loyalty to their family and the church, they generally avoid group separatism or an ethnic advocacy group. Although fraternal and social organizations do offer ethnic interactional opportunities, most Filipinos seem more desirous of broader participation in nonethnic associations.

The Asian Indians

Asian Indians were a minuscule presence in the United States until the 1960s, when more than 27,000 immigrants arrived. By 1980, they had become a population of 362,000, increasing to 815,000 by 1990. Averaging 38,000 new immigrants annually in recent years, Asian Indians have become the fourth-largest Asian group and will soon overtake Japanese Americans. California is home to the largest cluster of Asian Indians, with other high population totals found in New York, New Jersey, Illinois, and Texas.

Most Asian Indian immigrants are Hindi-speaking, but many others arrive who speak Gujarati, Punjabi, or Bengali. Racial ambiguity marks their acceptance pattern. Their skin color ranges from light brown to almost black, although most of the immigrants in the United States are of a light hue. Americans perceive them as racially different but have difficulty categorizing them. Defined as "White" sometimes, "Asian" other times, and "brown" or "Black" still other times, Asian Indians tend to classify themselves "White" and identify with the majority group.

About half of all working Asian Indians are in managerial or professional occupations, more than any other group in the United States, including Whites. About 20 percent of the nation's convenience stores, gas stations, or family-managed hotels and motels are operated by Asian Indians, giving them a family-labor economic niche. This ethnic group has the smallest proportion of its members in low-paying, low-status jobs.

The Japanese

In 1970, Japanese Americans constituted the largest Asian American group, totaling 591,000.[8] Although they increased to 701,000 in 1980, they dropped to third behind the Chinese and Filipinos. In 1990, Japanese Americans numbered 848,000, and they continue to sustain modest increases with an average of 6,000 new immigrant annually.

As with other Asian groups, the largest concentration of Japanese Americans resides in California. Other high population areas include New York, Hawaii, Texas, and Washington. The Japanese presence is augmented by nonimmigrants, intracompany transferees who arrive with their families on two- or three-year assignments. Almost 15,000 arrive annually.

Although a significant presence in some states, Japanese Americans are the most widely dispersed of all Asian groups throughout the fifty states. They are the most highly educated of all American groups, including Whites, and their economic success has enabled assimilation to continue at a rapid pace. Younger Japanese Americans seem more interested in their structural assimilation, as indicated by their high rates of outgroup dating and marriage. Despite occasional outbreaks of "Japan bashing" because of trade competition and Japanese corporate takeovers of some U.S. companies, this group shows less desire than most racial and ethnic groups to retain or revive its cultural ties to its past.[9]

The Koreans

Korean Americans have been one of the fastest-growing Asian immigrant groups in the United States, but in the past six years their annual immigration totals have steadily declined from about 34,000 in 1988 to almost 19,000 in 1992. Their U.S. population has grown from 70,000 in 1970, to 355,000 in 1980, and to 799,000 in 1990. More than 65,000 new immigrants have arrived since that count and, with their continued high migration and fertility rates, they may exceed one million by the end of the century.

Foreign-born Korean Americans live in all fifty states, from a low of slightly more than 500 in North Dakota to a high of over 210,000 in California. Among first- and second-generation Korean Americans, one out of three lives in California, one of nine in New York, and about 4 percent live in each of the following states: New Jersey, Texas, Virginia, Washington, and Maryland.

About 70 percent are Christians, mostly Methodist and Presbyterian. If they do not have their own church building, Korean congregations rent a facility in a same-faith established church and hold separate worship services and social programs. Church affiliation is about four times greater than in Korea, because the church serves also as a communal bond for ethnic identity and culture.[10]

Koreans can be found in a variety of occupations, but one striking aspect is their self-employment rate of about 12 percent, far greater than any other group. One out of eight Korean Americans is a business owner. These family-owned businesses are found in both cities and suburbs, more likely serving other minority customers or mainstream Americans than fellow Koreans. Through use of the *kye,* a rotating-credit association, many Korean merchants are able to secure funds to start a business, expand, or get through times of cash shortages.[11]

The Vietnamese

American involvement in the Vietnam War played a major part in Vietnamese migration, in their coming both as refugees and immigrants. From about 8,000 in 1970, they ballooned to 262,000 in 1980 and then increased to 615,000 in 1990. Given current trends, it is not unreasonable to anticipate their U.S. presence to exceed 750,000 by the end of the century.

Foreign-born Vietnamese live in all fifty states, from less than 100 in Wyoming to more than 275,000 in California. One out of two Vietnamericans lives in California, with one in ten in Texas, and other sizable numbers in Virginia, Washington, New York, and Pennsylvania.

One unique aspect of Vietnamese culture that demonstrates why we should not generalize about Asians is their cultural orientation that one's destiny is shaped by astrology and *phuc duc,* the good or bad fortune inherited through the deeds of five generations of one's family. These beliefs tend to make first-generation Vietnamericans stoic about their lives, thus unlikely to be demonstrative or militant against injustices. This belief lessens in the Americanization of the next generation.

Their acculturation is similar to other Asian groups, however.[12] The older adults, particularly the women who are less likely to be in work situations interacting with outgroup members, display little grasp of English or American ways but the children and younger adults, more exposed to American life, learn quickly. Scholastic achievement by Vietnamese youth is strong, well above the national average.

Other Asian Americans

More than 240,000 Laotians, 147,000 Cambodians, and 130,000 Thai also call the United States home. Many are refugees and more likely to live on welfare or in near-poverty conditions. These adults thus rebuke the "model minority" stereotype of Asian American success. Also comprising part of the cultural diversity of Asian Americans are Afghanis, Burmese, Indonesians, Malaysians, and Pakistanis (the largest of these five groups), whose number in the aggregate is well over 300,000, with about half of them living in California.

Black Americans

Because enormous diversity exists among Black Americans, only an ignorant person could generalize about "the Blacks." Use of the term "African American" is somewhat problematic for our discussion, because we are focusing on diversity within the racial classification and want to distinguish between those who are American born of long-ago African ancestry, those who are recent African immigrants, and those who are from a Caribbean background or elsewhere.[13]

Even within these three main groupings, enormous diversity exists in the lives of the different social classes of American-born Blacks, and in the languages, cultures, and adjustment patterns of Black immigrants from the different countries. Moreover, as with other racial groups, social stratification creates separate worlds for the American born, and ingroup loyalty and social isolation among many first-generation Americans often keeps them apart from others.

American society is far from eliminating racism as a serious social problem, and Black Americans, still disproportionately represented among the nation's poor, have all the attendant problems of that sad reality. Billions of dollars have been spent on social welfare programs and economic incentives, and yet one-third remain trapped as part of a growing underclass.

Yet this is not the complete picture. Black America is really two societies, one poor and the other nonpoor. Thanks to civil rights legislation and other social reforms, remarkable gains have been made, especially in education and occupational representation. Nevertheless, a disturbing gap remains between Black Americans and White Americans.

American-Born Blacks

One of the more encouraging social indicators for Black Americans, as reported by the Census Bureau, is educational attainment, but even here the message is mixed.[14] From a high school dropout rate of 22 percent in 1970, that figure is presently down to 11 percent, compared to 10 percent for Whites. In 1970, 4 percent of Blacks and 11 percent of Whites completed college; by 1993, this level was achieved by 12 percent of Blacks and 23 percent of Whites, or a tripling of the Black rate to a doubling of the White rate.

Black enrollment in college has increased from 25 percent in 1975 to 28 percent in 1991. However, this increase has not kept pace with that of White students, which grew from 35 percent to 44 percent in the same period. So, although more Black Americans achieve higher educational levels, the gap is actually widening between the two races.[15]

Black representation in managerial and professional specialties grows steadily, now at about 14 percent for males and 19 percent for females. About 18 percent of the males and 40 percent of the females are in technical, sales, or administrative support positions.[16]

For Black females, this is a dramatic change in occupation patterning from just a little over one generation ago, when two out of five worked in domestic service.[17] As of now, Black and White females are less different from one another than are the males. About 70 percent of Black males work in blue-collar jobs as compared to over one out of two White males working in white-collar jobs.

Continued increase in the number of Black elected officials is another positive indicator. With 38 of 435 representatives in the 103rd Congress, Blacks are nearing a total proportionate to their population ratio, although only one U.S. Senator is of their race. Almost 8,000 elected Black officials now serve in the U.S. or state legislatures, in city or county offices, in law enforcement or education. This number has grown consistently for more than twenty-five years.[18]

On the negative side are the data for Blacks living in the central cities: higher rates of poverty, unemployment, infant mortality, miscarriages, and mortality than Whites. Of particular concern is the steadily rising number of single-parent families. Of the 7.9 million Black families in 1993, 47 percent were headed by women and 6 percent by men, for a total of 53 percent single-family households, compared to a total of 18 percent White single-parent families.

Adding strength to Black American families is the extended family household. About 60 percent of children with only the mother present live in the home headed by a grandparent and, among teenage mothers, this figure increases to 85 percent, allowing for greater child care.[19]

The Africans

Immigration from Africa remained low until the 1950s, when about 14,000 immigrants arrived. This number doubled to about 29,000 in the 1960s, more than doubled to 81,000 in the 1970s, and again in the 1980s to 177,000. Annual immigration averages about 27,000 annually at present. Ethiopia, Nigeria, and Ghana are the primary sending countries of Black Africans. Nigerians constitute the largest group, with about 92,000 claiming Nigerian ancestry in the 1990 census, compared to 35,000 Ethiopians and 20,000 Ghanians.

African immigrants face two handicaps while trying to make a cultural adjustment to life in the United States.[20] In their homelands they were a racial majority, but here they are not. In various social and work settings, many encounter racism for the first time. Second, because of their cultural distinctions, many Africans do not identify with American Blacks, nor they with them. Successful American Blacks interested in helping the less fortunate of their race usually concentrate on the American-born poor, not on newcomers from Africa. As a matter of preference and necessity, the African immigrants seek out one another for mutual support and refuge.

A high percentage of the Africans are educated and possess occupational skills enabling them to obtain economic security quickly. As Ira de Augustine Reid and, more recently, Muruku Waiguchu have observed, because of the cultural gulf and social class distinctions, most prefer to retain their African identity rather than blend in with the Black American community.

The Haitians

In the 1950s, the first significant number of Haitian immigrants came, about 4,400 well-educated, upper-class citizens fleeing the Duvalier regime. The 1960s saw almost 35,000 mostly middle-class Haitians arrive. Since then, 56,000 immigrants in the 1970s, 138,000 in the 1980s, and more than 70,000 since 1991 have primarily been poorly educated, unskilled, lower-class individuals.[21]

Haiti is the poorest country in the Western Hemisphere and its people have suffered even more under a brutal regime. In addition to the legal immigrants, thousands of others flee their land in flimsy boats, causing a controversial U.S. policy of turning back, detaining, and/or refusing admittance to the undocumented aliens.

About 91 percent of all Haitian Americans, most of whom are Roman Catholics, are concentrated in just four states: New York (40 percent), Florida (36 percent), Massachusetts (8 percent), and New Jersey (7 percent). Most live in social isolation in tightly clustered neighborhoods. Speaking Haitian Creole, most have a very limited command of English. They usually work in low-paying jobs in service industries or as farm laborers.

The Jamaicans

Jamaican Americans are the largest non-Hispanic group from the Caribbean now living in the United States.[22] Of the approximately 450,000 here, about 80 percent are foreign born. Each decade their immigration totals have increased: about 75,000 in the 1960s, almost 138,000 in the 1970s, and more than 208,000 in the 1980s. Still averaging more than 20,000 immigrants annually, they continue to grow as a sizable minority group.

Almost two-thirds of all Jamaican Americans live in New York. Florida is home to another 30 percent, with other large Jamaican populations found in New Jersey, Connecticut, California, Maryland, Massachusetts, and Pennsylvania.

Jamaica itself is a pluralist island society with three racial layers, containing a small White elite, a brown middle and working class, and a lower tier of Blacks who comprise four-fifths of the population. Most of the immigrants are from this latter group.

First-generation Americans speak Jamaican English, which includes rapid speech patterning and a clipped accent. They adapt rather easily to American society, although first-time encounters with racism cause surprise and embitterment in some. Reggae music and West Indian food stores are two of the more noticeable cultural crossovers. The second generation appears to be integrating into society as Black Americans, not maintaining their cultural identity.

Hispanic Americans

Hispanic is a broad term that encompasses the *Hispanos* of the Southwest whose family roots predate the nation's expanding borders, U.S. nationals like the Puerto Ricans, Latino immigrants and refugees, and their descendants. This generic term suggests a common Spanish language and cultural influence, but is deceptive because it ignores the Portuguese Brazilians and the many cultural and class distinctions among the various Spanish-speaking nationalities.

Although some non-Hispanic Americans view the Hispanic American population as a collectivity of similar groups, their differences are consequential enough to prevent the evolution at this time of a cohesive entity. Cultural orientations, social class divisions, and first-generation American ingroup loyalties create considerable diversity within this rapidly growing ethnic group, presently comprising about one-tenth of the total U.S. population.

Central and South Americans

Excluding the Mexican Americans to be discussed shortly, about 2.7 million people residing in the United States today are first- or second-generation Americans from Central or South America.[23] Salvadorans are the largest group, with about 640,000, followed by Colombia with about 420,000, and Guatemala with about 315,000. Other larger groups include those from Nicaragua (235,000), Ecuador (215,000), Peru (210,000), Honduras (155,000), and Panama (102,000).

California claims the most Central and South Americans, about one-third of the total. Other leading states are New York, Florida, New

Jersey, Texas, Virginia, Illinois, and Maryland. These Latino groups usually settle in large metropolitan areas, especially in Los Angeles, San Francisco, Houston, New York City, Chicago, New Orleans, Miami, and Washington, DC.

Central and South Americans are very diverse and defy generalization, except to say they tend to be better educated and less susceptible to poverty than all other Latinos except Cubans and also fall behind Anglos in both categories. Otherwise, differences in the economic development in their homelands, their rural or urban backgrounds, social class, or racial composition make for numerous dissimilarities. Besides the 75,000 Brazilians who speak Portuguese, almost all other Central and South Americans here speak Spanish, although there are differences in dialect.

Cuban Americans

Since 1961, more than 640,000 Cubans have come to the United States, and those of Cuban ancestry now exceed one million. Two out of every three Cuban Americans live in Florida. Another 8 percent of Cuban Americans live in New Jersey, with an additional 7 percent each in New York and California. Texas and Illinois also contain significant Cuban American populations.[24]

In Miami, the Cubans have stamped a positive imprint. Its "Little Havana" section is now a six-hundred-block area, and over 25,000 Cuban-owned businesses operate in the Miami metropolitan area. The Cuban influence has transformed Miami from a winter resort town to a year-round commercial center with linkages throughout Latin America, making it into a leading bilingual cultural center.

Cubans have a lower fertility rate and a much higher proportion of people sixty-five years old and over than other Hispanic groups. They also have a lower unemployment rate, higher median family income, and greater middle-class composition. Cubans are politically active, showing a strong preference for the Republican party.

Dominican Americans

A major sending country of recent immigrants is the Dominican Republic, which shares the island of Hispaniola with Haiti. Immigration from there had been very small until the 1960s, when more than 93,000 arrived. A chain migration followed, bringing another 148,000 in the 1970s, and more than 252,000 in the 1980s. Current annual immigration has been more than 41,000 and shows no signs of slowing down.

Ninety-two percent of the more than 550,000 Dominicans living in the United States have settled in just four states. Almost 70 percent reside in New York, about 10 percent in New Jersey, and 6 percent each in Florida and Massachusetts.

Their large numbers and settlement patterns have enabled the Dominicans to establish viable ethnic neighborhoods, often adjacent to Puerto Rican ones. Although the two groups coexist and essentially keep to themselves, intergroup marriages and consensual unions are becoming common. Low educational attainment and limited job skills result in high unemployment rates and poverty-level living standards among many Dominicans.

Mexican Americans

The Mexican presence in the Southwest predates the area becoming part of the United States, and Mexico's adjacent border has encouraged both short-term and permanent migration for work and a better life.[25] It is therefore not surprising to learn that about two-thirds of all Mexican Americans live in this region today. Almost 6.5 million Mexican Americans live in California, about 4 million in Texas, more than 600,000 in Arizona and Illinois, and more than 330,000 in New Mexico.

All fifty states contain appreciable numbers of Mexican Americans. The largest of these concentrations living outside the Southwest is in Illinois (625,000). Some of the other states with sizable numbers include Colorado (280,000), Florida (175,000), Washington (160,000), Michigan (140,000), New York (100,000), Oregon (90,000), and Kansas (80,000).

Nine out of ten reside in metropolitan areas, and some of them are realizing the American Dream in rising educational levels, occupational opportunities, and incomes. However, Mexican American gains as a group have not kept pace with Anglo gains because of the large influx of unskilled, poorly educated newcomers. Almost half of urban Mexican Americans live in central cities, where life in the barrio is one of substandard housing, high rates of unemployment, poverty, school dropouts, crime, and gang violence.

One source of strength for Mexican Americans is the family. Their divorce rate is well below the national level, and the percentage of their family units headed by both a husband and wife is comparable to the national average.

Puerto Rican Americans

Of the total Puerto Rican population of 2.7 million living on the mainland, New York continues as the leading center with about 1.1 million, followed by New Jersey with more than 304,000. Nearby states also have large concentrations: Massachusetts, 146,000; Pennsylvania, 143,000; Connecticut, 140,000. Elsewhere, Florida has 240,000; Illinois, 147,000; California, 132,000; and Ohio, 46,000.[26]

In comparison to other Hispanic groups, Puerto Ricans have the lowest median family income, the highest poverty rate (about 40 percent) and the highest proportion of female-headed families (about 50 percent). Puerto Ricans have a higher educational attainment level on average than Mexicans, but lag far behind non-Hispanic Americans. As with the Mexican American urban poor, the Puerto Rican urban poor live in areas of limited job opportunities, making them more vulnerable to welfare dependency.[27]

Some segments of the Puerto Rican community are doing well. Almost 40 percent of all Puerto Rican families earn as much or more than the national median family income level, and about 10 percent have incomes that classify them as affluent.

North Africans
and Southwest Asians

Immigration from Islamic countries of North Africa and Southwest Asia has been of such sustained strength that these ethnic groups have become a visible presence in many states. More than 182,000 immigrants arrived in the 1970s, followed by the next wave in the 1980s that increased to almost 343,000. If the present trend continues, that will be surpassed in the 1990s. Not all are Muslims, particularly the many Christians from Lebanon and Coptic Christians from Egypt.

Although the single largest concentration of Arab Americans is the more than 250,000 living in southern Michigan, the largest proportion of the approximately 1.7 million Americans claiming Arabic ancestry in the 1990 census is the 40 percent living in the Northeast. About 28 percent live in the Midwest, 20 percent in the South, and 12 percent in the West. About one-fourth of all Arab Americans, about 400,000, are of Lebanese descent. Syrians are the next largest group, exceeding 130,000. Other sizable groups are Egyptians, Assyrians, and Palestinians.[28]

Largest of all groups, but neither Arab nor Arabic-speaking are the Iranians. With their distinct culture and *Farsi* language, about 60 percent of the more than 235,000 Iranian Americans live in California. Other large enclaves are in the New York and Washington, DC metropolitan areas. Many are middle-class professionals and their children are becoming extensively Americanized, despite their parents' efforts to preserve their culture.

Turks also are neither Arabs nor Arabic-speaking but tend to settle near other Arabic and Islamic immigrants in working-class urban neighborhoods. Along with their Arabic neighbors, they work as tradesmen and laborers.

Native Americans

The 1990 census showed a 38 percent increase in Native Americans, rising from 1.4 million in 1980 to almost 2 million. Much of this increase results from a birth rate almost twice the national average. Some of it may also be because it is now fashionable to claim Native American ancestry or else gain certain advantages in affirmative action, education, jobs, loans, and merchandising.

The quality of life varies from tribe to tribe. Some reap large profits from gambling casinos, but others languish in poverty. Nationwide, the Native American poverty rate hovers at two-and-one-half times the national average. Equally depressing are the statistics showing Native American life expectancy about ten years less than the national average. Their death rates from diabetes, liver disease, tuberculosis, and alcohol-related accidents are two to three times the national average.[29]

Twelve percent of Native Americans are aged 10 to 19, compared to 9 percent of other U.S. racial/ethnic groups. Yet compared to those same minority groups, fewer Native American teens will graduate from high school (55.4 percent vs. 66.5 percent), and fewer still will complete college (7.4 percent vs. 16.2 percent), given current patterns.[30]

Disputes over water rights, fishing rights, natural resources, landfills, and upwind or upstream pollution of tribal lands continue in many states. With more than seven hundred Native Americans as lawyers by 1990, legal efforts to honor treaty rights have been more numerous and successful than in earlier years.[31]

Those successes have led officials to respect the growing power of Native Americans. For instance, after losing seventy-six out of eighty court battles with various Native American tribes, the state of Washington broke new ground and dealt with the tribes as if they were governments. Reaching agreement on salmon management, they now also cooperate on health policy, child-welfare agreements, and water rights. Wyoming, Colorado, and New Mexico have also negotiated directly with tribes in their borders to avoid and possibly lose costly court battles.

As the Native Americans increase their clout, anti-Native American groups such as the Citizens Equal Rights Alliance (CERA) and Stop Treaty Abuse (STA) campaign to stop them.[32] Claiming the exercise of treaty rights is not in tune with contemporary society, they pursue a course of disruption until all citizens can equally use resources on Native American lands. Understandably, large development corporations support these organizations.

Beyond the Horizon

A new wave of immigrants flock to American shores, carried by hope to pursue the same dreams of a better life that motivated millions of other immigrants before them. A new generation of native-born Americans, the descendants of those older immigrants, observes the present immigration with apprehension, concerned and alarmed about what they fear undermines the American culture and character. That was the past nativist reaction to previous immigrations also.

Some demographers, historians, and politicians point with alarm to tomorrow's reality, given today's trends. Misgivings about the multiple losses of White numerical superiority, preeminence of Western culture and the Judeo-Christian heritage, and preservation of the existing social order are heard from many sections of the country. There is distress over group separatism and use of languages other than English. On another front, feminist advocacy also draws negative responses in some quarters.

Some of the resistance is from well-intentioned individuals who view the changes as altering the nation's identity too dramatically. Some of that concern is rooted in racial fears, as the White majority sees its numerical superiority, its economic and political dominance threatened by the continued arrival of so many non-White immigrants.

At the heart of most of these feminist, ethnic, and racial issues is the struggle for power. Challenges to the status quo—as vocal and visible minority groups seek economic, political, and social power—prompts resistance by those unwilling to yield their advantages. Their real fears of loss of hegemony are masked in dire predictions about loss of societal cohesion.

Multiculturalism is evident in the land once again and we can find many examples of both accommodation and conflict. Which trend will prevail? Will our future be one of greater discord or greater unity? What does lie beyond the next horizon?

Fortunately, we have some clues from our past and present that may offer us a glimpse of that future. In the next three chapters we shall seek that understanding.

8

Intergenerational Comparisons

Each generation of Americans experiences anew the influx of immigrants arriving in pursuit of the American Dream. Each new generation also contains native-born Americans who not only have been denied fulfillment of that dream but witness newcomers who succeed where they do not. This has been the case since colonial beginnings and appears likely to continue far into the future. It is an old story and yet incredibly fresh each time to those who live or observe it.

When we examine what has prompted people, past and present, to forsake their homelands and begin new lives in this country, we find a remarkable consistency in their motives.[1] Many have entered on their own initiative, lured by the promise of a better life. Others were recruited by labor agents, enticed by advertisements or the media, or else encouraged to leave by their own governments, which sought to lessen social unrest or economic distress. Still others, forced to flee their native lands as refugees, had little choice.

Whatever the reason, whenever the time, the United States has always served as a destination for these adventurous, desperate, or determined people. Yet despite the immigrant ancestry of most Americans, many times in the past and present they have wanted to pull in the welcome mat for new immigrants.

Why Are Voices Raised Against Immigration?

Too often the native born have reacted with fear and anxiety, perceiving some groups as "unassimilable" and their presence in large numbers as a threat to societal cohesion.[2] Other Americans are apprehensive about these groups' possible integration, believing such an eventuality would somehow destroy or undermine the "purity" of the American character.

So it was with Rufus King, the American ambassador to England, who wrote in 1797 to Secretary of State Timothy Pickering that the Irish immigrants would "disfigure our true national character."[3] Ever since, others have expressed concerns about this or that group of immigrants as wrong for the nation's well-being. The most recent example, as mentioned in Chapter 1, is in *Alien Nation*, Peter Brimelow's diatribe against the racially and culturally distinct newcomers now coming to the United States who, he claims, do not assimilate.

Religious, Racial, and Cultural Issues

Sometimes these reactions reveal a religious bias: against Quakers, Shakers, or Catholics in the eighteenth century; against Catholics, Jews, or Mormons in the nineteenth century; or against Catholics, Jews, or Sikhs in the early twentieth century. Other negative responses reflect a racial bias: against African and Native Americans throughout the nation's history; against Asians and dark-complexioned southern Europeans in the late nineteenth and early twentieth centuries. There have been other varieties of bias: religion *and* race (Rastafarian), culture *and* religion (Irish, Italian). As the twentieth century draws to a close, new nativist voices express the old fears about other religiously, racially, or culturally different newcomers: the Muslims, Asians, or Latinos.

Economic Competition

Past or present targets have also induced alarm because others see them as a danger to their own livelihood. This perceived economic threat may result from the scarcity of jobs, affirmative action hiring or promotion policies, or the recruitment of cheaper labor or strikebreakers. Since the mid-nineteenth century, employers have often used newly arrived groups, including migrating Black Americans, to keep wages low or to break a strike.

The resulting ethnic antagonism can be of three types. Native-born Americans may resent the immigrant influx, as when West Coast labor unions in the late nineteenth and early twentieth centuries fought against Asian workers. An interethnic rivalry may develop, such as the importation of Syrian Lebanese immigrants in an effort to break the three-hundred-mill shutdown in the Paterson, New Jersey region in 1913, caused by striking European immigrant textile workers. The third variation of an immigrant economic threat can be posed by same-group members. Economist Vernon Briggs, for example, has shown the negative influence on employment conditions for legal Mexican Americans by undocumented Mexicans working in the food and fiber industry.

The "Tipping Point"

Sometimes biases are so deeply ingrained that people will respond negatively to the presence of even one member of a despised outgroup. More often, however, if the number of outgroup members is few, people tend to be more receptive to less-alike strangers, or at least indifferent or begrudgingly tolerant. When the outgroup numerical increase reaches the tipping point, hostile responses become more likely. As Luigi Laurenti's classic study on property values and race revealed, that tipping point has no exact number; it is a perceptual stage where the ingroup believes "too many" of "those people" are in their midst and "something needs to be done."[4]

Today Isn't Yesterday, or Is It?

If ten generations of Americans have followed similar patterns of response to immigrants who have subsequently blended into the mainstream, why can't we recognize that fact and be less fearful about today's newcomers?

Today's nativists dismiss any effort to compare past immigrant concerns with their own. Past objectors, they argue, were narrow-minded bigots opposed to people who have since proven their ability to assimilate. They contend that today we are "inundated" with racially different Asians who lack a Judeo-Christian heritage, whose culture differs radically from ours. Hispanics, they add, hold on to their language and customs, thereby presenting a real threat to the cohesiveness of American society.

With the 1990s poised to become the decade of the greatest number of immigrants ever to arrive (possibly over ten million), and with almost nine out of ten from Third World countries, nativists consider current immigration as a serious threat to the population composition of American society as we have long known it.[5] Moreover, the nation has not satisfactorily dealt with the unemployment and poverty of its native-born Americans, they contend, to continue to admit large numbers of immigrants, which would intensify further an already difficult problem.

Questions about America's racial mix, unemployment, and poverty do offer some new wrinkles to old arguments and need to be addressed. However, despite nativist disclaimers of new and different elements, these arguments share many commonalities with those of similar-minded alarmists of previous generations.[6] All have seen newcomers as a threat to the "purity" of the American character and to the stability and economic welfare of the society. All have seen the newcomers as inferior additions and complained about their retention of language and customs. All have assumed acculturation and assimilation would not occur. As Rita J. Simon states,

> These have been the arguments used against all of the "current cohorts" from the time the new immigrants began arriving, first from Ireland, then a decade or two later from Southern, and Eastern Europe. . . . Contemporary immigrants are no less popular than the immigrants who began coming to this country after the Civil War and for all the years in between. The only popular or valued immigrants are those who came long ago, whenever "long ago" happened to be.[7]

I would suggest that when nativists argue today's situation is far different from past years, their perception has been affected by the Dillingham Flaw. This appears to be the case because they tend to view past fears as ignorant or irrational nativism against White ethnics who actually shared far more similarities with their hosts than any differences. However, what we perceive today as their mutual similarities were not viewed as such in those times. It is the perception back then, not the perception today, that matters when examining past behaviors.

How Can We Learn the Truth?

So are things different today or not? We need some comparative data to determine where the truth lies. To relate the present with the past, I'll focus on several aspects of nativist fears: the significance of immigration totals, the foreign-born presence, racial population changes, and assimilation.

Immigration Rate

One important indicator of the impact of immigrants on a society is the immigration rate. This measurement tool allows for comparisons of different eras and enables us to specifically address vague nativist fears that America is being overwhelmed by a large influx of foreigners. It

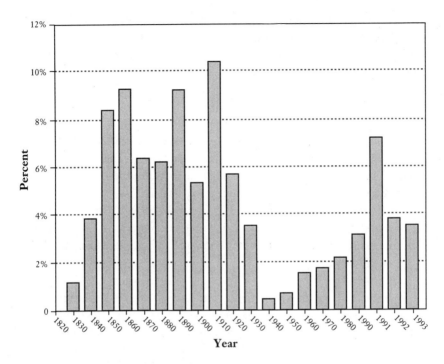

Figure 8.1. *Immigration Rate, 1820-1993*

Source: U.S. Immigration and Naturalization Service, *1993 Statistical Yearbook* (Washington, DC: Government Printing Office, 1994).

thus serves as a concrete aid in objectively describing a reality that may or may not differ from perceptions.

The immigration rate per 1,000 persons in the general population is computed by dividing the sum of the annual immigration totals by the sum of annual U.S. population totals for the same number of years.[8] Collection of such data began in 1820 when new regulations required shipmasters to submit passenger lists to customs officials.

What is particularly useful about this measurement tool is that it allows us to relate immigration totals to population totals in a way that provides a comparative means for analysis. Immigrant totals for any particular year or decade become more relevant if we know the size of the population the newcomers are joining. To be more specific, if 1 million people enter a society that totals 10 million people, the immigrants' presence will be more keenly felt than if 1 million people enter a society that has a population of 250 million.

The 1980s were the second highest decade in the total number of immigrants arriving (7.3 million compared to 8.8 million in 1901-1910).

However, in terms of immigration rate, the 1980s—which also include undocumented aliens granted permanent residence under the 1986 amnesty program—actually rank eleventh out of the seventeen decades (see Figure 8.1). Immigrants in the 1980s were less than one-third the proportion found between 1901 and 1910 and numerically less as well.

The year 1991, with its 1.8 million immigrants and 7.2 percent immigration rate, is an anomaly. It includes the greater part of those undocumented aliens already living in the United States who were granted permanent residence under the Immigration Reform and Control Act of 1986. In 1992, the total dropped almost 50 percent to about 974,000 immigrants and a 3.8 percent rate. In 1993, another drop in the totals to about 904,000 resulted in an immigration rate of 3.5 percent. These figures may serve as more accurate indicators of immigration for the rest of this decade, assuming no changes in immigration laws or patterns.[9]

Legislation in 1990 set a limit of 700,000 immigrants for 1992 to 1994 and of 675,000 thereafter. Because immediate family members are not included in these caps, annual figures will actually be higher, as they were in 1993. If current patterns continue, we can project a total of 10 to 11 million immigrants arriving in the 1990s, making it the decade with the largest number of immigrants in the nation's history.

Such a projection can provoke that nativist alarm mentioned earlier. However, because the population also increases through natural processes, examining the immigration rate provides a more accurate measure of what is really happening. Because Census Bureau projections of the total population in the year 2000 range from about 270 million to about 282 million, and because annual immigration limits are set by law, we can project the immigration rate for this last decade of the twentieth century. By this ascertainment, the 1990s immigration rate will fall somewhere between 3.5 percent and 4.1 percent, ranking this decade tenth of eighteen.

What are we saying? First, we are saying that the earlier waves of immigrants in each of the decades between 1840 and 1920 had greater significance in affecting the nation's population composition. By this we mean that the ratio of immigrants to the population receiving them was greater in the past. Such a higher ratio thereby means that those immigrants from 1840 to 1920 proportionately and visibly changed America's population mix to a greater degree than the recent immigrants have.

We are also saying that a major factor in examining the immigration rate is immigration law. The 1990 law now in effect has a ceiling of 675,000 immigrants annually, beginning in 1995. Because the general population will experience natural increases annually while the immigration cap remains constant, the immigration rate must therefore decline in the years to come. Until new legislation raises that immigration cap, we can expect a steady reduction in the immigration rate, one measurement of alien impact on the host society.

Immigration Rate Caveats

Although the immigration rate is a helpful comparative measurement, it cannot stand alone. Too many other factors need to be considered as well. For example, the United States is now a postindustrial society. Many manufacturing jobs no longer exist that immigrants with few skills and limited command of English could once attain. The ability of a nation to absorb its newcomers thus depends on how well they can find their niche in the workplace, as well as on the proportion of immigrants to the total population.[10]

Some states—such as California, Texas, Florida, and New York—receive such a large volume of immigrants that they are severely overburdened in education and social welfare costs. Nationwide, the data are much more positive. In the 1980s, some eleven million working immigrants earned over $240 billion annually, paying more than $90 billion in taxes, far more than the estimated $5 billion that immigrants received in welfare.[11]

Another factor in considering the immigration rate is how much immigration contributes to population growth in an era of declining birth rates. Using a formula of births plus immigration minus deaths and emigration, the Population Reference Bureau reported in September 1994 that immigrants currently account for 20 percent of U.S. population growth.[12] Demographer Leon F. Bouvier says immigration will thus affect the nation's future ethnic population mix, a topic that will be discussed in the last chapter.

Foreign-Born Population

A companion set of data to immigration rates is the foreign-born population in various time periods, because they represent the cumulative totals of immigrants residing in the United States. Therefore, by determining what percentage of the general population is foreign born at any given time, we can discern the extent of their presence as a basis for comparing the past with the present.

Data on the foreign born were not gathered until the 1850 census.[13] That year marked the close of the first decade with more than 1 million

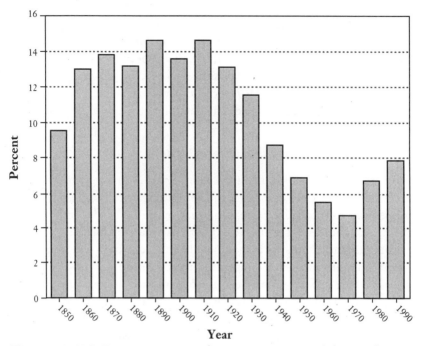

Figure 8.2 *U.S. Foreign-Born Population as a Percent of the Total Population, 1850-1990*

Source: U.S. Bureau of the Census, *Historical Statistics of the United States, Part I,* Series A105-118 (Washington, DC: Government Printing Office, 1976); *Statistical Abstract of the United States 1994* (Washington, DC: Government Printing Office, 1994).

immigrants, 1.7 million to be exact. (In the 1830s there were about 600,000 and about 143,000 in the 1820s.) So 1850 serves as an good starting point for examining times of higher immigration.

Past Patterns

Because immigration rates were higher in the past than in the present, as we have just seen, it is therefore not surprising to see in Figure 8.2 that the foreign-born segment of the population has been higher in ten of the past fifteen decennial censuses, consecutively from 1850 to 1940.

In Figure 8.2 we can see that the percentage of foreign born living in the United States between 1860 and 1920 was much greater than in 1990. In the 1890 and 1910 census, one in seven was foreign born; in 1860, 1870, 1880, 1900, and 1920, it was one in eight. In 1990, about one in twelve was foreign born, a decidedly smaller proportion in a time when immigration fears find frequent expression in the media.

At the turn of the century, most cities in the Northeast contained a foreign-born population that comprised two-thirds to three-fourths of the cities' total populations. In contrast, the cities in 1990 with the most foreign-born populations were Miami at 33.6 percent, Los Angeles at 27.1 percent, and New York at 19.7 percent. Although these are significant proportions, they pale alongside the data of eighty to ninety years ago.

Recent Patterns

From another viewpoint, the approximately 19.8 million foreign born identified in the 1990 census are the largest numerical total ever, but in proportion to the entire population that figure ranks eleventh among the fifteen decades for which this information is available.

Because these statistics do not include American-born children being raised in immigrant family households, the proportion of those living in various ethnic subcultures has been greater, especially among past generations when family size was typically larger than today. Regardless of acculturation and ethnogenesis patterns, different languages, customs, and traditions from the old country have always prevailed to some extent among a sizable part of American society, more so in the past than the present.

At its lowest point in 1960, the foreign-born component has since been moving upward again, reflecting the recent increases in the immigration rate. Similarly, the foreign-born percentages will continue to rise for a while but will eventually level off and decline, for the same reasons enumerated for the immigration rate.

Race in America

Race relations in the United States have had a violent, exploitative past and an often-troubled present. Racism finds many forms of expression ranging from verbal put-downs to killing, producing many disturbing consequences not only for its victims but also for the society itself in economic, health, and social welfare costs.

At first, only Whites among the native born enjoyed the privileges of citizenship and voting rights, and only White aliens could become naturalized citizens. In time, following the pain of the Civil War, the Fourteenth Amendment (1868) granted citizenship to anyone born or naturalized in the United States, and the Fifteenth Amendment (1870) extended voting rights to every male regardless of race or color. After an arduous struggle, non-White exclusion yielded under force of law to inclusion.

Advances against other areas of exclusion—notably in education, employment, housing, and public accommodation—occurred only a generation ago, growing out of the civil rights movement of the 1960s.[14] Gaining legal rights and political participation did not necessarily mean social acceptance, however. Just as Crèvecoeur overlooked the disenfranchised racial American minorities of his time, so too have many White Americans avoided any inclusion of non-Whites in their daily lives. Lack of interaction helps perpetuate stereotypes and allows racial prejudice and discrimination to thrive.

Although succeeding generations of America's people of color have made significant gains in education, employment, income, and political participation, problems remain. Many forms of institutionalized racism have been eliminated, but structural discrimination—the differential treatment of racial groups that is entrenched in our social institutions— remains. Three out of ten African and Hispanic Americans still live in poverty, three times that of Whites, a ratio that has been consistent during the lifetime of most readers of this book.

Racism manifests itself in negative reactions to the number of immigrants in general who are non-White, or of one race such as Asians, of one group such as Haitians. It finds expression also in fears that American society's racial mixture is changing too dramatically.

Changes in Racial Composition

If we look at some of the data about past and present racial groups in the United States, we can dispel some of the generalizations and unfair comparisons (the Dillingham Flaw) that engender some of the unfavorable responses to the presence of people of color. Our focus will be once again on proportional representation within the total population over the years. Is the non-White to White ratio greater than ever? Exactly how is our society changing in its racial mixture?

After increasing proportionately since 1790 and peaking in 1940 at 89.8 percent, the nation's White population has since been steadily decreasing, as Figure 8.3 reveals. At this point, however, the 1990 percentage of 83.9 is still a greater portion of the total population than the 79.3 percent of Whites living in the United States in 1790 or the 81.3 percent total in 1840.[15]

There was a smaller percentage of Whites in 1790 because there was a greater percentage of Blacks. Then, African Americans constituted almost one out of five residents, at 18.9 percent. That was the peak year for African Americans. Thereafter, elimination of the slave trade in 1808

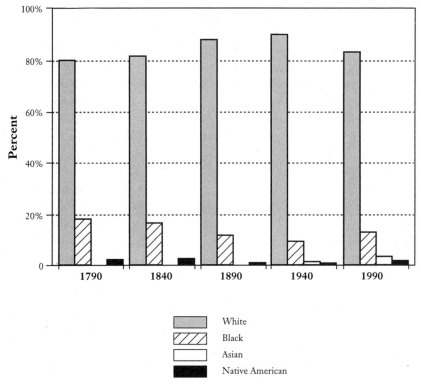

Figure 8.3. *U.S. Population by Race as a Percent of the Total Population*

Source: U.S. Bureau of the Census, *Historical Statistics of the United States, Part I,* Series A91-104 (Washington, DC: Government Printing Office, 1976); *Statistical Abstract of the United States 1994* (Washington, DC: Government Printing Office, 1994).

and mostly White immigration slowly but steadily reduced African American apportionment within the society.

Even though the percentage of African Americans continually declined until reaching its lowest point in 1940 at 9.8 percent, their percentages did not drop below current figures until 1890. Before then African Americans comprised a greater share of the total population.

Since 1950, their ratio has been slowly climbing from 9.9 percent to 12.3 percent in 1990. Part of that increase is due to the presence of more than 1 million residents of West Indian ancestry and more than 300,000 immigrants from Africa.

Virtually nonexistent in the United States in 1790, Asians have been steadily increasing in numbers and proportion since their first tallies in the 1860 census. Since the liberalization of immigration regulations in 1965, their growth has been dramatic and their visible concentration in certain regions of the country—particularly on the East and West Coasts and in the Chicago metropolitan region—makes their 3 percent total of the population seem much greater to residents of those areas.

After experiencing a calamitous decline in population from first contact with Europeans until the twentieth century, Native Americans have a high birth rate and are now steadily increasing their numbers. Their recent population growth has stabilized their proportional place in American society at 1 percent.

The Significance of the Data

What can we conclude from this information? Perhaps one surprise is that the United States is more White today than it was in the late eighteenth century. It was also more Black until 1890 than it is today. However, it is also true that the White population percentage of the total is shrinking and the Black population percentage is increasing. Also, the increase in Asians, Hispanics (who can be of any race), and Native Americans— when combined with the increase in African Americans—means that the United States today is more of a multiracial society than ever before, even though Whites presently exceed the proportion of the total that they maintained in 1790.[16]

What will the changing racial composition mean for the future of race relations? As the ratio of Whites declines, Whites will no doubt become more aware of their race instead of just paying attention to the visibility of other racial groups. Will this lead to greater understanding or to a racial backlash? This is part of the challenge before us.

In the last chapter we shall explore more fully the implications of current birth and migration rates on the future of American society, including racial composition.

Mainstream Americans

Rarely are cultures or societies static entities. In the United States, the continual influx of immigrants has helped shape its metamorphosis. Part of this tempering has been the evolving definition of the mainstream ingroup, or identifying who was "really an American."[17]

Early Conceptions

In the initial conception of mainstream Americans, the English comprised virtually all of this ingroup. Gradually this ingroup expanded from

English American exclusivity to British American or White Anglo Saxon Protestant, thus including the Scots-Irish and Welsh previously excluded. This reconceptualization was triggered by the rapid Americanization of these groups after the American Revolution and by nativist reaction to the first large-scale wave of immigrants whose culture and religion and, in the case of the Irish, their peasant class set them apart from the mainstream.

The Conception Changes

By 1890, the "mainstream American" ingroup did not yet include many northwest European Americans. Although some multigenerational Americans of other than British ancestry had blended into the mainstream, millions had not. These Americans remained culturally pluralistic, their separateness resulting from race, religion, or geographic isolation. In addition, more than nine million foreign born—one in seven, perhaps one in five if we include their children—also lived outside this mainstream society.

In 1890, the "melting pot" had not yet absorbed the 80,000 Dutch, 200,000 Swiss, or 1.2 million Scandinavians in the Midwest, most of whom had arrived after 1870.[18] Likewise, the 150,000 French immigrants, 200,000 Cajuns in Louisiana, and 500,000 French Canadians in New England and the Great Plains remained culturally, linguistically, and religiously separated from the larger society. So too did many of the 8 million Germans in the rural Midwest or concentrated in many large cities.

Their poverty and Catholic faith kept 6 million Irish in the Northeast and 300,000 Mexican Americans in the Southwest in social isolation. About 7.5 million African Americans, 248,000 Native Americans, and 110,000 Asians also lived as mostly impoverished racial minorities separate from the mainstream.

Race, culture, and/or social class origins shaped group relations in the United States in 1890, keeping the nation a patchwork quilt of cultural diversity. All three variables influenced perceptions, receptivity, and interactional patterns.

In the 1890s, the tide of immigration began to change. The turning point came in 1896 when immigrants from northern and western Europe were surpassed by immigrants from the rest of Europe. These "new" immigrants eventually redefined mainstream American, bringing those of northern and western European origins (including Australian and Canadian) into this classification in contrast to the newer, "less desirable" newcomers. However, that redefinition did not manifest itself fully for several more decades. In 1890, with many Germans and Irish not yet structurally assimilated, those Americans still looked upon as typifying mainstream Americans essentially remained those of British ancestry.

The Newest Conception

By 1970, a new turning point in immigration had been reached, with Third World immigrants outnumbering European immigrants. Once again, partly through a reaction to this change and partly due to acculturation, education, and upward mobility, the concept of "mainstream American" expanded. It included this time anyone of European origin, thus setting them apart from the people of color now arriving in great numbers, as well as the still nonintegrated African Americans and Native Americans.[19]

Mainstream American Caveats

Figure 8.4 illustrates these mainstream American and outgroup classifications. Admittedly, these groupings are somewhat arbitrary. For example, some non-English were clearly mainstream Americans in 1790, such as Welsh Americans William Floyd, Button Gwinnett, Thomas Jefferson, Francis Lewis, and Lewis Morris—all signers of the Declaration of Independence. However, there still were many eighteenth- and nineteenth-century segregated Welsh settlements of Quakers, Baptists, or Congregationalists scattered in numerous regions where Welsh-language newspapers and even books helped maintain a distinct ethnic minority group. Similarly, nineteenth-century German industrialists such as H. J. Heinz, Frederick Weyerhauser, John J. Bausch, and Henry Lomb typified non-British individuals who wielded considerable power and influence; yet most Germans remained socially isolated in rural or urban subcommunities.

The 1990 mainstream category is also an arbitrary oversimplification because it overlooks the religious and cultural differences among White ethnics that set them apart from fully assimilated European Americans. For example, mainstream Americans view the Amish, Mennonites, and Hasidic Jews as culturally distinct groups living within their own subcultures outside the mainstream. The categories cannot therefore be taken literally.

Even so, these categories still serve a useful purpose. They address the perception, acceptance, social distance, and therefore the basis on which people react positively or negatively to physically or culturally distinct others. Some people included in the mainstream group may not

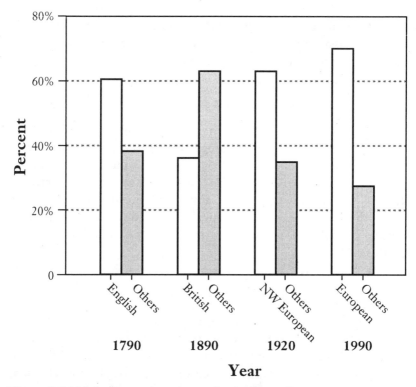

Figure 8.4. *Mainstream Americans, by Ancestry Group*

Source: Based on data from U.S. Bureau of the Census, *Historical Statistics of the United States, Part I,* Series A91-104 (Washington, DC: Government Printing Office, 1976); *Statistical Abstract of the United States 1994* (Washington, DC: Government Printing Office, 1994).

actually be a part of it and vice versa, yet these groupings offer an approximation of who is seen as "American" and who still remains an outsider. The social distance scores reported by Emory Bogardus and other researchers since 1926 are a helpful indicator of these groupings.[20] Comparatively, the studies reveal a lessening of social distance among all groups over the decades, but nevertheless a consistent clustering of non-White groups is farther away in social acceptance than White ethnic groups.

One can, of course, create other configurations and numbers. For example, one could introduce social stratification as a variable and make an effective argument for social class designation affecting mainstream acceptance and thereby altering the ingroup-outgroup memberships. Such a position has some merit although it opens the door for counter-arguments involving racism and structural assimilation that would affect acceptance regardless of social class. Even so, with a smaller proportion of people living in poverty today than in 1890, and less in 1890 than in 1790, the pattern shown in Figure 8.4 of an increased proportion of mainstream Americans over the centuries will likely remain and perhaps be even greater in the future.

These statistics serve to guide our understanding and are not an absolute identification. Avoiding the Dillingham Flaw and identifying mainstream Americans through the eyes of each period's contemporaries, we find that the expanding American identity has resulted in a greater ingroup totality today than ever before. Despite recently expressed fears about America becoming a polyglot society of dissimilar peoples (a historically recurring anxiety), the nation's mainstream group has expanded, not contracted. Brimelow is simply wrong in his claim that assimilation is no longer a goal among immigrants. The dual realities of pluralism and assimilation continue as they always have.

Another important point needs to be made. Women were long excluded from the societal mainstream. Although some instances of female independence in land ownership, inheritance, and voting rights did occur in colonial America, for the most part women remained subordinate to men and were denied those rights. Not until passage of the Nineteenth Amendment in 1920 did women universally gain the right to vote. It would be another forty years before other areas of sexual discrimination would be successfully challenged.

Women have achieved many gains in their struggle for equality and acceptance as equals in all areas of human endeavor. Parity has not been accomplished in many arenas—particularly in income, political representation, and upper-level occupational positions—but no one can deny that women's status in society has notably improved from just one generation ago. With numerous areas still requiring change, we can nonetheless say that at long last women are also moving into the category of mainstream Americans.

The "Wall"

What do we learn from this focus on mainstream Americans? As the nation's population mix has changed over the generations, so too has its definition of national cultural identity. Groups once excluded, once considered unassimilable, and even sometimes reviled, became included. In time, this socially constructed new reality seemed natural, especially with the appearance of a new group perceived as "different" and/or as economic competitors. A long, sometimes conflict-ridden process unfolded. Eventually, the newer group also became part of the ingroup and it was replaced by another outgroup.

The concept of an expanding mainstream American identity can be compared to the walled medieval cities. Only so many inhabitants could fit within the protective wall that surrounded the city. The lack of available space forced newcomers to settle outside in *fauborgs* (the first suburbs) where they could participate in the city's daily activities although they were not really a part of the city itself.

Hawking their wares like merchants inside the city's gates, they no doubt were resented by some as economic competitors. When trouble came in the form of marauders, all united in a common cause, but the new-comers were more likely to suffer the most in loss and destruction of their property outside the walls. In time, as the outsiders became a more integral part of the city, a new encircling wall would be built farther out and the old wall was torn down. With the previously excluded inhabitants now safely ensconced within the city's new walled perimeter, others would soon settle outside and begin the process anew.

The wall is an apt metaphor. In intergroup or gender relations, too often we still build protective walls of isolation, avoidance, or exclusion. Whether physical or social, walls do more than separate people: they limit one's field of vision, they restrict movement, and they create a "they" and "we" mentality that inspires conflict. Walls of prejudice keep people apart from one another, making those on one side more susceptible to victimization, as those *fauborg* dwellers once were. Just as economic growth brought the medieval walls down, so too does it help bring down our walls of prejudice. Conversely, economic decline helps erect walls between groups as people compete for jobs.

The social barriers we erect can sometimes be just as insurmountable and long-lasting as many of those medieval walls still standing these many centuries later. Sometimes though, those walls can be scaled, their gates opened, the ramparts destroyed. It is a paradoxical tribute to the dynamics of American society that its cultural identity walls of exclusivity have been weak enough to be overcome several times, thereby producing a stronger nation and a more vibrant American character than could have existed without such expansiveness.

Perception and Reality

Americans' perception of the foreign-born population is affected by how they become aware of the diversity that is in the United States. The growing presence of first-generation Americans in previously homoge-neous suburban locales brings a changed reality into the residents' taken-for-granted world. How that translates into interaction patterns will determine the positive or negative reactions. On the other hand, news about illegal aliens almost always triggers a negative response. Whether it is a story about the *Golden Venture,* a ship smuggling in Chinese aliens that ran aground off the New Jersey coast in 1994, or one of many other stories about illegal aliens entering the United States, Americans resent people who violate their laws and cost them money.

Legal and Illegal Aliens

Concern over illegal aliens is nothing new. After passage of the Chinese Exclusion Act in 1882, Americans faced the problem of Chinese illegally entering the United States through British Columbia. Today, with a porous border with Mexico, illegal crossings are constant. Federal agents apprehend more than 1 million aliens each year, but an estimated 200,000 successfully elude detection.[21]

Controversy over these undocumented aliens—particularly with the education, health, and social welfare costs they create—distorts the public image of legal immigrants. When a 1992 *Business Week*/Harris Poll found that 68 percent of all Americans thought immigration was bad for the country, they frequently cited reasons such as being unskilled and using too many government services.[22] These are more likely to be associated with illegal aliens than immigrants whose skills or family sponsorship clear them for admission legally. Unfortunately, many Americans do not make a distinction between these two very different groups of newcomers.

Today's Patterns in Perspective

Many Americans believe we live in the midst of the greatest immigration ever. In actual numbers, that appears to be true, but in relation to the total population, the current immigration rate is lower than that of the eighty-year period stretching from 1840 to 1920. Those higher rates meant a much greater ratio of immigrants to the population than at present.

Similarly, today's foreign-born population, so easily visible, is in fact far less in relation to the native-born population than in ten of the last fifteen censuses. Put plainly, we have a much lower foreign-born ratio today than we have had throughout most of the past 150 years.

We are indeed becoming a more multiracial society and we have more Africans, Asians, and Hispanics than ever before. The trend toward more people of color will continue, but the present racial composition of American society consists of a smaller proportion of non-White Americans than in 1790. However, Whites are declining as a percentage of the total and, if they feel threatened economically and politically, they could act to reverse or slow down this demographic change. Perhaps California, where Whites are first most likely to become a minority, will become the bellwether state for a national response, with passage of Proposition 187, which denies government-funded education and health care services to illegal aliens, merely the opening volley.

Acculturation, assimilation, and ethnogenesis have resulted in a greater inclusiveness of previously excluded groups into the mainstream American category. Up until now, however, that process has not included people of color. If the process is to continue, a sea of change in racial attitudes will be required to allow today's outgroup members to become part of the American mainstream.

Our discussions about the statistics relating to immigration, foreign-born census counts, and racial proportions have all addressed aspects of the pluralism that has been, and continues to be, the reality of the United States. Commentary on the expanding definition of mainstream Americans points to the ongoing assimilation process that continues throughout the generations. So, although dispelling some of the myths that immigration will get out of hand or that the proportion of foreign born is higher than ever, the data also offer quantitative insights for avoiding the Dillingham Flaw. Peter Berger was right. Things are not necessarily as they seem. The pluralism of today in many ways does not surpass that in our nation's past, and assimilation is not endangered by numbers because it has successfully continued as a dynamic force under more overwhelming proportionate numbers of years ago.

Left unsaid in this discussion is whether the agendas of separatist multiculturalists create a real danger to societal cohesiveness, regardless of comparative statistics. We turn next to that topic.

9

Is Multiculturalism a Threat?

On several occasions, under sponsorship of the U.S. Information Agency, I have traveled throughout Canada and Europe to give public lectures and media interviews on multiculturalism as well as confer with officials. Wherever I went, I found enormous interest in the subject—manifested in large audience turnouts and extensive questioning—often to the surprise of U.S. Embassy personnel accompanying me.

One should not be surprised. Those countries are also experiencing a large influx of dissimilar immigrants and the topic of multiculturalism intrigues those societies as it does ours. More to the point, multiculturalism scares many of them just as it does many Americans. Those expressing concern share an anxiety about loss of cultural homogeneity and national identity.

Multiculturalism is taught in academia, debated in government, promoted by ethnic leaders, reported by the media, and discussed among the citizenry. Few are indifferent to a subject with so many proponents and opponents. Some see multiculturalism as the bedrock on which to build a society of true equality, but others see multiculturalism as a sinkhole that will swallow up the very foundation of American society.

At its very core, the pro- and anti-multiculturalist debate is a polarization of the centuries-old dual American realities of pluralism and assimilation into competing forces for dominance. As this book has shown, pluralism has been a constant reality in the United States since colonial times, and assimilation has been a steady, powerful force as well. There have always been both assimilationist and pluralist advocates as well as both nativist alarmists and minority separatists.

Resentment and hostility about multiculturalism result from several factors. Rapid communication and televised images have heightened public consciousness of the diversity within American society, but without placing it in the continuity of the larger historical context. Government policies and programs, particularly those dealing with bilingualism, become controversial when viewed as more than transitional aids by both pluralists and assimilationists. Vocal advocates for each position arouse strong feelings in their listeners by suggesting an "either-or" stance of supposedly diametrically opposing forces.

What raises reactions toward multiculturalism to a firestorm level are still other factors. First are the radical positions either anti-immigrant or racist, or else anti-White male or nonintegrationist.[1] Another is revisionist history or literary anthologies that downplay "DWMs" (dead White males) or else Western civilization, and heavily emphasize women, people of color, and non-Western civilization. Add furor over political correctness—whether in the guise of speech or behavior codes, curricula offerings, or selective emphases. The result is controversy of a (dare I say it?) white-heat intensity.

Multiculturalism is a stance taken by pluralists. Does that mean it imperils the process of assimilation? The answer is, basically, no, but the explanation is a complicated one. Multiculturalism, as I mentioned in the first chapter, is a newer term for cultural pluralism, not a new phenomenon. Large foreign-speaking communities, foreign-language schools, organizations, houses of worship, and even pluralist extremists are not new to American society. Is, then, the new version not to be feared any more than its precursor, or is this more than a "new suit"? Is this thing we call multiculturalism a clear and present danger? Before we can address this concern, we need to understand exactly what multiculturalism is.

The Umbrellas
of Multiculturalism

Multiculturalism does not mean the same thing to everyone. Even the multiculturalists do not agree with one another as to what they are advocating. Before we can address the advantages or disadvantages of a multicultural society, therefore, we need to understand these differing viewpoints.[2]

The Inclusionists

During the 1970s, multiculturalism meant including material in the school curriculum that related the contributions of non-European peoples to the nation's history. In the next phase, multiculturalists aimed to change all areas of the curriculum in schools and colleges to reflect the diversity of American society and to develop in individuals an awareness and appreciation for the impact of non-European civilizations on American culture.[3]

Inclusionists would appear to be assimilationists, but they are more than this. Assimilationists seek elimination of cultural differences through loss of one's distinctive traits that are replaced by the language, values, and other attributes of mainstream Americans. Although inclusionists share assimilationists' desire for national unity through a common identity, they also promote a pluralist or multiculturalist perspective. This finds expression by recognizing diversity throughout American history and of minority contributions to American art, literature, music, cuisine, scientific achievements, sports, and holiday celebrations.

In the 1990s, this viewpoint has perhaps found its most eloquent voice in Diane Ravitch.[4] She too emphasizes a common culture but one that incorporates the contributions of all racial and ethnic groups so that they can believe in their full membership in America's past, present, and future. She envisions elimination of allegiance to any specific racial and/or ethnic group, with emphasis instead on our common humanity, our shared national identity, and our individual accomplishments.

Inclusionist multiculturalists thus approach pluralism not as if groups each stand under their own different-colored umbrellas, but all share one multicolored umbrella whose strength and character reflect the diverse backgrounds but singular cause of those standing under it together.

The Separatists

Multiculturalists who generate the most controversy advocate "minority nationalism" and "separate pluralism." They reject an integrative approach and the notion of forming a common bond of identity among both the distinct minority groups and mainstream Americans. Instead of a collective American national identity, they seek specific, separate group identities that will withstand the assimilation process. This form of multiculturalism is the most extreme version of pluralism.

To achieve their objective and create a positive group identity, these multiculturalists seek to teach and maintain their own cultural customs, history, values, and festivals but refuse to acknowledge those of the dominant culture. For example, some Native Americans raise strong objections to Columbus Day parades and Afrocentrists downgrade Western civilization by arguing that it is merely a derivative of Afro-Egyptian culture, a claim that is not historically accurate.[5]

Separatist multiculturalists do not want to stand with others under one multicolored umbrella. Not only do they wish to be under their own special umbrella, they want to share it only with their own kind and let them know why it is such a special umbrella. One may walk the same ground in the same storm, but shelter can only be found under a group's personal umbrella.

The assimilationists are particularly infuriated about the separatists' position because such emphasis on group identity promotes what Arthur Schlesinger calls "the cult of ethnicity." In *The Disuniting of America* (1991), a book widely discussed in both Europe and North America, Schlesinger warns that the Balkan present may be America's prologue.[6]

It is precisely that devastating warfare in the Balkans between Bosnians, Croatians, and Serbs in the former Yugoslavia that has prompted so many voices in Canada, Europe, and the United States against multiculturalists who espouse separate pluralism. The "balkanization of society" is the most common expression that critics of multiculturalism use to suggest the threat to the social fabric is supplied by a divisive policy promoting group identity over individual or societal welfare.

When Hispanic leaders from groups such as the League of United Latin American Citizens (LULAC) insist on "language rights," the maintenance of the Spanish language, and Latino culture at public expense, the assimilationists warn of an emerging "Tower of Babel" society.[7] When Afrocentrists such as Molefi Asante and Leon Jeffries emphasize the customs of African cultures over those of the dominant culture, their stress on African ethnicity provokes disapproval from critics such as Schlesinger who complain they drive "even deeper the awful wedges between races" (p. 58) by exaggerating ethnic differences.

Before we address these concerns in the next section, let us first identify a third type of multiculturalist.

The Integrative Pluralists

You may recall the observation in Chapter 1 that in 1915, Horace Kallen used the metaphor of a symphony orchestra to portray the strength through diversity of American society.[8] Just as different groups of instruments each play their separate parts of the musical score but together produce beautiful music of blends and contrasts, so too, he said, do the various populations within pluralist America. Kallen's idea of effective functional integration but limited cultural integration, however, was essentially a Eurocentric vision and reality. People of color were mentioned only incidentally and were typically not allowed to sit with, let alone join, the orchestra.

Harry Triandis not only added an interracial component to this view of integrative pluralism in 1976, but he also suggested the majority culture is enriched by "additive multiculturalism."[9] By this he meant that one can get more out of life by understanding other languages, cultural values, and social settings. He hoped for society becoming more cohesive by finding common superordinate goals without insisting on a loss of Black identity, Native American identity, Asian or Hispanic identity. Arguing that mainstream Americans, secure in their identity, need to develop new interpersonal skills, Triandis maintained that the essence of pluralism is the development of appreciation, interdependence, and skills to interact intimately with persons from other cultures. He added,

> The majority culture can be enriched by considering the viewpoints of the several minority cultures that exist in America rather than trying to force these minorities to adopt a monocultural, impover-ished, provincial viewpoint which may in the long run reduce creativity and the chances of effective adjustment in a fast-changing world. (p. 181)

This argument of cultural enrichment from diverse subcultures found another form of expression in *Beyond the Culture Wars* (1992) by Gerald Graff.[10] He suggests that exposure to differing cultural views will revitalize education by creating the dynamics of dialogue and debate. As Socrates once encouraged his students to search for truth through intellectual clashes, so too, Graff maintains, can multicultural education help students overcome relativism and become informed about different positions.

Ronald Takaki echoes Graff's idea by recommending that the university become the meeting ground for different viewpoints.[11] American minds, he believes, need to be opened to greater cultural diversity. American history, like America itself, does not belong to one group, says Takaki, and so a change in the status quo is needed. Instead of a hierarchy of power headed by a privileged group, greater cross-cultural under-standing and interconnected viewpoints are necessary.

Integrative pluralists envision a multitude of distinctive umbrellas each sheltering a different group, but with the umbrellas' edges attached to each other so that collectively they cover everyone. Guided equally by the many handles of the interconnected umbrellas, one can look around to see where another group is coming from within the framework of the whole.

Roses and Thorns

Cultivated for almost five thousand years, roses were known to the Persians, Greeks, and Romans. One of our most popular flowers, they now come in more than eight thousand varieties. Yet as beautiful and romantic as most people find roses to be, their thorns can hurt.

Roses seem a particularly apt analogy in any discussion about multiculturalism. Both require warmth and nurturing to bloom fully. The stronger their roots, the more they thrive. A variety of species is common to both, yet universal treatment gives vibrancy to all. Both also contain beauty and danger. Focusing only on the rose when reaching for it usually brings flesh into painful contact with a thorn; focusing narrowly on racial or cultural differences often causes the pain of isolation or conflict.

Some proponents of multiculturalism (the separatists) want only to focus on one variety of "rose" among many, but other advocates (the inclusionists) stress the commonality in origin that so many kinds of "roses" share. The third group of multiculturalists (the integrative pluralists) emphasize the overall beauty of "roses" of different colors and varieties sharing the same "garden." The critics of multiculturalism, however, seem only to see its "thorns."

Completely ignoring the thorns needlessly places one at risk. If we look only at the thorns, we miss the beauty of the rose. If we pay heed to the thorns or remove them, as florists so thoughtfully do for their customers, then they cannot hurt us and our appreciation for the rose remains unspoiled. In the rest of this chapter, we shall look first at the thorns, the negative side of multiculturalism, and then at the roses, or positive aspects.

The Thorns
of Multiculturalism

The thorns of multiculturalism are primarily those of immigration, language, culture, and race. Other smaller ones could undoubtedly be named, but these are the most important, because some Americans find them a threat to American society.

The "Immigrant Thorns"

Make no mistake about it. Continuing high immigration fuels the debate over multiculturalism, but this subject is about much more than simply past contributions or the preservation of one's heritage. It is about power struggles among groups. It is about economics, jobs, social welfare, and tax dollars.

The large numbers of immigrants arriving each year are likely to instill antipathy in many native-born White and Black Americans toward any manifestation of foreign origins through multicultural policies or programs. With over seventeen million immigrants arriving since 1971, a sizable proportion of the American public thinks too many immigrants live in this country. Such anti-immigration sentiments have been heard in the land almost continually since large numbers of Irish Catholics began entering the United States in the early nineteenth century.

Public opinion polls conducted by the Roper Center in 1981 and 1982 found two-thirds of all Americans favored a decrease in immigration.[12] That heavy anti-immigration response should be understood in the context of the 1980-1982 recession and the influx of over 200,000 Vietnamese "boat people" and 125,000 Cuban "Marielitos" within this two-year period.

A 1992 *Business Week*/Harris Poll revealed 68 percent of all respondents saying the present immigration is bad for the country.[13] Forty-seven percent of Blacks and 62 percent of non-Blacks wanted fewer immigrants to come. In the same year, a poll of almost 3,000 Americans of Cuban, Mexican, and Puerto Rican descent, conducted by the Latino National Political Survey, found two-thirds agreeing that there were too many immigrants in the United States. Obviously, anti-immigration sentiments are not confined to any one group.

One multigenerational pattern about public response to immigration needs mentioning. Contemporary immigrants of any time period have almost always received negative evaluations by most native-born Americans, many themselves descendants of earlier immigrants once castigated by other native-born Americans. With the passage of time, people view these now "old" immigrant groups as making positive contributions to the cultural and socioeconomic well-being of society, because they transfer their negative perceptions to new immigrant groups.

Numerous anti-immigration organizations have emerged to lobby for restrictive laws to curtail immigration. The largest of these are the American Immigration Control Foundation (AICF), the Federation for

American Immigration Reform (FAIR), and the Center for Immigration Studies (CIS).

Although these and other anti-immigrant groups vary somewhat in the intensity of their views, they all see the present immigration as a threat to the United States. Their opposition rests on their belief that immigrants either take jobs away from Americans, often from poor people who are forced onto welfare, or else the immigrants go on welfare themselves. Either way, these groups insist, the immigrants drive up social welfare costs. Other arguments include the assertion that immigrants strain law enforcement resources, contribute to an overpopulation problem through their higher birth rates, and deplete natural resources.

Some states—such as California, Florida, Illinois, New Jersey, New York, and Texas, which are the destinations of 80 percent of all immigrants—clearly feel the impact of immigration more than other states. In early 1994, the New York State Senate Committee on Cities issued a report claiming that legal and illegal immigrants cost that state more than $5 billion a year in welfare, education, and criminal justice services.[14] Such reports and claims of high costs to the taxpayer provide ready ammunition for immigration critics.

If multiculturalism means favoring an immigration that places a financial hardship on the American worker and taxpayer, then many Americans oppose multiculturalism.

The "Language Thorns"

Foreigners speaking a language other than English have been a thorn in the side of many Americans for more than two hundred years. In 1750, Benjamin Franklin expressed concern about the prevalence of the German language in Pennsylvania, and George Washington wrote to John Adams in 1798 against encouraging immigration because, among other things, the new arrivals "retain the language . . . which they bring with them."[15] No doubt these men spoke not only for themselves but for a great many of their contemporaries as well.

Such complaints have reverberated down through the generations to the present day. They are now also louder and more numerous, given current migration trends. Two out of every three immigrants speak Spanish and, as a result, more than eighteen million Americans five years old and over speak Spanish. Another five million speak an Asian or Pacific Island language. Education officials expect over five million children speaking more than 150 languages to have entered the nation's public schools by the time this decade ends.

With the prevalence of so many non-English-speaking youngsters and adults, Americans have done more than complain. For example, Japanese American S. I. Hayakawa, a former U.S. Senator from California and former president of San Francisco State University, founded U.S. English, an organization dedicated to making English the nation's official language, eliminating or reducing bilingual education programs, and abolishing bilingual ballots, government documents, and road signs.[16]

English-only laws were introduced in dozens of state legislatures in the late 1980s. Although thirteen states had rejected English-only legislative proposals by 1990, eighteen states passed such legislation. Other states were considering similar proposals until a federal judge in 1990 struck down Arizona's state constitutional amendment, ruling that it violated the First Amendment. Advocates of language pluralism expect the judicial ruling to serve as the precedent for other state challenges, but the controversy over language usage continues.

Many Americans who are impatient with those unable to speak English contend that anyone living in this country should speak its language. Believing that our schools provide the "heat" for the melting pot, they are particularly irked about bilingual education programs.

Critics see bilingual programs as counterproductive because they reduce assimilation and cohesiveness in American society and simultaneously isolate ethnic groups from one another. Opponents use the phrases "ethnic tribalism" and "classrooms of Babel" to argue that bilingual education fosters separation instead of cultural unity.[17] When LULAC leaders and others say that language and cultural maintenance programs should be public expenses, the monolingual adherents see red.

If multiculturalism means English proficiency is not a priority, then many Americans oppose multiculturalism.

The "Cultural Thorns"

Almost eighty thousand new immigrants—about 85 percent of them Asian or Hispanic—now arrive each month in the United States. Ethnic resiliency in language, ingroup solidarity, and subcultural patterns are all sustained and enhanced by the steadily increasing size of each new immigrant group.

Without this constant infusion of newcomers, the twin processes of ethnogenesis and acculturation would inexorably lessen each group's cultural isolation. Group members would gradually learn to speak English and function more fully within the larger society. Even if such factors as limited education, poor job skills, and discrimination were present to prevent economic mainstreaming, greater cultural fusion would most likely occur over time.

Instead, we have large-scale immigration from Asian and Latin American countries revitalizing ethnic subcommunities with their language usage and cultural patterns. Differences in physical appearance, non-Western traditions and religious faiths—together with the prevalence of languages other than English, especially Spanish—suggest to some Americans that unless immigration is significantly curtailed, American culture and society are in danger of fragmenting.

What makes the cultural thorns even sharper is the new ethnic presence in our suburbs. Once the almost exclusive sanctuary of homogenized Americans, many suburbs are now the residential areas of choice for tens of thousands of first-generation Americans of non-European origin, who are mostly Asian. Well-educated business and professional persons, seeking out desirable communities with excellent school systems, have brought racial and ethnic diversity to towns unaccustomed to such a multiethnic mix, sometimes erecting a mosque or Sikh temple with its unique architecture in contrast to other structures in the community.

It is not simply the presence of visibly distinct newcomers that creates tensions. These first-generation Americans live in the community but they are not part of it, for they seldom interact with neighbors. Instead they maintain an interactional network within their own group scattered throughout the area. This informal social patterning is reminiscent of other immigrants who have lived in recognized territorial subcommunities but, because these middle-class suburban ethnics live among homogenized Americans, their lack of involvement in community life encourages social distance and grates on others' sensibilities.

Besides a normal first-generation immigrant preference to associate with one's own people, some pragmatic elements deter suburban ethnic social interactions. Often the wife, filling the traditional gender role as keeper of home and hearth, has limited command of English and feels insecure about conversing with neighbors. The husband, usually at work for long hours, has little free time, except to spend with the family.

Joining social organizations is a strong American orientation, as noted by Tocqueville and many others. Possessing neither time nor yet fully acculturated, few Asian Americans get involved in such typical suburban activities as parent-teacher organizations, team sports coaching, or scouting leadership. In time, this will probably change, but the present noninvolvement maintains Asian social distance from other Americans in their local communities.

In response, suburbanites often view the Asians as not giving, only taking from the community. This reaction is especially acute when Asian American children, reflecting the high motivation and goal achievement instilled in them by their parents, appear overrepresented in garnering awards and gaining recognition in scholarships and music.

If multiculturalism means maintenance of an alien culture and lessening community cohesiveness, then most Americans oppose multiculturalism.

The "Racial Thorns"

Except for extremist groups like the Ku Klux Klan, the National Association for the Advancement of White People (NAAWP), and neo-Nazis, few talk openly of race in their opposition to multiculturalism. Nevertheless, race is an important component of the multiculturalism debate.

The United States may be a less racist country than in earlier years if civil rights legislation, public opinion polls, and the social indicators of education, occupation, income, and elected officials serve as a barometer. Yet racism still exists, perhaps less intensely in some areas than others, but it remains nonetheless. It can be found in numerous conversations, avoidance responses, subtle acts of discrimination, and a myriad of interaction patterns.

Institutional racism—the established laws, customs, and practices which systematically reflect and produce racial inequities in American society—is, however, a more significant factor than individuals committing overt racist actions. Biases remain built into the social structure, causing many individuals unknowingly to act without deliberate intent to hinder the advancement of non-Whites.

Although the Commission on Civil Rights in 1981 identified areas in which affirmative action could take aim at institutional racism (job seniority rules, nepotism-based recruitment or union membership, bank credit practices, culturally biased job performance tests), some of these remain problem areas. De facto housing segregation and disparities in school funding for urban and suburban schools are other examples of the multigenerational continuation of a subtle, structural racist practice. The pervasiveness of institutional racism remains both an obstacle in the path of upward mobility to many racial minority group members and a basic impediment to better interracial relations.

As successful as this country has been in assimilating national minorities, it has been far less successful in assimilating racial minorities.

African and Native Americans are still not fully integrated as mainstream Americans. Because we have never fully resolved our centuries-old twin problems of race relations and racial integration, the growing presence of people of color from Third World countries exacerbates the matter.

Racial animosity continues in Black-White conflicts, most just publicized locally but some getting national attention, such as a group of Whites beating Blacks in New York's Howard Beach section, or the beating of Rodney King by Los Angeles police officers. We also find racial strife between Blacks and Asians, Blacks and Hispanics, Hispanics and Whites, or even multiracial battles as occurred in the 1992 Los Angeles riot.

Racial tensions have heightened in some areas because of the influx of racially distinct, "clannish" strangers into neighborhoods unaccustomed to their presence. When this occurs in previously homogeneous middle-class suburbs, the reactions may be more subtle but the resentment is real and finds expression in avoidance responses, zoning regulations, and verbal complaints within one's circle of family, friends, and neighbors.

If multiculturalism means an increased racial presence and/or increased racial power that puts their own racial group to any disadvantage, then most Americans oppose multiculturalism.

The Roses of Multiculturalism

Roses bud, bloom, and wither away. Rosebuds give us the promise of new beauty about to arrive, and when the flowers are in full bloom, their contribution of beauty to our lives has to be experienced to be fully appreciated. Gradually, though, the roses wither and their petals gracefully fall to the ground, covering the dark earth with their various colors. With modest pruning, the gardener can coax other roses to appear and repeat the process again and again.

Multiculturalism is not a rose that will wither in the United States, which has always been a land of diversity and destination for millions of immigrants. However, some "blooms" of ethnicity do wither as, for example, we witness what Richard Alba calls "the twilight of ethnicity" among European Americans.[18] Moreover, what appears to some people as thorns may actually be roses instead. Let us extend our metaphor of roses to the four types of thorns just discussed.

The "Immigrant Roses"

If a nation's strength lies in its people, then America's strength clearly lies in the diversity of its people. Immigrants from all over the world have come here and, in one way or another, each group has played some role in the nation's evolution into its present superpower status.

Past immigrants built our cities, transportation systems, and labor unions, and enabled us to come of age both agriculturally and industrially. Many of today's immigrants have revitalized our cities, helped our high-tech industries remain competitive, and pumped billions of dollars annually into the national economy through their businesses, occupations, and consumerism. Combating negative stereotyping, societal ostracism, and fear about their growing size, each immigrant group then and now has worked hard to survive and put down roots. Viewed as a threat, each has proven to be an asset. Although most might accept that pronouncement about the first two waves of immigration, how true is it of the current immigration? One answer can be found in a 1992 *Business Week* report that, in the 1980s, the economic benefits of immigrants to the nation far outstripped their costs; some eleven million working immigrants earned over $240 billion a year, paying more than $90 billion in taxes, far more than the estimated $5 billion immigrants received in federal welfare.[19] Although the immigrant roses bloom, others do not often appreciate their beauty; it is the exceptional individual who admires immigrants when they are immigrants. Only after the immigrant rose withers and its falling petals mingle with the soil that contains all our roots do we look back and cherish the bloom that was part of our heritage.

The "Language Roses"

Unlike the people of most nations who are at least bilingual, most Americans are monolingual. This limitation encourages ethnocentrism and provincialism and places the business community at a disadvantage in the global marketplace. Mastery of a second language enhances one's mental mobility, enriching cultural insights and perspectives.

If Americans were to become proficient in a second language, encouraged to do so by the Asian and Latino population cohorts now living here, the result could easily be a society reaching greater maturity and tolerance in its intergroup relations. Most Europeans have long been at least bilingual and their cultures and societal cohesion have not suffered. Bilingual advocates argue bilingualism would not undermine American culture either, only enrich it.

For those who do not "buy into" bilingualism for all citizens, the public opinion polls and scientific studies about English language acquisition offer comforting news. Echoing similar newspaper polls and studies in California, Colorado, and elsewhere, a 1990 *Houston Chronicle* poll showed 87 percent of Hispanics believed it was their "duty to learn English" as quickly as possible.[20] A few years earlier, a study by the Rand Corporation determined that 98 percent of Latino parents in Miami felt it was essential for their children to become competent in English. Such attitudes reach fruition according to the data, as indicated by Rodolfo de la Garza in 1992, who reported that most U.S.-born Latinos and Asians use English as their primary language.[21] Teachers and other schoolchildren everywhere give corroborating testimony to this fact.

Despite all fears of Asian and Hispanic immigrants posing a threat to the English language, assimilation is still, as Nathan Glazer (1993) asserts, "the most powerful force affecting the ethnic and racial elements of the United States."[22] As the American Jewish Committee states, "The use of additional languages to meet the needs of language minorities does not pose a threat to America's true common heritage and common bond—the quest for freedom and opportunity."[23]

To allay further the anxieties of those who fear that the large Hispanic American presence is an unprecedented threat simply because of its size, we do have a comparable example in the nation's past. We can draw a parallel with the almost 4.9 million Germans who entered the United States between 1841 and 1900, a number roughly comparable to all Hispanic immigration since 1971. In doing so, we need to keep in mind the total U.S. population was much smaller then (23.1 million in 1850 and 62.9 million in 1890, compared to 203.3 million in 1970 and 248.7 million in 1990). Radio, television, and movies—ubiquitous English-learning media in the twentieth century—were unknown to the Germans in the eighteenth century.

Although we could speak of regions within states such as in Pennsylvania or small cities such as Hoboken, New Jersey, where Germans outnumbered others and maintained their language and culture for decades, we shall focus on an even more massive region. In the mid- to late-nineteenth century, so many hundreds of thousands of Germans lived in the area between Cincinnati, Milwaukee, and St. Louis that it became known as the "great German triangle."[24]

Because so many German children attended public schools in the German triangle, the states passed laws permitting all academic subjects to be taught in German whenever the demand was sufficient to warrant it. Ohio passed its statute in 1837; the others followed in the 1840s.

Consider for a moment the profundity of this action. In major cities, as well as in rural regions, the states of Ohio, Missouri, and Wisconsin (as well as other states) authorized German as an official language for *all* classroom instruction! Cultural diversity, including that of language, was not only tolerated, but also encouraged.

The use of German in the public schools served a purpose other than academic instruction. It was intended to preserve the whole range of German culture, even more so after the unification of Germany in the 1870s. With an increased pride in their origins, German immigrants and their children developed a greater sense of their ethnicity than they possessed before their emigration. Because language enhanced their sense of being German, the German Americans continued to speak their language in their schools, homes, churches, and in everyday business transactions.

As extensive German immigrant settlement in the region continued decade after decade, German-language instruction in all subjects continued in the public schools. Such was the case in the private schools as well. By 1910, more than 95 percent of German Catholic parishes had parochial schools taught in German, and more than two thousand parishes conducted German-language services, much to the consternation of the Irish American church hierarchy.

During World War I, patriotic hysteria to drive the "Hun" language out of the schools prompted states such as Ohio and Nebraska to pass laws prohibiting instruction in German in all schools, public and private. A legal challenge to this action reached the U.S. Supreme Court in *Robert Meyer v. Nebraska* (1923).

Although the Court upheld the states' right to determine public school instruction in English only, its ruling on private and parochial schools was an important one with regard to language rights. Ruling that all state laws prohibiting the teaching and use of German in private or parochial schools were in violation of the Fourteenth Amendment and therefore unconstitutional, the Court declared that the rights of both parents and private/parochial schools to teach their children in a language other than English was within the liberty guaranteed by that amendment.

Despite the institutionalization of academic instruction in German, the steady influx of large numbers of German immigrants, and more than sixty years of German language maintenance, German language usage declined. That process had already begun by 1885, as indicated by

German American leaders who complained that the younger generation was losing the German tongue and that parents no longer insisted on their children studying German in the schools.

As with other ethnic groups, English gradually replaced the homeland language, even among the millions of Germans so heavily concentrated in regions such as the German triangle. The German language rose once bloomed mightily in the United States, but it has withered, its petals drifting downward and blending with others that fell earlier. Perhaps the Spanish language is another such rose.

The "Cultural Roses"

The United States contains a variety of persistent subcultures, people who steadfastly adhere to their own way of life as much as possible, resisting absorption into the dominant culture. These are usually religious groups—such as the Amish, Hutterites, Mennonites, Hasidim—or groups whose ancestors predate the United States, such as the Native Americans and Spanish Americans in the Southwest. One could also make a case for a persistent subculture seeming to exist among one-third of the Black Americans mired in poverty for multiple generations. Until society finds an effective means to end their deprivation, these hard-core Black poor will continue to subsist within a subculture necessary for their survival.

Most racial and ethnic groups, however, are part of a convergent subculture that gradually disappears as its members become integrated into the dominant culture. For some, their "cultural roses" bloom longer than others but, at some point, the roses do wither. Beside the Germans just discussed, we have dozens of other examples of once-vibrant ethnic subcultures, ones that contemporary native-born Americans considered both persistent and a threat to the dominant culture, that converged into the mainstream.

Ethnic subcultures do not undermine the dominant culture. The United States has always had ethnic subcultures and, when their strength and vitality grow, they often contain separatist advocates. It is not uncommon for outsiders to become anxious about subgroup loyalties posing a danger to the larger society. Theodore Roosevelt's famous remark that "there is no room in this country for hyphenated Americanism"[25] spoke to the same fears of subversion of American culture that Schlesinger has addressed as the "disuniting of America."

When immigrants come to the United States, they come to join us. In forsaking their ancestral lands, they pay us the highest compliment:

they want to spend the rest of their lives with us in a country where they hope to realize their dreams of a better life. They come to be a part of us, an "us" they have imagined our being after exposure to thousands of pictures, films, television shows, stories, letters, and rumors. They come to join us, not keep separate from us. It may take some time, longer than some Americans' patience but, for most, that integration into the dominant culture occurs.

The falling petals of fading cultural roses also mingle with the soil containing all our roots. American society, reflecting its multicultural past and present, keeps on being enriched with architecture, art, creative works, cuisine, music, and other cultural contributions from the diversity of its people.

The "Racial Roses"

Here we have a rare species of rose, for its bloom in a multiracial setting in the United States is difficult to produce. Too much of our past and present has been filled with racial animosity, exploitation, and violence. As I said earlier, we have never fully resolved the twin problems of race relations and racial integration in our society.

Part of our problem has been our cultural mindset. With a simplistic "White" and "non-White" racial classification system, we have insidiously enmeshed race within our social structure. We have created and consistently reinforced an "us" and "them" mentality that manifests itself in social distance, differential treatment, deprivation, and suffering. Furthermore, our monoracial categories ignore the multiracial backgrounds of millions of African Americans, Filipinos, Latinos, Native Americans, and "Whites."

As changing demographics make an increased multiracial society more evident to Americans, perhaps we shall see the weeds of racism removed (particularly the rooting out of institutional discrimination) and the blooming of the racial roses. Such a change will not be easy. Yet, as the non-White segment of the American population increases, so may the multiracial component of the American identity. If no longer relegated to the periphery, racial groups will be more at the center, and at the center one finds both power and integration.

Increased racial tensions remain a distinct possibility and we certainly find examples of that today. However, with the greater sharing of power that must come, that very same sharing of power could also cause greater racial acceptance.

At the risk of being accused of wearing rose-colored glasses in depicting the racial roses, I would suggest that if we can get the racial roses to bloom in this land—get to that point where each of the races displays its full beauty—then we can look pass that point to the next horizon. When the racial rose petals fall and mingle with the soil common to us all, we will have moved past race as a divisive aspect of our society. This was Martin Luther King Jr.'s dream, that one day his children would be judged by the content of their character instead of the color of their skin.[26]

Is Multiculturalism the Enemy?

On the battlefield of multiculturalism, pluralists and assimilationists wage war, but neither side will vanquish the other. As always, both forces will remain an integral part of American society. The United States will remain a beacon of hope to immigrants everywhere, keeping the rich tradition of pluralism alive and well. Assimilationist forces, as consistently demonstrated for centuries, will remain strong, particularly on immigrant children and their descendants. Multiculturalism will no more weaken that process any more than the many past manifestations of ethnic ingroup solidarity have.

Social observers of different eras—Alexis de Tocqueville, Gunnar Myrdal, and Andrew Hacker, among others—have commented on the separate racial worlds within the United States. These separate worlds are not the result of multiculturalist teachings. Only when we break down the remaining racial barriers, eliminate institutional discrimination, and open up paths free of obstacles to a good education and job opportunities for everyone will racial integration improve. Afrocentrist schools do not undermine a cohesive American society any more than Catholic schools, yeshivas, or other religious schools do. Multiculturalism is not the enemy; systemic racism is.

10

Beyond the Horizon

Nativists' reactions against increased American diversity were often not just a response to what they perceived as a clear and present danger to America as they understood it. Beside their concern about the growing presence of those undesirable strangers in their midst, they also worried about their impact on the future of American society.

A limerick from the early twentieth century captures that worry in lines that WASPs, feeling threatened by the influx of so many unlike others, did not find amusing:

> In nineteen and seventy-five,
> crowds swarmed like bees 'round a hive,
> To see in a tent
> An American gent,
> The very last Yankee alive.[1]

Numerically, WASPs have been a minority group for some time now, but they are hardly an endangered species. Still, their reduced presence and projections about their further shrinkage, along with all non-Hispanic Whites, have rekindled fears about the loss of dominance implied in the above limerick.

One final word about the limerick: "Yankee" is one of those interesting words that helps us understand the expanding mainstream category discussed in Chapter 8. It once meant a New Englander, but by the time of the Civil War, it had changed to indicate a Northerner. Since World War I, "Yankee" has simply meant any American. At the time of this limerick, however, its usage was understood to be a reference to its earlier connotation of an Anglo American, much like Mark Twain's popular work, *A Connecticut Yankee in King Arthur's Court*, which was first published in 1889.[2]

In recent years, various demographers and social observers have offered their projections and scenarios about America's future. As the twentieth century draws to a close, we can anticipate an onslaught of media attention to this subject.

The Dawning of a New Century

We stand on the threshold of a major calendar change. Soon we will mark not only the passing of a hundred years but also of a thousand years. This combination of a forthcoming new century and millennium has the futurists busy prognosticating about life in the twenty-first century. These predictions, as usual, range from the ridiculous to the sublime. Some will be accurate and others not. No one really knows what the future holds. We can only make educated guesses.

Those living when the United States entered the nineteenth century could not have foretold with precision new immigration patterns, or that the nation's size would triple, or that such technological advances as electric generators and lights, steam locomotives and ships, the telegraph and telephone, the reaping machine, vulcanized rubber, dynamite, radio, and moving pictures would revolutionize the way we live.

Similarly, those witness to the beginning of the twentieth century could not accurately envision atomic energy, jet engines, radar, transistors, test tube babies, or the changing waves of immigration. How civilization will change in the twenty-first century or what world events will affect migration is really unknown, but that doesn't stop many from suggesting the possibilities.

Sometimes the predictions seem uncanny. Two centuries ago Secretary of State John Jay remarked, "The Mediterranean is the ocean of the past, the Atlantic the ocean of the present, and the Pacific the ocean of the future."[3] With California now our largest state and with the economic strength of Japan, the increasing industrialization of other Asian countries, and signs of China's opening markets, Jay's prophecy seems quite accurate.

World Population Growth

The Population Reference Bureau reported in 1994 that, even though fertility rates are dropping worldwide, world population growth may grow from about 6 billion in 1999 to between 8 and 11 billion by 2030, depending on fertility and mortality rates. In the midrange projection, Southern Asia will have the biggest increase, adding 1.2 billion more people. All of the developing countries are expected to at least double in population size by 2030.[4]

Developing countries will account for a greater share of the world population by 2030, representing between 85 and 87 percent of the world's total. Africa's share will increase most rapidly, from 12 to 19 percent, and industrialized countries will shrink from 22 to 14 percent of the world's total population.

The significance of these patterns lies in their impact on immigration to the United States and this country's subsequent change in population composition. The inability of a country to support its large population has been an important push factor in emigration elsewhere. As population pressures mount in developing countries in the oncoming years, so will immigration pressures.

Current projections show continued high birth rates in most African, Asian, and Latin American countries outpacing their ability to provide a decent quality of life. In many of these nations the fertility rate is dropping, but the population continues to rise startlingly because of the high proportion of their populations under the age of sixteen.

With so big a segment entering the child-bearing years, a built-in factor exists for further population expansion because none of these countries are anywhere near zero population growth where two adults have only two children. Mexico, for example, tripled its population between 1950 and 1990, increasing from 27 million to 85 million. By the turn of the century, it will be at about 103 million and perhaps reach 154 million within thirty years. As our next-door neighbor and largest sending country, Mexico seems destined to send us millions more immigrants in the next few decades.

U.S. Population Predictions

When it comes to projections about the future of American diversity, the Census Bureau has offered a portrait of society at midpoint in the next century. The government demographers base their forecast on the continuance of current trends. They assume the birth rate will remain fairly low and life expectancy will increase slightly, but immigration will continue to average 950,000 annually from the same sending countries as now.

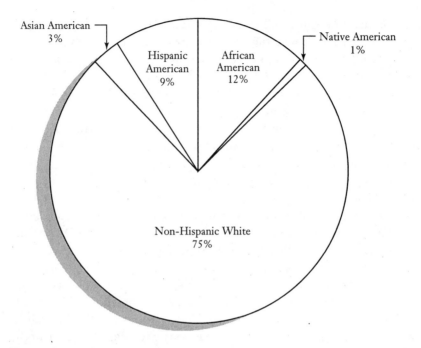

Figure 10.1. *U.S. Population in 1990*

Source: U.S. Bureau of the Census, *Current Population Reports,* Series P25-1092 (Washington, DC: Government Printing Office, 1992); *Statistical Abstract of the United States 1994* (Washington, DC: Government Printing Office, 1994).

These assumptions may be reasonable, but they are by no means certain. We can no more anticipate the actualities and ramifications of social change a half century from now than could past Americans witnessing the advent of the nineteenth and twentieth centuries. Actually, high-, middle-, and low-range projections exist to give us a continuum of future possibilities. Even so, these projections rest on assumptions that may or may not hold true. What follows are the midrange projections from the Census Bureau.[5]

Hispanic Americans

Hispanic Americans could increase their share of the population from 22.4 million, or 9 percent, in 1990 to 21 percent in 2050, when they will number about 81 million. This would be a population growth three-and-a-half times their size in 1990. The projections show the Latinos surpassing African Americans in 2013, 42.1 million to 42 million, to become the nation's largest minority group.

African Americans

African Americans numbered about 30.5 million in 1990, or 12.3 percent of the total. By 2050, they may be approximately 62.2 million, or 16 percent of the total population. If this occurs, they will double their present numbers.

Native Americans

Of the almost 382 million Americans projected in 2050, almost 5 million will be Native Americans. This would be a 150 percent increase over their near 2 million headcount in the 1990 census. However, their share of the total would remain at its present 1 percent.

Asian Americans

In 1990, there were about 7.5 million Asian Americans, comprising 3 percent of all Americans. They are expected to more than quintuple by 2050 and reach 41.1 million, giving them an 11 percent share of the total population.

Non-Hispanic White Americans

If all these groups increase proportionately within the total population, then the only group left—non-Hispanic Whites—must decrease. From their present 75 percent portion of the population, calculations for 2050 show a decline to 53 percent.

The Alarm Bells Ring

These projections have triggered alarm bells not just among nativists who have consistently opposed liberal immigration policies but also among some pluralists who believe in the value of diversity. Demographer Leon F. Bouvier is one such example.[6] In *Peaceful Invasions* (1992) he worries about projections showing the United States growing at a faster rate than other industrial nations. With about half this growth anticipated to be from immigration, Bouvier suggests immigration restrictions are needed to strengthen America's economic stability, cultural cohesion, and quality of life.

To achieve these goals Bouvier argues for a reduction of immigration to 450,000 annually to reduce the intensity of the racial shift. A lower

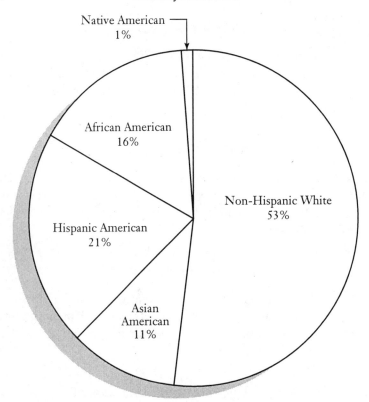

Native American
1%

African American
16%

Hispanic American
21%

Asian
American
11%

Non-Hispanic White
53%

Figure 10.2. *Projected U.S. Population in 2050*

Source: U.S. Bureau of the Census, *Current Population Reports,* Series P25-1092 (Washington, DC: Government Printing Office, 1992); *Statistical Abstract of the United States 1994* (Washington, DC: Government Printing Office, 1994).

ceiling, he maintains, will also enhance cultural adaptation and not cultural separatism by cutting back the source of ethnic vitality. Without the sizable continued inflow of low-level workers, he further believes that American industry will be forced to improve technologically to compete internationally in the twenty-first century.

Anti-immigration organizations, such as those mentioned in the last chapter (AICF, FAIR, CIS), also seize Census Bureau projections to argue for dramatically lowering the number of immigrants permitted to enter. Most argue that although large-scale immigration may have been beneficial to the nation at one time, it no longer is the case, given the size and complexity of today's society.

Resetting the Alarm

Alarms keep us from oversleeping. Sometimes though, we set them too early or, forgetting to turn them off, they awaken us on the wrong day, causing us to lose sleep needlessly. We need to be careful that we set our alarms properly so that we do not fall victim to a false alarm.

Today's decisions affect tomorrow's outcomes, so it is important to be vigilant about the consequences of our actions as we attempt to define what kind of society we wish to become. The problem is that too many actions often have unintended consequences. Just look at how immigration changed far differently than the sponsors of the 1965 immigration act expected. Trying to ascertain the future of immigration or population composition is no easy task.

A source of this nation's strength has always been in its people, including the positive contributions to our society and culture from tens of millions of immigrants. Millions more from around the world would like to move to the United States if they could. Yet even though immigrants are a valuable addition, this country could not possibly absorb all who want to come. Some limits are necessary and a key part of the current debate is what those limits should be. Only a few subscribe to the radical position of open borders without any restrictions whatsoever.

Because some of the anti-immigration arguments are predicated on Census Bureau projections, several points need to be made that might possibly aid us in determining if the alarm has been set too early. The crux of the matter rests on the accuracy of the predictions. Because we cannot know whether or not the predictions were indeed accurate until the time arrives, the only viable approach at this time is to identify what variables could affect even the most conservative scenario of U.S. population projections. In this way we can understand the matter more fully and have additional insights for the formulation of public policy.

Certainly more restrictive immigration laws would affect the projections. Anti-immigration lobbying groups, economic unrest, and public sentiment are influential variables that could influence legislation to reduce immigration totals and thereby alter the population composition.

Homeland conditions in the sending countries are a key factor in determining their emigration rates. Unless Mexico and the other developing countries boldly expand their economies, mounting population pressures will encourage a high exodus to receiving nations such as the United States. However, the world is a rapidly changing place in technology, cultural diffusion, and global interdependence. Perhaps the social change sweeping the world will alter circumstances in Third World countries significantly enough to affect their emigration rates.

Multinational conglomerates operate not out of compassion but for profit. These developing nations offer them major opportunities for expansion and increased profits. We may expect them to open even more new factories and offices in these Third World countries to expand their labor and consumer markets. As they do, it is to be hoped that the expanding economies will improve life opportunities in those countries.

Perhaps the next fifty years will also bring such an infusion of aid from developed countries to developing ones that their quality of life will reach satisfactory levels for their citizens. Why should the developed nations do this? Although humanitarian reasons might be a partial motivation, such aid would be in their own self-interests because improved conditions in these countries would likely reduce the influx of immigrants from those countries.

If these Third World nations develop sufficiently, the demographic transition already evident may accelerate, lowering fertility rates sufficiently to stabilize population growth in the mid-twenty-first century. Such a scenario would mean the lessening of causes for migration and consequently a change in the immigration patterns experienced by the United States.

The Dillingham Flaw in Reverse

In our previous discussions of the Dillingham Flaw, we spoke of using oversimplified categorizations and imposing present-day sensibilities on the past when such perceptions did not exist in those times. We can also apply the Dillingham Flaw when the same errors are committed by anyone looking into the future.

How can we be certain that today's group categories will still be valid in the mid-twenty-first century? Right now, most White Americans bear witness to mixed European ancestry, but two generations ago those Americans of southern, central, and eastern European backgrounds were far more likely to be of a single national lineage and religion. Group identity then was not the same as group identity today, because large-scale intermarriage has generated such a blending of peoples that "Whites" and "European Americans" have become synonymous in language usage.

In the early twentieth century, Italian, Polish, and Slavic Americans were once members of distinctive ethnic groups lacking economic, political, and social power. They displayed all the characteristics of a minority group in their ascribed status, endogamy, unequal treatment, and visibility. For the most part, today they are part of the societal mainstream, now displaying the traits of civic, marital, and structural assimilation. As their integration nears completion, *European American* serves as a generic term for heritage, not for everyday ethnicity, subcultural participation, or minority status.

European immigrants still arrive, and they begin the acculturation process anew, as earlier European arrivals once did. Most European Americans, however, are two or more generations removed from the ethnic experience. They are, for the most part, homogenized into a mainstream American identity, with ethnicity simply now an appreciation for their roots, occasionally marked by symbolic celebrations.

Yesterday's categories for European ethnic Americans no longer fit today's Americans of mixed European ancestry. As we'll discuss shortly, today's racial categories already fail to cover some of today's Americans. How, then, can we know with any certainty what are the right categories for tomorrow's Americans?

Using today's categories for Americans living in 2050 can easily be an unwitting application of the Dillingham Flaw in reverse. Projecting our perceptions and the existing social distance between groups onto a distant future carries a presumption that they will remain the same. Yet the only constant in life is change, and so our categories may be inadequate or irrelevant to our descendants.

Factors Influencing Change

Other demographic patterns exist to help us anticipate the future beside the fertility, mortality, and migration rates used by the Census Bureau. Some of these, particularly those dealing with marriages and children, give cause for being cautious in predicting group composition in 2050.[7] We can detect some growing patterns that suggest different group categories in the future.

Interethnic Marriages and Children of Mixed Ancestry

Just as European nationality groups have blended together extensively through intermarriage in a multigenerational progression toward assimilation, so too may we expect Hispanic Americans to do the same. This process has been underway for decades and increasing steadily over the years.

Hispanics, who can be of any race, are increasingly marrying other Latinos of different national origins. Over 3.4 million married Hispanic couples now fit this category, compared to 1.9 million in 1980. This pattern continues to expand, especially among Hispanic Americans born in the contiguous forty-eight states.

Even more revealing is the outmarriage pattern. One sign of closing social distance and the final stage of assimilation is the widespread intermarriage of minority group members with those of the mainstream group. In 1993, over 1.2 million Hispanic Americans married someone of non-Hispanic origin, up 35 percent from 891,000 in 1980. That number roughly approximates about 7 percent of the adult Hispanic American population, not an overwhelming proportion but nonetheless a growing one.

Given the past history of other groups assimilating and the current assimilationist patterns of so many second-generation Hispanic Americans, we may reasonably expect two things. First, a greater increase in Hispanic outmarriages is inevitable. Second, Hispanic achievement of social, economic, and political power—together with widespread intermarriage—will enlarge the mainstream American category once more to include them. One might even speculate that these two trends could become so universal that one day Hispanic American will be no more a separate ethnic category than Italian, Polish, or Slavic now is.

Interracial Marriages and Biracial Children

Elimination of the racial barrier in the United States by 2050 may or may not occur, but a present-day trend suggests that the present-day simplistic racial categories are already obsolete. In 1994, there were more than 3 million biracial children in the United States, and this number is climbing as a result of an increasing interracial marriage rate.

Since 1970, the total number of interracially married couples has almost quadrupled, growing from 310,000 to about 1.2 million in 1993. The Black/White married couple category increased from 65,000 to 242,000, itself almost a quadrupling. Interracial couples of Whites married to a spouse other than Black (mostly Asian) grew from 233,000 to 920,000, and interracial couples of Blacks married to a spouse other than Whites increased from 12,000 to 33,000. Although the number of Black/White intermarriages is only about one-fourth that of other White-racial combinations, the 242,000 is significant. Such continued increases and their biracial offspring should generate pressure for the deconstruction of race as we know it and its subsequent reconstruction.[8]

Many other Americans also have a multiracial ancestry, such as virtually all Latinos and Filipinos and many Native Americans and Native Hawaiians have.[9] Among Black Americans with a multigenerational history in the United States, experts estimate that somewhere between 30 to 70 percent are multiracial, and so too are a sizable proportion of those classified as Whites.

Race always has been primarily a social construct, not one simply rooted in biological features.[10] It is defined differently in different societies, with racial boundaries blurred or distinct depending on geographical, cultural, and political factors. In the United States today, arbitrary or single-race classifications no longer apply to an increasing number of Americans. Recognizing a changing America, the Census Bureau has revised its categories several times for its decennial headcounts but, until now, its "select one only" format has prevented many from identifying with their mixed racial parentage.

Perhaps the day is not too far distant when the American people and their government will either broaden racial categories to include gradations between Black and White as Brazil does, or create new official census categories like "Eurasian," "Afroindian," and "Amerlatino," or simply allow people to check multiple racial categories.

The Challenge
of Racial Diversity

Despite questions about categories or the accuracy of the demographic projections, America is clearly becoming a more multiracial society than ever before.[11] What does this mean for race relations? American society is less racist than in the past, but racism still saturates the land. Discrimination and violence sometimes show that race relations are deteriorating rather than improving.

Racial tensions, confrontations, and violent acts continue to occur in many geographic locales. Sometimes it is a Black-White conflict, perhaps in New York City, or it is a Cambodian-Latino fight maybe in Stockton, California. Possibly it is Blacks clashing with Korean merchants in Chicago or elsewhere, or with Hispanics in Miami. As in Washington, DC in 1991, it could be Hispanics rioting after a Black female police officer shot a Salvadoran immigrant. Or, as in Los Angeles in 1992, it could be a multiracial riot, with Latinos and Blacks preying on Whites, Koreans, and other Asian Americans.

Increased racial diversity poses a crisis for American society in the Chinese and Greek meaning of the word *crisis*. In those languages, crisis means both danger and opportunity.

The danger lies in race relations worsening. Will African Americans accept the presence and competition of Asians and Latinos? Will Asians and Latinos accept each other because they often share urban territories? Will Whites peacefully accept the growing presence of Asians in their suburban neighborhoods? Will Whites calmly accept their diminishing status as non-White groups steadily grow proportionately in strength?

The opportunity lies in a heightened awareness about the pluralist reality of American society. The predominance of an Anglo American assimilationist model has worked to the disadvantage of those considered different or unassimilable. Understanding the American tradition of racial diversity could lead to an appreciation of its existence and ultimately to greater societal cohesion. Such a possibility would make the United States as powerful a world model for brotherhood as its political system has served as a government model for over two hundred years.

Among the range of race relations possibilities, then, lies increased tensions and violence at one end of the continuum and interracial harmony at the other. Obviously, we should strive to attain the latter and avoid the former. America's real future may fall short of the ideal, but that is not reason enough to stop trying to fulfill the dream of Martin Luther King Jr.

Increased Religious Diversity

Earlier immigrant waves changed the United States from an almost exclusively Protestant nation into a country of three major faiths: Protestant, Catholic, and Jewish. Because religion is so closely intertwined with ethnicity, current migration patterns offer clues about the religious preference of future Americans, if present trends continue.

Protestants now account for about 56 percent of the total population, and Catholics for about 26 percent. Jews comprise about 2 percent, Muslims slightly less, and about 4 percent profess other religious faiths. Eleven percent express no religious preference.

Because Latin America and Asia are the major sending regions for about 85 percent of all immigrants to the United States, we can identify

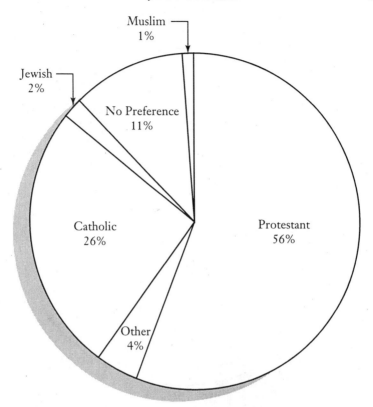

Figure 10.3. *U.S. Religious Membership in 1990*

Source: U.S. Bureau of the Census, *Current Population Reports,* Series P25-1092 (Washington, DC: Government Printing Office, 1992); *Statistical Abstract of the United States 1994* (Washington, DC: Government Printing Office, 1994).

the prevailing religions in those countries and project them onto those entering the country. Realizing also that immigrants tend to have a higher birth rate than native-born Americans and that some religions are more zealous in seeking religious converts, demographers can factor in those variables as well when projecting the future of religious affiliations.

Latin America and the Philippines are mostly Catholic and, as major sources of new immigrants accounting for more than half the total, they will help Roman Catholics increase dramatically in size. By 2050, Catholics may increase from one-fourth of the American population to one-third. They might also constitute the majority of residents in such heavily populated states as California, Florida, Texas, and New York.

Another rapidly growing religious group are the Muslims. Appealing to many African, Middle Eastern, and Asian Americans, Islam is becoming a more noticeable presence as mosques now pepper the American

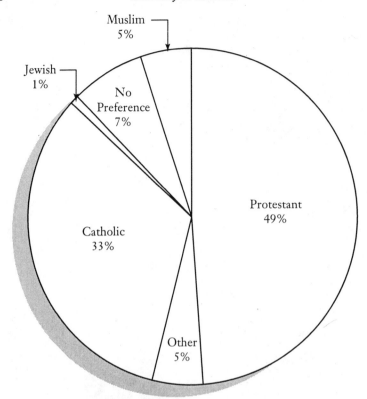

Figure 10.4. *Projected U.S. Religious Membership in 2050*

Source: U.S. Bureau of the Census, *Current Population Reports,* Series P25-1092
(Washington, DC: Government Printing Office, 1992); *Statistical Abstract of the United
States 1994* (Washington, DC: Government Printing Office, 1994).

landscape. Within a few years, Muslims will surpass Jews to become the
third-largest religious denomination in the United States. By the middle
of the next century, Muslims may account for 5 percent of the American
population while Jews decrease to about a 1 percent share of the
population.

Other Eastern religions—particularly Buddhists, Hindus, and Sikhs—
should continue to grow substantially in the United States. By 2050,
they may comprise 1 to 2 percent of American society. Protestants, on
the other hand, will likely drop below 50 percent. Mainstream denominations seem destined to decline the most as fundamentalist denominations continue to gain new converts.

One should not assume cultural homogeneity will prevail among the
two rapidly growing Catholic and Muslim faiths. Both may comprise many

unassimilated minorities. Catholics will be found among multigenerational Americans of European and African ancestry and among such newer groups as Haitians, Filipinos, Indochinese, Latinos, and others. Muslims will include native-born African, Arab, and Asian Americans, as well as immigrants from those regions.

Religious diversity is becoming ever more pronounced throughout the land. If Census Bureau projections hold true and American Protestants fall below 50 percent, then no religious faith will be dominant in the United States. We shall be a land where all faiths are minorities. When no religion was dominant at the time of the nation's founding, we benefited from the separation of church and state doctrine. Perhaps a future of all minority religions foretells a time of even greater ecumenism and tolerance.

The Mainstreaming of Women

American society has embarked on an irreversible path toward gender equality. As we discussed in Chapter 7, great strides have been achieved since the 1960s, but much remains to be accomplished before parity with men is a reality. When women achieve social, economic, and political power equal to men, they will then be fully integrated into the society, or mainstreamed.

All the indicators point toward further progress. Within ten years the U.S. Department of Education projects the number of women enrolled in institutions of higher education will increase from 7.9 million to over 8.7 million.[12] The U.S. Department of Labor projects the female labor force participation rate to rise from its present 58 percent to 63 percent by 2005.[13] An increasing number of women continue to choose college majors and careers that were in mostly male domains previously. More women are becoming lawyers and judges, seeking elected political office, and moving into positions of power and influence.

As these trends continue and as women's higher expectations grow, we may anticipate the experiences of women to be as different from now in 2050 as today's women find their opportunities in contrast to those in 1950. Furthermore, the "glass ceiling" of limited upward mobility that women currently experience in many work settings may well become a twentieth-century relic if present-day trends and challenges to its practice continue.

The Ever-Changing Mosaic

The metaphor of a mosaic to describe American society is helpful in many ways. When we examine a mosaic up close, it is easy to see the individual tiles with their different colors. It is also easy to see the flaws—those individual tiles that are chipped, cracked, or spotted. We cannot help but notice the mortar between the tiles that separates (joins?) them.

Up close we see everything and we see nothing. It is another version of failing to see the forest for the trees. We are able to focus on the individual differences of the tiles but, until we step back, we are unable to grasp the beauty of the big picture that the tiles collectively present to us. When we do step back, the borders between the tiles fade as they blend into one another. The flaws we were so critical about are meaningless now in appreciating the beauty of colors and design the artist has provided for our enrichment and enjoyment. The whole is the sum of its parts, to coin a phrase.

In a very real sense, the United States is a mosaic of men and women of different colors, religions, and national origins. We are a microcosm of the world itself. We have become what Ben Wattenberg calls the "first universal nation."[14]

And yet one aspect of the mosaic metaphor does not fit us at all. A mosaic is something fixed, static, unchanging, and we have never been that. Tens of millions of people from all over the world have come to this country, made it their home, and invigorated it with their energy and determination. From its colonial diversity to its present-day diversity, the United States each year has experienced new arrivals and new changes to its population mix.

If we are a mosaic, then we are an ever-changing one. Some might prefer to call us a kaleidoscope to allow for continually changing patterns, but I prefer the idea of an ever-changing mosaic. Looking into a kaleidoscope is an individual experience, but gazing at a mosaic can be a shared one, and shared experiences are what the metaphor is partly about. Moreover, the mosaic metaphor extends the analogy further in enabling us to compare its close-up flaws to the criticisms often directed against nonmainstream groups.

Whether one uses the metaphor of an ever-changing mosaic or a kaleidoscope to describe its people, the United States continues to manifest a dynamic cultural pluralism that has always marked its existence, even in colonial times. Although it has a greater mix of races and nationalities today, the United States is, in some ways, actually less multicultural than it was in the past. What we are experiencing today in large-scale immigration and minority group (including female) challenges to the status quo is part of the continuing dynamics of a nation evolving to make its reality resemble more of its ideals.

Despite fears about divisiveness, the mainstream group is larger than ever before. Despite male apprehension about the feminist movement, women are becoming a more integral part of the mainstream and dispelling many myths as they do. Despite concerns over language retention, today's immigrants want to learn English and do so no slower than past immigrants and perhaps even more quickly because of the mass media. Despite nativist anxieties about non-Westerners not blending in, Asians are demonstrating their desire to integrate by having the highest naturalization rates among all of the largest sending countries.

Multiculturalism is neither new nor a threat to the stabilization and integration of American society. Extremists come and go, but the core culture remains strong, the American Dream prevails, and men and women seek to be part of it, bringing with them the diversity that *is* America. Multiculturalism, then, is an old, continuing presence that strengthens not weakens, enriches not diminishes, nourishes not drains a civilization whose character and temperament have long reflected the diversity of its people.

Notes

Chapter 1

1. Arthur M. Schlesinger Jr., *The Disuniting of America: Reflections on a Multicultural Society* (Knoxville, TN: Whittle Communications, 1991); Peter Brimelow, *Alien Nation: Common Sense About America's Immigration Disaster* (New York: Random House, 1995).

2. Hispanic leaders' views on language maintenance appear in Linda Chavez, "Hispanics vs. Their Leaders," *Commentary,* October 1991, 47-49.

3. Diane Ravitch's much-discussed views appeared in her article, "Multiculturalism: E Pluribus Plures," *American Scholar 59* (1990): 337-54.

4. Peter Berger's thoughts are expressed in his wonderful sociological primer, *Invitation to Sociology* (Garden City, NY: Doubleday, 1963), 23. Another classic on perception and reality is Peter L. Berger and Thomas Luckmann, *The Social Construction of Reality* (New York: Doubleday, 1963).

5. The comparison of multiculturalism and cultural pluralism by Nathan Glazer and Peter Rose appear in the special issue edited by Peter I. Rose, "Interminority Affairs in the U.S.: Pluralism at the Crossroads," *The Annals of the American Academy of Political and Social Science,* 530 (1993). The two articles are Nathan Glazer, "Is Assimilation Dead?" 122-36; Peter I. Rose, "Of Every Hue and Caste," 187-202.

6. Horace Kallen, "Democracy versus the Melting Pot," *Nation,* 18 February 1915, 190-94; *Nation,* 25 February 1915, 217-20.

7. Peter Rose, "Of Every Hue and Caste," *The Annals of the American Academy of Political and Social Science,* 530 (1993): 193.

8. Horace Kallen, *Culture and Democracy in the United States* (New York: Boni and Liveright, 1924).

9. The posthumous publication of Robert E. Park's writings is *Race and Culture: Essays in the Sociology of Contemporary Man* (New York: Free Press, 1950).

10. Milton Gordon's seminal work on assimilation is *Assimilation in American Life* (New York: Oxford University Press, 1964).

11. Stephen Steinberg, *The Ethnic Myth* (New York: Atheneum, 1981).

12. Crevecoeur's famous statement appears in *Letters from an American Farmer* (1782; reprint, New York: Albert and Charles Boni, 1925), 54-55.

13. Observations about Crevecoeur's omission of racial minorities appear in Vincent N. Parrillo, *Strangers to These Shores* (Boston: Houghton Mifflin, 1980), 98, and in all subsequent editions; Nathan Glazer's "Is Assimilation Dead?" *The Annals of the American Academy of Political and Social Science,* 530 (1993): 124.

14. Emerson's recorded thoughts appear in *The Journals and Miscellaneous Notebooks of Ralph Waldo Emerson,* ed. Ralph H. Orth and Alfred K. Ferguson (Cambridge, MA: Belknap, 1971), 9: 299-300.

15. James A. Henretta et al., *America's History Since 1865* (Homewood, IL: Dorsey Press, 1987), 588.

16. Frederick Jackson Turner, *The Frontier in American History* (New York: Henry Holt, 1920), 351.

17. Israel Zangwill, *The Melting Pot: Drama in Four Acts* (New York: Macmillan, 1921), 33.

18. The intermarriage findings of Richard D. Alba are reported in "The Twilight of Ethnicity Among Americans of European Ancestry: The Case of the Italians," in *Rethinking Today's Minorities,* ed. Vincent N. Parrillo (Westport, CT: Greenwood Press, 1991).

19. The study by Stanley Lieberson and Mary C. Waters is *From Many Strands* (New York: Russell Sage, 1988).

20. Lisa Neidert and Reynolds Farley reported their findings in "Assimilation in the United States: An Analysis of Ethnic and Generation Differences in Status and Achievement," *American Sociological Review* 50 (1985): 840-50.

Chapter 2

1. An excellent, highly readable overview of Native American civilizations is Peter Farb, *Man's Rise to Civilization as Shown by the Indians of North America from Primeval Times to the Coming of the Industrial State* (New York: E. P. Dutton, 1968).

2. A good source for information about Whites' perceptions of Native Americans is Robert F. Berkhofer Jr., *The White Man's Indian: Images of the American Indian from Columbus to the Present* (New York: Knopf, 1978).

3. The original source of Edward Sapir's observations is "The Status of Linguistics as a Science," *Language* 5 (1929): 207-14. Other references include the "Selected Writings of Edward Sapir," in *Language, Culture and Personality,* ed. David G. Mandelbaum (Berkeley: University of California Press, 1949); J. B. Carroll, *Language, Thought, and Reality: Selected Writings of Benjamin Lee Whorf* (Cambridge: MIT Press, 1961).

4. Wilcomb E. Washburn offers succinct insights into Native American social structures in *The Indian in America* (New York: Harper & Row, 1975), 25-65.

5. Helpful information about Southeastern Native Americans can be found in Jesse Burt and Robert B. Ferguson, *Indians of the Southeast: Then and Now* (New York: Abingdon, 1973).

6. A good source for further information about Northeastern Native Americans is Howard S. Russell, *Indian New England Before the Mayflower* (Hanover, NH: University Press of New England, 1980).

7. Native American response to culture contact is detailed in Nancy O. Lurie, "Indian Cultural Adjustment to European Civilization," in *Seventeenth-Century America,* ed. James M. Smith (Chapel Hill: University of North Carolina Press, 1959).

8. The Iroquois political consensus model is fully examined in Jack Weatherford, *Indian Givers: How the Indians of the Americas Transformed the World* (New York: Crown, 1988).

Chapter 3

1. Mildred Campbell, "Social Origins of Some Early Americans," in *Seventeenth-Century America,* ed. James M. Smith (Chapel Hill: University of North Carolina Press, 1959), 63.

2. Stephen Steinberg, *The Ethnic Myth* (New York: Atheneum, 1981), 10.

3. Bruce Catton and William B. Catton, *The Bold and Magnificent Dream: America's Founding Years, 1492-1815* (New York: Doubleday, 1978), 165, 166, 168.

4. Lawrence H. Fuchs' quotation comes from his extensive analysis of America's evolution into a multicultural society, *The American Kaleidoscope: Race, Ethnicity, and the Civic Culture* (Hanover, NH: Wesleyan University Press of New England, 1990), 12.

5. Maxine Sellers, *To Seek America: A History of Ethnic Life in the United States* (New York: James S. Ozer, 1977), 37.

6. Stephen Steinberg, *The Ethnic Myth* (New York: Atheneum, 1981), 8.

7. Gary B. Nash, ed., *Class and Society in Early America* (Englewood Cliffs, NJ: Prentice Hall, 1970), 19.

8. Diversity in colonial cities receives fine treatment in Gary B. Nash, *The Urban Crucible: Social Change, Political Consciousness, and the Origins of the American Revolution* (Cambridge, MA: Harvard University Press, 1979). Older books covering this topic include the following: Stella H. Sutherland, *Population Distribution in Colonial America* (New York: Columbia University Press, 1936); Oscar T. Barck Jr. and Hugh T. Lefler, *Colonial America* (New York: Macmillan, 1958).

9. U.S. Bureau of the Census, *Historical Statistics of the United States, Part II,* Series Z 20-132 (Washington, DC: Government Printing Office, 1976), 1168-72.

10. Martin Van Buren's quotation can be found in Donald B. Cole, *Martin Van Buren and the American Political System* (Princeton, NJ: Princeton University Press, 1984), 14.

11. John Randolph's criticism is mentioned in John C. Fitzpatrick, ed., *The Autobiography of Martin Van Buren* (New York: DaCapo, 1973), 9. Another fine treatment of this subject is John Niven, *Martin Van Buren: The Romantic Age of American Politics* (New York: Oxford University Press, 1983).

12. The process of ethnogenesis is discussed more fully in Richard D. Alba, "Models for Viewing American Catholicism," chap. 1 in *Italian Americans: Into the Twilight of Ethnicity* (Englewood Cliffs, NJ: Prentice Hall, 1985), 9-12; Andrew M. Greeley, *The American Catholic: A Social Portrait* (New York: Basic Books,

1977); Vincent N. Parrillo, *Strangers to These Shores*, 4th ed. (New York: Macmillan, 1994), 39; Lester Singer, "Ethnogenesis and Negro Americans Today," *Social Research* 29 (1962): 419-32.

13. Further information about *Gullah* can be found in Carl Bridenbaugh, *Myths and Realities: Societies of the Colonial South* (Baton Rouge: Louisiana University Press, 1952); Peter H. Wood, *Black Majority: Negroes in Colonial South Carolina* (New York: Knopf, 1974).

14. One gets a good sense of the regional subcultures in Lawrence Fuchs' "True Americanism: The Foundations of the Civic Culture," chap. 1 in *The American Kaleidoscope: Race, Ethnicity, and the Civic Culture* (Hanover, NH: Wesleyan University Press of New England, 1990). Other sources include Richard Hofstadter, *America at 1750* (New York: Knopf, 1971); James H. Kettner, *The Development of American Citizenship, 1608-1870* (Chapel Hill: University of North Carolina Press, 1978).

15. Some excellent analyses of colonial women can be found in Nancy Woloch, *Women and the American Experience* (New York: McGraw-Hill, 1984); Laurel Ulrich, *Good Wives: Image and Reality in the Lives of Women of Northern New England, 1650-1750* (New York: Random House, 1982).

16. One of the best books on social class in colonial America is Gary B. Nash, *Class and Society in Early America* (Englewood Cliffs, NJ: Prentice Hall, 1970).

17. James A. Henretta et al., *America's History to 1877* (Homewood, IL: Dorsey Press, 1987), 54-55.

18. Ibid, p. 93.

19. A classic study on the Great Awakening is Edwin S. Gaustad, *The Great Awakening in New England* (New York: Harper & Row, 1957).

20. Daniel J. Boorstin, *The Americans: The Colonial Experience* (New York: Vintage, 1958), 179.

21. Statistics about denominational churches are taken from a composite drawn from three sources: James A. Henretta et al., *America's History to 1877* (Homewood, IL: Dorsey Press, 1987), 130; Dexter Perkins and Glyndon G. Van Deusen, *The United States of America: A History*, 2d ed. (New York: Macmillan, 1968); Oscar T. Barck Jr. and Hugh T. Lefler, *Colonial America* (New York: Macmillan, 1958), 398.

22. The 1741 "Negroe conspiracy" receives treatment from Gary B. Nash in *The Urban Crucible: Social Change, Political Consciousness, and the Origins of the American Revolution* (Cambridge, MA: Harvard University Press), 108; Oscar T. Barck Jr. and Hugh T. Lefler, *Colonial America* (New York: Macmillan, 1958), 306.

23. Michael Kammen, *People of Paradox: An Inquiry Concerning the Origins of American Civilization* (New York: Knopf, 1972), 49.

24. James Stuart Olson, *The Ethnic Dimension in American History* (New York: St. Martin's Press, 1979), 51.

Chapter 4

1. Abigail Adams' letter is quoted in Vincent N. Parrillo, *Strangers to These Shores*, 4th ed. (New York: Macmillan, 1994), 496.

2. Eliza Wilkinson's letter is quoted in James A. Henretta et al., *America's History to 1877* (Homewood, IL: Dorsey Press, 1987), 196.

3. Information about *The Contrast* is from Arthur H. Quinn, *Representative American Plays* (New York: Appleton-Century-Crofts, 1957), 45.

4. Comments about American painters, as well as their comments about Jefferson's inaugural address, are from Stanley Elkins and Eric McKitrick, *The Age of Federalism* (New York: Oxford University Press, 1993), 190.

5. Biographical information about Noah Webster is drawn from "Noah Webster," in *The New Encyclopaedia Britannica*, ed. Peter B. Norton (Chicago: Encylopaedia Britannica, 1990), 12: 550.

6. Helpful insights into independence movements within American churches can be found in James A. Henretta et al., *America's History to 1877* (Homewood, IL: Dorsey Press, 1987), 258-60; Sidney A. Ahlstrom, *A Religious History of the American People* (New Haven, CT: Yale University Press, 1972); Martin Marty, *The Protestant Experience in America* (New York: Dial Press, 1970).

7. The data reported by Jackson T. Main are found in "The Economic Class Structure of the North," chap. 1 in *The Social Structure of Revolutionary America* (Princeton, NJ: Princeton University Press, 1965).

8. Gary B. Nash, *The Urban Crucible: Social Change, Political Consciousness, and the Origins of the American Revolution* (Cambridge, MA: Harvard University Press, 1979), 257.

9. James A. Henretta's study originally appeared as "Economic Development and Social Structure in Colonial Boston," *William and Mary Quarterly,* 3d ser., 22 (1965): 75-92, and was reprinted in Gary B. Nash, *Class and Society in Early America* (Englewood Cliffs, NJ: Prentice Hall, 1970), 133-49.

10. Data on birth and women working come from the U.S. Bureau of the Census, *Historical Statistics of the United States, Part II,* Series Z 20-132 (Washington, DC: Government Printing Office, 1976).

11. Max Weber's classic work is *The Protestant Ethic and the Spirit of Capitalism,* trans. Talcott Parsons (New York: Scribner, 1974). Karl Marx's original essay on religion can be found in Lloyd D. Easton and Kurt Guddat, eds., *Writings of the Young Marx on Philosophy and Society* (New York: Doubleday, 1967). More recent related works are Louis Harap, "Marxism and Religion: Social Functions of Religious Belief," *Jewish Currents,* 36 (1982): 12-17, 32-35; John Wilson, *Religion in American Society: The Effective Presence* (Englewood Cliffs, NJ: Prentice Hall, 1978).

12. Meredith B. McGuire, *Religion: The Social Context* (Belmont, CA: Wadsworth, 1981), 186.

13. Vincent N. Parrillo, *Strangers to These Shores,* 4th ed. (New York: Macmillan, 1994), 149.

14. Information about the census comes from the U.S. Bureau of the Census, *Historical Statistics of the United States, Part II,* Series Z 20-132 (Washington, DC: Government Printing Office, 1976), 1168.

15. The concept of internal colonialism was first espoused by Robert Blauner in "Internal Colonialism and Ghetto Revolt," *Social Problems* 16 (1969): 393-406.

16. Two excellent sources about the interactions of racial cultures include the following: Gary B. Nash, *Red, White, and Black: The Peoples of Early America* (Englewood Cliffs, NJ: Prentice Hall, 1974); Robert F. Berkhofer Jr., *The White Man's Indian: Images of the American Indian From Columbus to the Present* (New York: Knopf, 1978).

17. John C. Miller, *Crisis in Freedom* (Boston: Little, Brown, 1951), 41-42.

18. Mary C. Waters, commenting on recent immigrants, observes that "language is one of the first elements of the immigrant culture to disappear over the generations" in *Ethnic Options* (Berkeley: University of California Press, 1990), 116.

19. Both the Federalist and Noah Webster quotations appear in John C. Miller, *Crisis in Freedom* (Boston: Little, Brown, 1951), 51-52.

Chapter 5

1. Renowned linguistic expert Joshua Fishman discussed language retention in *Language Loyalty in the United States* (London: Moulton, 1966).

2. The gradual English language acquisition of immigrants is examined by Calvin Veltman, *Language Shift in the United States* (New York: Moulton, 1983).

3. Tocqueville's observations are from his classic, *Democracy in America,* revised by Francis Bowen and edited by Phillips Bradley (1835; reprint, New York: Knopf, 1960), 359-360.

4. Harriet Martineau's comments come from *Society in America,* ed. Seymour Martin Lipset (1837; reprint, Garden City, NY: Anchor Books, 1962), 183.

5. Frederika Bremer's remarks are quoted in Carl Wittke, *We Who Built America,* rev. ed. (Cleveland: Case Western Reserve University Press, 1967), 207-208.

6. Frederick Law Olmsted, *A Journey Through Texas, or a Saddle-Trip on the Southwestern Frontier* (1860; reprint, New York: Burt Franklin, 1969), 169-183, 276-278.

7. Charles Dickens, *American Notes* (1842; reprint, Greenwich, CT: Fawcett, 1961), 201.

8. An account of early nineteenth-century New Orleans is given in Carl Wittke, *We Who Built America,* rev. ed. (Cleveland: Case Western Reserve University Press, 1967), 318.

9. A good overview of the Irish American experience is Marjorie R. Fallows, *Irish Americans: Identity and Assimilation* (Englewood Cliffs, NJ: Prentice Hall, 1979).

10. Fine insight into diverse German settlements is Robert H. Billigmeier, *Americans from Germany: A Study in Cultural Diversity* (Belmont, CA: Wadsworth, 1974).

11. A penetrating insight into the immigrant German Catholic Church under nativist attack is Jay P. Dolan, *The Immigrant Church: New York and German Catholics, 1815-1865* (Baltimore: Johns Hopkins Press, 1975).

12. Henretta et al., *America's History to 1877* (Homewood, IL: Dorsey Press, 1987), 359.

13. Tocqueville's witnessing the forced migration of Native Americans is recorded in Volume I of *Democracy in America,* rev. ed., ed. Phillips Bradley (New York: Knopf, 1960).

14. Still one of the best books on the expulsion of Native American tribes is Dale Van Every, *Disinherited: The Lost Birthright of the American Indian* (New York: Avon Books, 1966). The forced removal of Native Americans is also recounted in Edward H. Spicer, "American Indians," in *Harvard Encyclopedia of American Ethnic Groups,* eds. Stephan Thernstrom, Ann Orlov, and Oscar Handlin (Cambridge, MA: Belknap, 1980), 58-114.

15. A useful book about enslaved Black culture is Eugene D. Genovese, *Roll Jordan Roll: The World the Slaves Made* (New York: Pantheon, 1974). See also John Blassingame, *The Slave Community* (New York: Oxford University Press, 1974).

16. Henretta et al., *America's History to 1877* (Homewood, IL: Dorsey Press, 1987), 417.

17. An overview of the role of organized religion among African Americans from slavery to the present is given in C. Eric Lincoln and Lawrence H. Mamiya, *The Black Church in the African American Experience* (Durham, NC: Duke University Press, 1990).

18. Stanford M. Lyman examines Chinese organizational life in *Chinatown and Little Tokyo* (Millwood, NY: Associated Faculty Press, 1986) and in his earlier work, *Chinese Americans* (New York: Random House, 1974).

19. The colonization of Mexicans living in the Southwest is explained by Ellyn R. Stoddard in *Mexican Americans* (New York: St. Martin's Press, 1994), 66-69, 206-212. See also Wayne Moquin and Charles Van Doren, eds., *A Documentary History of the Mexican Americans* (New York: Praeger, 1971).

20. Perhaps the most thorough description of the participation of women in benevolence and reform is Keith Melder, *Beginnings of Sisterhood: The American Women's Rights Movement, 1800-1850* (New York: Schocken, 1977).

21. A graphic portrait of mob violence and political activism during the days of the Know-Nothings is Carleton Beals, *Brass Knuckle Crusade,* rev. ed. (New York: Hastings House, 1960). See also John Higham, *Strangers in the Land: Patterns of Nativism, 1860-1925* (New York: Atheneum, 1971).

Chapter 6

1. Data on railroad track miles are reported in James A. Henretta et al., *America's History Since 1865* (Homewood, IL: Dorsey Press, 1987), 515.

2. Edna Bonacich's split labor market theory first appeared in "A Theory of Ethnic Antagonism: The Split Labor Market," *American Sociological Review* 37 (1972): 547-59.

3. Stephen Steinberg, *The Ethnic Myth* (New York: Atheneum, 1981), 38.

4. One of the best introductions to working women is Alice Kestler-Harris, *Out to Work* (New York: Oxford University Press, 1982). Leslie Woodcock Tentler, *Wage-Earning Women: Industrial Work and Family Life, 1900-1930* (New York: Oxford University Press, 1979) is a thoughtful treatment of the impact of industrial work on female identity.

5. A good source on city growth is Constance McLaughlin Green, *The Rise of Urban America* (New York: Harper & Row, 1965). Specific data on urban industrial output can be found in James A. Henretta et al., *America's History Since 1865* (Homewood, IL: Dorsey Press, 1987), 549, 551.

6. Robert Blauner, *Racial Oppression in America* (New York: Harper & Row, 1972), 62.

7. George M. Fredrickson, *White Supremacy: A Comparative Study in American and South African History* (New York: Oxford University Press, 1981), 130.

8. James S. Olson mentions the "grandfather clause" in *The Ethnic Dimension in American History* (New York: St. Martin's Press, 1979), 300.

9. Fine sociological insight into the North's largest Black community in the 1890s is W. E. B. DuBois, *The Philadelphia Negro: A Social Study* (New York: Schocken, 1967).

10. Observations about Black economic advances can be found in Robert Higgs, *Competition and Conflict: Blacks in the American Economy, 1865-1914* (Chicago: University of Chicago Press, 1980), 125-28.

11. Two helpful works that include information about the early Asian presence are Harry H. L. Kitano and Roger Daniels, *Asian Americans: Emerging Minorities* (Englewood Cliffs, NJ: Prentice Hall, 1988); Stanford M. Lyman, *The Asian in North America* (Santa Barbara, CA: ABC-CLIO, 1977).

12. Senator Blaine's remark comes from the *Congressional Record* (14 February, 1879) and quoted in Vincent N. Parrillo, *Strangers to These Shores,* 4th ed. (New York: Macmillan, 1994), 277.

13. Roger Daniels, *The Politics of Prejudice* (New York: Atheneum, 1969), 20.

14. A documentary history of anti-Chinese prejudice is Cheng-Tsu, *Chink!* (New York: Meridian, 1972).

15. Gary R. Hess offers insight into the little-researched early Asian Indian presence in "The Forgotten Asian Americans: The East Indian Community in the United States," *Pacific Historical Review* 43 (1974): 583-94.

16. Further information about Mexican Americans can be found in Joan W. Moore and Harry Pachon, *Mexican Americans,* 2d ed. (Englewood Cliffs, NJ: Prentice Hall, 1976); Nancy Gonzalez, *The Spanish Americans of New Mexico: A Heritage of Pride* (Albuquerque: University of New Mexico Press, 1967); Leonard Pitt, *The Death of the Californios: A Social History of Spanish-Speaking Californians, 1848-1890* (Berkeley: University of California Press, 1966).

17. Native American loss of land and other aspects of tribal disintegration are discussed in Curtis E. Jackson and Marcia J. Galli, *A History of the Bureau of Indian Affairs and Its Activities Among Indians* (San Francisco: R & E Research Associates, 1977). The most-cited work on late nineteenth-century White-Native Ameri-

can relations is Dee Brown, *Bury My Heart at Wounded Knee* (New York: Holt, Rinehart & Winston, 1971).

18. Statistics on Native American populations come from the Racial Statistics Branch, Population Division, U.S. Bureau of the Census, "American Indian, Eskimo, and Aleut Populations in the United States," unpublished data provided to the author.

19. Government assimilation efforts are detailed in Frederick E. Hoxie, *A Final Promise: The Campaign to Assimilate the Indians, 1880-1920* (Lincoln: University of Nebraska Press, 1984).

20. A fine sociohistorical insight into Arabic immigrants is Philip M. Kayal and Joseph M. Kayal, *The Syrian-Lebanese in America* (New York: Twayne, 1975).

21. Examination of some of the northern and western European groups can be found in Charles H. Anderson, *White Protestant Americans: From National Origins to Religious Group* (Englewood Cliffs, NJ: Prentice Hall, 1970). Also recommended is Lawrence H. Fuchs, *The American Kaleidoscope: Race, Ethnicity, and the Civic Culture* (Hanover, NH: Wesleyan University Press of New England, 1990).

22. For a quick overview of the southern, central, and eastern European immigrants, see Vincent N. Parrillo, "Southern, Central, and Eastern Europeans," chap. 6 in *Strangers to These Shores,* 4th ed. (New York: Macmillan, 1994). Also highly recommended is Alejandro Portes and Reuben Rumbaut, *Immigrant America: A Portrait* (Berkeley: University of California Press, 1990).

23. Madison Grant, *The Passing of the Great Race,* (1916; reprint, New York: Arno Press and The New York Times, 1970).

24. An informative book about the expanding rights of women is Mary P. Ryan, *Womanhood in America: From Colonial Times to the Present,* 2d ed., (New York: Franklin Watts, 1979).

25. Jane Addams recounted her life's work in *Twenty Years at Hull House* (New York: Macmillan, 1914).

26. For an intimate portrait of the travails of the suffragettes, see Joyce Cowley, *Pioneers of Women's Liberation* (New York: Merit, 1969).

27. The APA is the subject of Donald J. Kinzner, *An Episode in Anti-Catholicism: The American Protective Association* (Seattle: University of Washington Press, 1964). The Klan in the urban

North is profiled in Kenneth Jackson, *The Ku Klux Klan in the City, 1915-1930* (New York: Oxford University Press, 1967).

Chapter 7

1. Educational statistics come from the National Center for Education Statistics, *Digest of Education Statistics* (Washington, DC: Government Printing Office, 1993).

2. Data about female elected officials come from the Center for the American Woman and Politics, Eagleton Institute of Politics (information releases, Rutgers University, 1994).

3. The study finding gender bias in the schools was reported by Barbara Kantrowitz, "Sexism in the Schoolhouse," *Newsweek,* 24 February 1992, 62.

4. The 1991 Department of Labor study was reported by Amy Saltzman, "Trouble at the Top," *U.S. News & World Report,* 17 June 1991, 40-48.

5. A good overview of the various Asian American groups can be found in Robert W. Gardner et al., "Asian Americans: Growth, Change, and Diversity," *Population Bulletin* 40 (Washington, DC: Population Reference Bureau, 1985).

6. Peter Kwong offers an excellent insight into economic conditions among Chinese Americans in *The New Chinatown* (New York: Hill and Wang, 1987).

7. Filipino occupational patterning is detailed in Pyong Gap Min, "Filipino and Korean Immigrants in Small Business: A Comparative Analysis," *Amerasia,* 13 (Spring 1987): 53-71. See also Antonio J. A. Pido, *The Filipinos in America* (New York: Center for Migration Studies, 1986).

8. Still the best portrait of Japanese Americans is Harry H. L. Kitano, *Japanese Americans: The Evolution of a Subculture,* 2d ed. (Englewood Cliffs, NJ: Prentice Hall, 1976).

9. Japanese cultural and structural assimilation is discussed in Harry H. L. Kitano and Roger Daniels, *Asian Americans: Emerging Minorities* (Englewood Cliffs, NJ: Prentice Hall, 1988); Robert M. Jiobu, "Ethnic Hegemony and the Japanese of California," *American Sociological Review* 53 (1988): 353-67.

10. A comprehensive portrait of Korean Americans is found in Ill Soo Kim, *New Urban Immigrants: The Korean Community in New York* (Princeton, NJ: Princeton University Press, 1981).

11. A good analysis of Korean entrepreneurship in comparison to Blacks is Robert L. Boyd, "Black and Asian Self-Employment in Large Metropolitan Areas: A Comparative Analysis," *Social Problems* 37 (1990): 268.

12. Cultural assimilation among the Vietnamese is examined in Paul J. Strand and Woodrow Jones Jr., *Indochinese Refugees in America* (Durham, NC: Duke University Press, 1985).

13. Sociologist John S. Butler traces the history of the terms that Black Americans have applied to themselves and contrasts their ethnic-racial identities with those of other Americans in "Multiple Identities," *Society* 8 (1970): 19-22.

14. One of the most widely read and cited works that analyzes the comparative status of African Americans today is that by political scientist Andrew Hacker, *Two Nations: Black and White: Separate, Hostile, Unequal* (New York: Scribner, 1992). The best sociological portrait is James E. Blackwell, *The Black Community: Diversity and Unity,* 3d ed. (New York: HarperCollins, 1991).

15. Educational statistics rates are reported in the U.S. Bureau of the Census, *Current Population Reports,* Series P 20-469 (Washington, DC: Government Printing Office, 1992) and in the *Statistical Abstract of the United States 1994* (Washington, DC: Government Printing Office, 1994), 157, 173.

16. Black occupational distribution data come from the U.S. Bureau of Labor Statistics, *Employment and Earnings* (January 1994) and from U.S. Bureau of the Census, "The Black Population in the United States," *Current Population Reports,* Series P-20-469 (Washington, DC: Government Printing Office, 1991), Table 2.

17. Andrew Hacker in *Two Nations: Black and White: Separate, Hostile, Unequal* (New York: Scribner, 1992) argues that Black females, unlike Black males, have achieved parity, because White males are less threatened by Black females than by Black males. His argument rests on the sexist bias in position and pay in the workplace.

18. Information on Black elected officials comes from the U.S. Bureau of the Census, *Statistical Abstract of the United States 1994*

(Washington, DC: Government Printing Office, 1994), Table 443: 284.

19. Family household data are reported in the U.S. Bureau of the Census, *Current Population Reports,* Series P20-477 (Washington, DC: Government Printing Office, 1992).

20. The cultural gulf between African-born and American-born Blacks received an early comparative analysis in Ira de Augustine Reid, *The Negro Immigrant* (1939; reprint, New York: Arno Press and The New York Times, 1969). See also Vincent N. Parrillo, *Strangers to These Shores,* 4th ed. (New York: Macmillan, 1994), 389-91.

21. A revealing study into the Haitian American community is Alex Stepick and Carol Dutton Stepick, "People in the Shadows: Survey Research Among Haitians in Miami," *Human Organization* 49 (1990): 64-77.

22. A still relevant profile of Jamaican society is M. G. Smith, *The Plural Society in the British West Indies* (Berkeley, CA: University of California Press, 1965).

23. Helpful insights about Central Americans are in Nora Hamilton and Norma Stoltz Chinchilla, "Central American Migration: A Framework for Analysis," *Latin American Research Review* 26 (1991): 75-110.

24. A detailed look at Cuban American migration and social institutions appears in Thomas D. Boswell and James R. Curtis, *The Cuban-American Experience* (Totowa, NJ: Rowman and Allanheld, 1984).

25. An intriguing overview of the Chicano experience is offered by Irene I. Blea, *Toward a Chicano Social Science* (New York: Praeger, 1988).

26. Two books are especially informative about Puerto Ricans: Joseph P. Fitzpatrick, *Puerto Rican Americans: The Meaning of Migration to the Mainland,* 2d ed. (Englewood Cliffs, NJ: Prentice Hall, 1987); Clara E. Rodriguez, *Puerto Ricans: Born in the U.S.A.* (Boston: Unwin Hyman, 1989).

27. A revealing insight into the Puerto Rican urban community can be found in Nicholas Lehman, "The Other Underclass," *Atlantic Monthly,* December 1991, 101-108.

28. Arab Americans are profiled in Alixa Naff, *The Arab Americans* (New York: Chelsea House, 1988).

29. Native American health information comes from the Indian Health Service, *Trends in Indian Health* (Rockville, MD: Government Printing Office, 1990); Robert W. Blum et al., "American Indian-Alaska Native Youth Health," *JAMA, The Journal of the American Medical Association* 267 (25 March 1992): 1637.

30. Educational data come from Gerard E. Gipp, "Promoting American Indian Education," *Education Digest,* November 1991, 58.

31. Native American legal efforts are described in "Dances With Lawyers," *The Economist,* 10 August 1991, A18.

32. Some of the organized resistance to Native American treaty rights is explained by Scott Kerr in "The New Indian Wars," *The Progressive,* April 1990, 22.

Chapter 8

1. Comments about motives for migration can be found more specifically in discussions on the "push-pull factors" in Vincent N. Parrillo, *Strangers to These Shores,* 4th ed. (New York: Macmillan, 1994), 168-69, 321, 419-20.

2. Nativist alarm about immigration can be found in John Higham's classic, *Strangers in the Land: Patterns of Nativism, 1860-1925* (New York: Atheneum, 1971).

3. James M. Smith, *Freedom's Fetters* (Ithaca, NY: Cornell University Press, 1956), 25.

4. The "tipping point" concept was first described by Luigi Laurenti in his classic study of integrated neighborhoods in *Property Values and Race: Studies in Cities* (Berkeley: University of California Press, 1960).

5. Immigration projections for the 1990s are based on data from the U.S. Immigration and Naturalization Service, *1993 Statistical Yearbook* (Washington, DC: Government Printing Office, 1994), Table 2: 28.

6. Anti-immigration arguments will be presented more fully in Chapter 9.

7. Rita J. Simon, "Old Minorities, New Immigrants: Aspirations, Hopes, and Fears," *The Annals of the American Academy of Political and Social Science,* 530 (1993): 65, 73.

8. The immigration rate formula and data come from the U.S. Bureau of the Census, *Statistical Abstract of the United States 1994* (Washington, DC: Government Printing Office, 1994), Table 5: 10.

9. Projections of total immigrants and the immigration rate for the 1990s were developed from known data for 1991-1992 from the U.S. Bureau of the Census, *Statistical Abstract of the United States 1994* (Washington, DC: Government Printing Office, 1994), Tables 3 and 5; U.S. Immigration and Naturalization Service, *1993 Statistical Yearbook* (Washington, DC: Government Printing Office, 1994), Table 3: 30; *1992 Statistical Yearbook* (Washington, DC: Government Printing Office, 1992), Table 5: 10.

10. Two good sources for information about the effects of changing employment opportunities are Bennett Harrison, *The Great U-Turn: Corporate Restructuring and the Polarizing of America* (New York: Basic Books, 1988); Barry Bluestone, *The Deindustrialization of America* (New York: Basic Books, 1982).

11. The taxes paid/welfare received data are from Michael J. Mandel and Christopher Farrell, "The Immigrants," *Business Week,* 13 July 1992, 114-22.

12. The formula for computing immigration as a percent of net change and the 1:4 ratio comes from Robert Warren, "Immigration's Share of U.S. Population Growth," *Population Today,* September 1994, 3.

13. Foreign-born population statistics come from U.S. Bureau of the Census, *Historical Statistics of the United States, Part I,* Series A 105-118 (Washington, DC: Government Printing Office, 1976), 14; *Statistical Abstract of the United States 1994* (Washington, DC: Government Printing Office, 1994), Table 54: 52.

14. Insights into the civil rights movement can be found in Aldon Morris, *The Origins of the Civil Rights Movement: Black Communities Organizing for Change* (New York: Free Press, 1984); Lewis M. Killian, *The Impossible Revolution, Phase II* (New York: Random House, 1975).

15. Racial population data are drawn from the U.S. Bureau of the Census, *Historical Statistics of the United States, Part I* Series A 91-104 (Washington, DC: Government Printing Office, 1976), 14; *Statistical Abstract of the United States 1994* (Washington, DC: Government Printing Office, 1994), Table 12: 13.

16. Among the many writings about the present status of African Americans, two particularly helpful sources are Andrew Hacker, *Two Nations: Black and White: Separate, Hostile, Unequal* (New York: Scribner, 1992); Reynolds Farley and Walter R. Allen, *The Color Line and the Quality of Life in America* (New York: Russell Sage, 1987).

17. An excellent insight into the evolution of American identity is Martin E. Spencer, "Multiculturalism, 'Political Correctness,' and the Politics of Identity," in Vincent N. Parrillo, ed., "Multiculturalism and Diversity" [special issue], *Sociological Forum* 9 (December 1994): 547-67.

18. The data about ethnic Americans in 1890 are drawn from James S. Olson, *The Ethnic Dimension in American History,* 2d ed. (New York: St. Martin's Press, 1994), 102-104.

19. Fine insight into how people become racialized as a social process that rests on the power of some to create and enforce concepts of race with little inherent meaning can be found in Michael Omi and Howard Winant, *Racial Formation in the U.S. from the 1960s to the 1980s* (New York: Routledge & Kegan Paul, 1986).

20. Social distance survey findings can be found in Emory Bogardus, "Comparing Racial Distance in Ethiopia, South Africa, and the United States," *Sociology and Social Research* 52 (1968): 149-56; Carolyn A. Owen, Howard C. Eisner, and Thomas R. McFaul, "A Half-Century of Social Distance Research: National Replication of the Bogardus Studies," *Sociology and Social Research* 66 (1981): 80-97.

21. Information about illegal aliens can be found in the U.S. Immigration and Naturalization Service, *1993 Statistical Yearbook* (Washington, DC: Government Printing Office, 1994), 155-56.

22. The public opinion poll about immigration appears in Michael J. Mandel and Christopher Farrell, "The Immigrants," *Business Week,* 13 July 1992, 114-22.

Chapter 9

1. John Leo, regular columnist for *U.S. News & World Report,* often criticizes the radical multiculturalists and politically correct activists. On the issue of revisionist history, for example, see "The Hijacking of American History," *U.S. News & World Report,* 14 November 1994, 36.

2. A good example of the debate raging between multiculturalists of differing viewpoints is "Multiculturalism: An Exchange," *American Scholar,* 59 (Spring 1991), in which Molefi Kete Asante and Diane Ravitch both expressed their views and attacked the others'. Their comments are also found in Ronald Takaki, ed., *From Different Shores: Perspectives on Race and Ethnicity in America,* 2d ed. (New York: Oxford University Press, 1994), 283-95.

3. A detailed portrait and analysis of the phases of multiculturalism can be found in Martin E. Spencer, "Multiculturalism, 'Political Correctness,' and the Politics of Identity" in Vincent N. Parrillo, ed., "Multiculturalism and Diversity" [special issue], *Sociological Forum* 9 (December 1994): 547-67.

4. The oft-cited article by Diane Ravitch that launched so much discussion about inclusion versus separatism is "Multiculturalism: E Pluribus Plures," *American Scholar* 59 (1990): 337-54.

5. The Afrocentrist position has been espoused by Molefi K. Asante in *The Afrocentric Idea* (Philadephia: Temple University Press, 1987); "Putting Africa at the Center," *Newsweek,* 23 September 1991, 46.

6. Arthur M. Schlesinger Jr., *The Disuniting of America: Reflections on a Multicultural Society* (Knoxville, TN: Whittle Communications, 1991).

7. The LULAC leadership advocacy for language rights is explained by Linda Chavez in "Hispanics vs. Their Leaders," *Commentary,* October 1991, 47-49.

8. Horace Kallen's symphony orchestra metaphor appeared in "Democracy versus the Melting Pot," *Nation,* 18 February 1915, 220.

9. The interracial and additive multiculturalism ideas can be found in Harry C. Triandis, "The Future of Pluralism," *Journal of Social Issues* 32 (1976): 179-208.

10. Gerald Graff, *Beyond the Culture Wars: How Teaching the Conflicts Can Revitalize American Education* (New York: Norton, 1992).

11. Ronald Takaki's position is best stated in his article, "Multiculturalism: Battleground or Meeting Ground?" *The Annals of the American Academy of Political and Social Science,* 530 (1993): 109-21.

12. The Roper polls are reported in Rita J. Simon, "Old Minorities, New Immigrants: Aspirations, Hopes, and Fears," *The Annals of the American Academy of Political and Social Science,* 530 (1993): 62-63.

13. The 1992 poll appeared in Michael J. Mandel and Christopher Farrell, "The Immigrants," *Business Week,* 13 July 1992, 114-22.

14. Information about the New York State Senate Report, "Our Teeming Shores," comes from Chris Carola, "Study: Immigrants Cost N.Y. Billions," *The Record,* 21 January 1994.

15. Franklin and Washington's comments are discussed in Vincent N. Parrillo, *Strangers to These Shores,* 4th ed. (New York: Macmillan, 1994), 145, 129.

16. Hayakawa's views are succinctly put in S. I. Hayakawa, "USA Needs to Have an 'Official' Language," *USA Today,* 11 November 1988.

17. An example of the "tribalism" and "Babel" charges can be found in Connie Leslie, "Classrooms of Babel: A Record Number of Immigrant Children Pose New Problems for Schools," *Newsweek,* 11 February 1991, 56-57.

18. The frequently mentioned *White ethnic twilight* concept comes from Richard D. Alba, *Italian Americans: Into the Twilight of Ethnicity* (Englewood Cliffs, NJ: Prentice Hall, 1985).

19. Data on the economic benefits of immigrants to the nation in the 1980s are from Michael J. Mandel and Christopher Farrell, "The Immigrants," *Business Week,* 13 July 1992, 114-22.

20. Vincent N. Parrillo, *Stangers to These Shores,* 4th ed. (New York: Macmillan, 1994), 553.

21. The studies about Latino parental attitudes about English are from *English as the Official Language,* a position paper issued in 1987 by the American Jewish Committee, New York. Rodolfo

de la Garza related the primary usage of English among second-generation Asians and Latinos in *Latino Voices: Mexican, Puerto Rican, and Cuban Perspectives on American Politics* (Boulder, CO: Westview, 1992).

22. Nathan Glazer, "Is Assimilation Dead?" *The Annals of the American Academy of Political and Social Science,* 530 (1993): 123.

23. *English as the Official Language,* a position paper issued in 1987 by the American Jewish Committee, New York.

24. Carl Wittke, *We Who Built America,* rev. ed. (Cleveland: Case Western Reserve University Press, 1967), 196-99; James S. Olson, *The Ethnic Dimension in American History* (New York: St. Martin's Press, 1979), 105-106.

25. Roosevelt's remark comes from a speech he gave in 1917 and preserved in Ralph Stout, ed., *Roosevelt in the Kansas City Star* (Boston: Houghton, Mifflin, 1921), 137.

26. Martin Luther King Jr.'s famous "I have a dream" speech was delivered on August 28, 1963, during the March on Washington for Jobs and Freedom. His actual words were, "I have a dream that my four little children will one day live in a nation where they will not be judged by the color of their skin but by the content of their character."

Chapter 10

1. The satiric limerick by J. M. Flagg appeared underneath a cartoon in *Life,* 12 January 1922, one year after passage of restrictive immigration legislation designed to combat the reality of such nativist fears.

2. Reconceptualization of "Yankee" is discussed by John J. Appel and Thelma Appel in detailed notes accompanying the slide collection, *The Distorted Image: Stereotype and Caricature in American Popular Graphics, 1850-1922,* Anti-Defamation League of B'nai B'rith.

3. John Jay's quote appears in Leon F. Bouvier, *Peaceful Invasions: Immigration and Changing America* (Lanham, MD: University Press of America, 1992), 149.

4. World population growth analysis is given in W. Lutz, *The Future of World Population* (Washington, DC: Population Reference Bureau, 1994).

5. U.S. Bureau of the Census, *Current Population Reports,* Series P25-1092 (Washington, DC: Government Printing Office, 1992); *Statistical Abstract of the United States 1994* (Washington, DC: Government Printing Office, 1994), Table 17: 17.

6. Bouvier's arguments are given in *Peaceful Invasions: Immigration and Changing America* (Lanham, MD: University Press of America, 1992), which contains a thoughtful analysis and provocative public policy recommendations.

7. Statistics of married couples of mixed races or origins come from the U.S. Bureau of the Census, *Statistical Abstract of the United States 1994* (Washington, DC: Government Printing Office, 1994), Table 62: 56.

8. Susan Kalish, "Multiracial Births Increase as U.S. Ponders Racial Definitions," *Population Today,* April 1995, 1-2. An excellent anthology of essays on biracial children is Maria P. P. Root, ed., *Racially Mixed People in America* (Newbury Park, CA: Sage, 1992).

9. Information about Americans of multiracial origins can be found in R. D. Alba and M. B. Chamlin, "A Preliminary Examination of Ethnic Identification Among Whites," *American Sociological Review* 48 (1983): 202-23; R. G. McRoy and E. Freeman, "Racial Identity Issues Among Mixed-Race Children," *Social Work in Education* 8 (1986): 164-74; C. M. Snipp, "Who Are American Indians? Some Perils and Pitfalls of Data for Race and Ethnicity," *Population Research and Policy Review* 5 (1986): 237-52; T. P. Wilson, "People of Mixed Race Descent," in *American Mosaic: Selected Readings on America's Multicultural Heritage,* eds. Y. I. Song and E. C. Kim (Englewood Cliffs, NJ: Prentice Hall, 1991).

10. A particularly helpful short essay about the social construct of race in America is Paul R. Spickard, "The Illogic of American Racial Categories," in *Racially Mixed People in America,* ed. Maria P. P. Root (Newbury Park, CA: Sage, 1992), 12-23.

11. Questions about the present classification system are being raised in many quarters. See, for example, Juanita Tamayo Lott,

"Do United States Racial/Ethnic Categories Still Fit?" *Population Today,* January 1993, 6-7.

12. U.S. Department of Education projections of college-enrolled women come from the National Center for Education Statistics, as reported in the U.S. Bureau of the Census, *Statistical Abstract of the United States 1994* (Washington, DC: Government Printing Office, 1994), Table 270: 177.

13. U.S. Department of Labor projections are also from the U.S. Bureau of the Census, *Statistical Abstract of the United States 1994* (Washington, DC: Government Printing Office, 1994), Table 615: 395.

14. The views of Ben Wattenberg are fully expressed in *The Birth Dearth,* 2d ed. (New York: Pharos, 1989).

Index